Oh, Shenandoah

The North Fork at Tumbling Run, near Fishers Hill
OIL ON PANEL, 6" X 8," OCTOBER 21, 2008 (PAINTING #94).

Oh, Shenandoah

PAINTINGS OF THE HISTORIC VALLEY AND RIVER
BY ANDREI KUSHNIR

with a foreword by Dana Hand Evans,
essays by Warren R. Hofstra and William M. S. Rasmussen,
historical vignettes by Jeffrey C. Everett,
and an afterword by Edward L. Ayers

George F. Thompson Publishing
in association with
the American Land Publishing Project,
Museum of the Shenandoah Valley,
and Shenandoah University

Late Spring, Shenandoah Valley from the Skyline Drive
OIL ON PANEL, 12" X 16," JUNE 2, 2001 (PAINTING #71).

Here I am in the centre of the Magnificent Valley
of the Shenandoah—and the great valley of Virginia.
And a glorious Valley it is . . .

—Washington Irving (1853)

Sir, our native, substantial, independent yeomanry,
constitute our pride, efficiency and strength;
they are our defense in war, our ornaments
in peace; and no population, I will venture to
affirm, upon the face of the globe, is more
distinguished for an elevated love of freedom—
for morality, virtue, frugality and independence,
than the Virginia peasantry west of the Blue Ridge . . ."

—Delegate Charles James Faulkner (1832)

*Oak Leaf Park, near Luray**
OIL ON LINEN, 14" X 18," OCTOBER 23, 2011 (PAINTING #95).
*See *Notes on the Paintings* (page 385).

To my wife, Raissa,
and our children, Basil and Larissa,
each one an explorer and adventurer

Contents

At the Gallery, Washington, D.C.
OIL ON PANEL, 8" X 8," MAY 2, 2013.

Foreword

by Dana Hand Evans

In 1999, the Museum of the Shenandoah Valley (MSV) acquired its first work of art, *View of Winchester, Virginia, 1856*, by Edward Beyer (1820–1865). The fact that a landscape of the Valley was its first acquisition testifies to the MSV's regard for the genre. As *View of Winchester* attests, a landscape can not only capture the scenic beauty of a particular place, but also serve as an important historical document of its time. Today, most of the structures shown in *View of Winchester* have long since disappeared and now exist only on this canvas.

When the MSV was approached with the idea of an exhibition featuring seventy-one of the 264 landscapes of the Shenandoah Valley painted *en plein air* by Andrei Kushnir during the last ten years, there was no hesitation. Kushnir is a distinguished painter who has exhibited his work nationwide, including in exhibitions in some of America's most distinguished museums. Then, too, for an exhibition of works featuring Valley scenes, there is no better venue than the MSV, whose mission is to preserve and enrich the cultural life and heritage of this historic and scenic region.

As you will see in the exhibition and on the following pages, Andrei Kushnir's work is stunningly beautiful. The landscapes in this book shimmer and glow with light and color. The vibrant images jump from the canvas and draw the viewer into the scenes they depict. Perhaps even more astonishing is how these works capture the essence of land and life in the Valley. While some of his paintings depict historically significant places, more often they depict the farmlands, forests, and waterways of the region. The artist also focuses on cultural, educational, and commercial structures that dot the land. Some of these scenes show places that are treasured by the locals but little known to the rest of the world.

As a result, those who are fortunate to live in this Valley, as am I, will look at every image and not only see it, but *feel* its familiarity. From the rolling farms to the tranquil river scenes, from a cluster of houses that form a village to a home on the hill that makes a statement, from an image of people at a county fair to that of bathers at a swimming hole, we *know* these scenes. We recognize them as part of the Valley we love, yet we are concurrently startled to see them captured with such vibrant truth and clarity.

This is not the first time the MSV has presented landscapes depicting the Valley. In 2008, the museum organized and exhibited "Garnet Jex: Harpers Ferry Landscapes." There are some remarkable similarities between that first exhibition of eighteen Valley landscapes and this one, "Painting the Valley: Works by Andrei Kushnir." Like Kushnir, Garnet Jex (1895–1979) lived and worked in Washington, D.C., but he frequently traveled to the Shenandoah Valley for inspiration and to paint. More expansive in its scope and displaying, for the first time, works by a living artist, "Painting the Valley" provides a fitting and engaging sequel to that earlier exhibition.

For this project, the MSV is pleased to be collaborating with George F. Thompson Publishing, Shenandoah University, and the American Land Publishing Project in publishing this book. We also are pleased that Bill Rasmussen, the Virginia Historical Society's lead curator, and renowned Shenandoah University professor Warren Hofstra have provided thoughtful historical essays, which complement the informative historical vignettes by land-preservation expert Jeff Everett and the insightful afterword by respected historian Ed Ayers. The in-depth and enlightened texts of these distinguished scholars shine new light on the history and culture of the Valley, even as the book is focused on the artistry of Andrei Kushnir, who has refined the tradition of *plein-air* painting for this region.

Finally, the MSV is particularly pleased that the works comprising this exhibition tell the stories of communities throughout this valley. We are hopeful that even those who have long lived here will experience revelations as they view these works. We also hope that this exhibition and accompanying publication will help those living outside the Valley understand better the scope and depth of the region's scenic riches and be encouraged to visit here, again and again.

As I write this text, the MSV's staff members are developing, among other programs in support of the exhibition, a workshop to teach art students the skill of plein-air painting. It is intriguing to consider that, perhaps amongst these students, the next artist to exhibit landscapes of the Valley in the MSV will be inspired. What scenes will she chose to depict? What hues will he select for the canvas as he stands atop a knoll and gazes at the rolling farmland or undulating river? What changes in the landscape will her or his scene record as urbanization and industry assume greater influence on local economies? Such is the power and poetry of *plein air*, a snapshot rendered in paint, interpreted through unique sensibilities and experiences, as eyes see fresh and hands move fast to capture the light, all to place the viewer in a place and time that will never be repeated.

And so I now invite you to enjoy the *plein-air* paintings of the Shenandoah Valley that await you in the pages of this book. This viewing experience may not be the same as actually living in this fabled, lovely region of the nation. But it *will* help you understand why those of us who *do* live here give thanks every day, for the simple and wondrous beauty of it all.

Afternoon, Overlook of the North Fork from the New Market Battlefield
OIL ON PANEL, 12" X 16," AUGUST 16, 2010 (PAINTING #1).

Shenandoah Shore (Breezy Day) along the South Fork, near Bentonville
OIL ON PANEL, 5"X 7," JULY 30, 2002 (PAINTING #137).

Oh, Shenandoah

Buchanan, with the Wilson Warehouse

OIL ON PANEL, 8" X 12," SEPTEMBER 23, 2014 (PAINTING #200).

The Shenandoah Valley: Legendary American Landscape

by Warren R. Hofstra

Shenandoah—few places resonate more profoundly in American culture than the Shenandoah Valley. It is one of the best-known places in America. The word itself sounds deep within the same metrical sensibilities of our mind where music resides. Likewise, images of the Valley reverberate with the emotions evoked by the great landscape painters throughout the history of Western art. As in the grand perspectives of Claude Loraine, Nicholas Poussin, and so many of their followers over more than three centuries, we can imagine the Great Valley as an idyll of some lost but still grandiose and nostalgic past.

Mention the Shenandoah Valley to anyone or say you live there, as I do, and the response, almost invariably, is "Oh, it's so beautiful there, isn't it?" The famous American writer Washington Irving once wrote that the Shenandoah Valley is "equal to the promised land for fertility; far superior to it for beauty."[1] Beauty and the Valley are connected not only in the minds of most Americans, but also in the cognizance of people throughout the world. I remember a chance encounter I had several years ago with a woman in Knockando, Scotland, where my wife and I were visiting on a walking, birding, and whisky tour of the beautiful valley of the River Spey. The woman asked, "Where is your home?" I said, "The Shenandoah Valley." She quickly praised its beauty, of course, but then asked, "Is it near Wyoming? I have a daughter who lives there." The beauty of the Valley was more prominent in her mind than its geographical location.

My own first encounter with the Shenandoah Valley came when I was a boy. My family had just moved to the suburbs of Washington, D.C., a placeless place in America's original megapolis even then. One spring afternoon, my mother announced to my sister and me, "We're not taking a family vacation this year." No surprise there; the closest we came to vacationing was visiting our relatives in Wisconsin during our summers. "This year we'll be taking short trips to three places in Virginia," my mother continued. We would visit George and Martha Washington's Mount Vernon and Colonial Williamsburg, as a matter of course, but then I witnessed a silent change in her demeanor as the muse of wonder enveloped her. We knew, young as we were, that we were in the presence of something I would now call the sublime. "The third place will be the Shenandoah

Valley," she said. She portrayed the Valley's beauty so compellingly in the warm tone of her voice and her vivid description of the river and its magnificent mountains that I could envision the gauzy haze of a Valley morning and feel the dew literally dropping from the apples that she described as the ambrosia of the region. I would have preferred a week or two on the Wisconsin farm of my aunts and uncles, but there was no resisting what was, to my mother, a sacred journey. Ironically, she had grown up in Chicago and never even been near the Valley. Seeing it, however, meant more to her than a reunion with her sisters. I was in awe.

So, too, was I awed by Andrei Kushnir when he invited me to write an introductory essay to his book of plein-air paintings of the Shenandoah Valley. I had known his work from other projects that were also deeply rooted in place—for example, his fifty views of a single farm, Valley View Farm, along Crooked Run in Virginia's Piedmont on exhibit in 2004 at the Virginia Historical Society in Richmond.[2] In these I had sensed a sublime appreciation of a place and the capacity of a remarkable artist to evoke the emotions of its beauty amid the ordinariness of a working farm. Kushnir, I knew, would grace the Valley, comprehending its natural beauty, taking in its long and storied history, and grasping the vernacular meanings of its very human landscapes. The everyday life of the region has always fired my imagination and driven my appreciation for its land and history. Let me explain.

Why do we know—or think we know—the place so well? Why do people, such as the woman I encountered in Scotland, extol its beauty while misplacing it by thousands of miles? Why do we idealize it, romanticize it, and yearn for it without having ever seen it? The Shenandoah Valley is an icon in our geographical comprehension of a whole continent, but why has it assumed this importance?[3]

The song "Oh Shenandoah," with all its melodic majesty, has certainly embedded the name in the minds of millions of listeners. It is one of America's best-loved songs, but its origins are uncertain. It was not a professional product of Tin Pan Alley songwriters and publishers. It first appeared in print in 1882, but it was widely popular as a riverboat song and a sea chantey long before that.[4] Elegiac in tone, it is the song of a wanderer yearning for home and the "rushing waters" of a beautiful river, a beloved place. Its lyrics varied, rendering its meaning ambiguous. In one early nautical version, the last line of the refrain reads, "Away, I'm bound away, far from this land of misery," denying the Missouri River (more than 700 miles to the west) its poetic due. Only one version of the song is clearly about the Shenandoah River and its valley, but, in the iconography of today's popular culture, it is that association which sticks. It is so evocative of the Valley that the Commonwealth of Virginia once considered adopting it as the state song.[5]

Almost as renowned is the 1965 movie, *Shenandoah*, starring Jimmy Stewart as Charlie Anderson, a farmer in the Shenandoah Valley during the Civil War. As a widower, Anderson governs six sons, a daughter, and a daughter-in-law, all of whom he supports on 500 acres of prime land. Wanting no part of the war or its causes, he counters one recruiting agent's claim that "Virginia needs all of her sons, Mr. Anderson," with the warning that these sons were his and that "they don't belong to the state." "We never asked anything of the state," he admonished, "and never expected anything. We do our own living and thanks to no man for the right." The film might have fallen into the dustbin of Hollywood has-beens if it had not been revived as a successful Broadway musical with 1,050 performances and two Tony Awards between 1975 and 1977. The resonant chords the movie's themes struck in libertarian politics have also assured its longevity. David Boaz, writing for the Cato Institute, referred to *Shenandoah* "as the best libertarian film Hollywood ever made." And, in 1994, its compelling story brought it a close second at the First International Libertarian Film Festival.[6]

The name of the Valley is also associated with the tragic fate of America's first dirigible, the U.S.S. *Shenandoah*. Christened in 1923 and named for the home place of the wife to the Secretary of the Navy, the great ship, more than two football fields long, took a maiden voyage down the Shenandoah Valley on Navy Day in October of that year. That trip was followed a year later with a much-celebrated journey from California to Washington, D.C., which was the first transcontinental flight across the United States made by a rigid airship. Then on September 3, 1925, while on a promotional mission to forty Midwestern cities with stops at various state fairs, the ship was caught in a violent updraft during a storm, broke apart, and crashed to Earth near Caldwell, Ohio. Fourteen of its forty-three crewmembers died, including the commander. Thousands of souvenir hunters combed the crash site, which today includes a museum that commemorates the event. The tragedy remains so memorable to the area that a nearby school was named Shenandoah High, and its sports teams are still called the *Shenandoah Zeps*.

As with the song's melancholy tale, Charlie Anderson's saga, or the epic demise of the *Shenandoah*, places become recognizable in stories that we tell about them. Well-known places bear a stock of stories that are widely appreciated and oft related. An iconic place is *sui generis*; it produces its unique stories with lives of their own. These stories travel broadly around a culture and become part of what it means to be literate in a culture. They jump cultures. They are protean, assuming new meanings with time and context. They are culturally productive, prolific, and fecund, but their universality evolves from specific origins. As an article of national faith, few Americans cannot recite the stories of Plymouth Rock, Jamestown, Bunker Hill, Valley Forge, Gettysburg, Yellowstone, Wounded Knee, Niagara Falls, Wall Street, Hyde Park, Pearl Harbor, Watts, and many more places in the geographic iconography of American life. Many of these places, however, are not what they seem: That Pilgrims disembarked on a rock in Plymouth Bay is a literary fabrication, Jamestown did not sink into the river to be evoked as a site of Southern nostalgia, and the battle of Bunker Hill was actually fought on a neighboring mound. No matter. As in myth or religion, belief is more consequential than verity, authenticity more meaningful than actuality. So how did the Shenandoah Valley assume such a status in the absence of any singular, history-making event? Certainly, the song explains a lot. So does the movie. But they may be more effect than cause.

The stock of stories about the Shenandoah Valley—stories that explain its iconic status in twenty-first-century culture—long predates the modern era. Consider the Knights of the Golden Horseshoe. Something of the beauty and promise of the river must have been on the mind of Alexander Spotswood, the colonial governor of Virginia in 1716, when he and a party of gentlemen—known as the "knights" in multiple recountings—crossed and camped along it during the first major scouting foray into the region by Europeans. They dubbed the river the "Euphrates"—evoking the cradle of Western civilization and the Garden of Eden. They luxuriated. They harvested and ate "very good grapes, and [saw] a vine which bore a sort of wild cucumber, and a shrub which bore a fruit like unto a current."[7] What followed was a libatious ritual of possession by Englishmen in a new land—a new Levant, an imagined Cathay:

> After dinner we got the men all together and loaded all their arms and we drunk the King's health in Champagne, and fired a volley; the Prince's health in Burgundy, and fired a volley; and all the rest of the Royal Family in Claret, and a volley. We drunk the Governor's health and fired another volley. We had several sorts of liquors, namely Virginia Red Wine and White Wine, Irish Usquebaugh, Brandy, Shrub, two sorts of Rum, Champagne, Canary, Cherry punch, Cider, Water &c.[8]

After all was over, the party returned to Williamsburg, and, by several accounts, the governor distributed golden horseshoe pins to the gentlemen to commemorate the shodding of their horses for the climb over the Blue Ridge. The memento stuck in the minds of Virginians for centuries, inspiring characters in numerous romances and the names of many organizations formed to re-enact the rituals of chivalry or buttress a feudal regime of race and slavery in the decades before the Civil War.[9] "Euphrates" slipped out of usage, but the exotic aura of the name was soon conferred upon "Shenandoah."

By the early 1730s, it had become common for the public documents of the Virginia colony to refer to the river and its valley as the "Shenandoah." Robert Brooke, who had accompanied Spotswood in his exploration, received official appointment as surveyor for "Lands on Sherrando River." In other references, the river appeared as the "Shenando," "Shenondore," or "Sherando." Other variants included "Chanador," "Tschanaator," "Jonontore," "Ifanundowa," "Chanandowa," "Isanandowa," and "Shevanoll."[10] Obviously, the form and spelling of the name were in considerable flux until "Shenandoah" became commonplace later in the eighteenth century. But the place was becoming widely known. Although the origins and meaning of the name remain a mystery, the earliest reference I found to a cognate for the river and its valley appeared in John Lederer's report on his three journeys of exploration in western Virginia in 1669–1670. Offering instructions to anyone undertaking similar ventures in the future, Lederer describes "two breaches" in the Appalachian Mountains: "One, as I am informed by Indians, at a place called *Zynodoa*."[11]

Another early reference appeared on a map drafted by Franz Louis Michel, a young Swiss merchant on a trip in the Virginia backcountry scouting for a colony of his countrymen. The colony never materialized despite Michel's explorations along the Shenandoah and Potomac River Valleys in 1707 and his subsequent petition to the English crown, but the map he enclosed depicted, among other landscape features and fanciful renderings of various wild creatures, the "Mountains of Cenuntua" bordering the Valley to the west. If the beauty and bounty of the Valley later became a cultural trope, it may be first owing to Michel and his fulsome description of the "good land where are great forest trees of oak, and where much game abounds."[12]

Rockbridge Vineyard, near Raphine
OIL ON PANEL, 16" X 24," APRIL 28, 2015 (PAINTING #227).

Spring Evening at Opequon

OIL ON PANEL, 6" X 8," APRIL 3, 2011 (PAINTING #153).

A half-century later, the Valley gained greater recognition among both Americans and Europeans following the Seven Years' War, also known as the French and Indian War. During the war, the Shenandoah Valley supported a population of more than 18,000 people, constituted Virginia's western frontier, and served as a buffer against marauding parties of French and Indian warriors. When in command of the Virginia Regiment, George Washington fixed his headquarters in the Valley town of Winchester because of its "centrical situation" and strategic importance. Already a public figure of some renown in both England and America, Washington observed that the Valley "secures the communication with the neighbouring colonies, as well as the trade, to the rivers of Rappahannock, Potomack &c, and though trifling in itself, a place of utmost importance to the country in general, being contiguous to that part of our frontiers."[13] According to unsubstantiated rumors circulating around the time of the American Revolution, Washington looked to the Valley as a last resort if the defenses of the Continental Army failed in the eastern theaters. Congress did exile Hessian prisoners of war to the Valley, and they became an indelible part of the region's folklore to the present day.[14]

More and more Americans experienced the Valley firsthand during the decades following the American Revolution. By 1800, the population exceeded 83,000, more than half of which had been added since 1775.[15] But during this same period the population of Kentucky had swollen to more than 220,000, and many new settlers traveled up the Valley to the Wilderness Road and Cumberland Gap route west. Due to the "rage for Kentucky," as the editor of a Winchester paper commented in 1789, "the number of families which have passed through this town for the last four or five weeks, on their way to that distant region is almost incredible."[16] Even today, many genealogists find that their family trees have deep roots in the soil of the Valley's history, and local genealogical repositories are constantly filled with numerous ancestor seekers.

The notion of the Valley as incomparably fertile and teeming with game became fixed in the literature about the region during the nineteenth century. Although undoubtedly ignorant of Michel's petition, Samuel Kercheval, highly regarded as the Valley's first historian, wrote during the 1830s that, "when the country was first known to the white people, [it] was one entire and beautiful prairie" and, "like the rich prairies of the west, afforded the finest possible pasturage for wild animals. The country abounded in the larger kinds of game." Although modern ecological studies of the Valley's natural vegetation at the time Europeans began surveying the land reveal a heavy oak-hickory forest and the absence of large game such as bison in the archaeological sites of native Indian settlements, Kercheval chose to evoke the imagery of prairie fertility and abundance just at the time Americans began exploiting the great prairies of the nascent frontier to the west.[17]

The prairie myth persists in the minds of Valley residents today. It evokes images of open grasslands occupied by nomadic Indians hunting great game. We know, however, that Indian peoples were few in the Valley by the eighteenth century—too few to maintain prairies with a fire regime. The sites of their prior occupations, however, are ubiquitous, and some can be traced to the first human settlements in the region. Most of these sites, however, are small, lack structural remains, and bespeak a transient people using the Valley as a means to get elsewhere. Kercheval reports seeing remnants of burial mounds, palisaded villages, and other signs of settled and substantial lifeways. Now obliterated by plow and shovel, they remain today only as tantalizing hints of what the pre-Euro-American landscape might have been.[18]

The celebrity of the Shenandoah Valley flourished during Kercheval's time, as the gush of numerous mineral springs with their reputed curative powers drew thousands of visitors to the Valley each "season." Kercheval himself exalted the idyllic charms of one spring situated in a "beautiful grove of young oak and other timber." At another set of springs, "everything the water passes through or over is beautifully lined with a bright yellow fringe of moss."[19] The sylvan delights of these lush places attracted artists who produced popular images of the Shenandoah Valley that hung in many working- and middle-class American homes. Most popular were the paintings reproduced in Edward Beyer's *Album of Virginia; or Illustration of the Old Dominion*, most of which were, ironically, sited in New Virginia, as the western region of the state was known.[20] It was at this time that Natural Bridge became one of America's most famous destinations for travelers, joining a short list of natural wonders, such as Niagara Falls near Buffalo and Mammoth Cave in Kentucky, that were capable of evoking sublime emotions in a credulous public.[21]

If its geographic centrality raised awareness of the strategic importance of the Shenandoah Valley during the imperial and revolutionary conflicts of the eighteenth century, then the American Civil War magnified its martial reputation many fold. Confederate General Thomas J. "Stonewall" Jackson's famed Valley Campaign of 1862 and the lithographs of this and subsequent engagements which appeared regularly in Northern newspapers made the Valley famous both as a theater of conflict and as a site of memory and commemoration ever since. Thomas Buchanan Read's poem, "Sheridan's Ride," written shortly after Major General Philip Sheridan saved the Union from defeat at the battle of Cedar Creek on October 19, 1864, became such a sensation in the North that its wild popularity was credited with Abraham Lincoln's reelection only weeks later. Northern school children memorized the poem for so many generations thereafter that many Americans can still recite it today.[22]

The armies of both North and South recognized that the Valley not only provided a premier route of invasion, but also supplied such prodigious quantities of foodstuffs to the Confederacy that laying it waste became a major objective of Union strategy. "Eat out Virginia clear and clean," Commanding Union General Ulysses S. Grant ordered Sheridan on appointing him to the Valley command in 1864, "so that crows flying over it for the balance of this season will have to carry their own provender with them." Remembered as "The Burning," the episode has come to stand for the devastation and desolation of modern warfare.[23] Sheridan's military experiences in the Shenandoah Valley proved to be of great consequence for the twentieth century when, in 1870, he advised Otto von Bismarck, Chancellor of the German Confederation, on waging American-style total war in the Franco-Prussian conflict.[24]

Diehard Confederates in the Valley today still deplore the enduring effects of scorched-earth warfare on the region's landscape and lament the long suffering of a people "uniformly" loyal to the South. Yet so divided was the Valley in the tug of war between North and South—appropriate for a region that had long been a great migration corridor between these adversaries—that one Civil War observer dubbed it the "debatable ground."[25] And, as early as the summer following the war's end in 1865, another described a "broad landscape, dotted with a thousand harvest fields . . . of growing corn." The Valley, he proclaimed, was "fast shaking off the ashes of war and spreading its summer treasures in the golden sunshine, and ere long General Sheridan's 'waste and howling wilderness' will again blossom as the rose."[26] The Agricultural Census backed up these claims. In 1870, all but one county in the Valley produced more wheat than it had ten years earlier before the outbreak of war. And, in the decades following, the Valley's farmers outproduced the Midwest in wheat on both a per capita and per acre basis.[27] If the Valley earned a wide reputation for Civil War heroics, it was due as much to the hard work of recovery as to the blood and tears of the fight itself.

This story of the debatable ground reborn as a garden was so compelling to Americans that the Shenandoah Valley became one of the premier destinations for tourists during the great age of railroad travel when trunk lines knit the continent together for the first time. During this period, the Baltimore and Ohio Railroad gained control of the entirety of the Valley route and published guidebooks with photographs and descriptions identifying the scenes that had so recently figured in a grueling conflict. Veterans came on the train unit by unit to relive the great trials of their youth. Not missing a beat in the economic rebound, in 1879 the Virginia Department of Immigration and Agriculture began to publish handbooks to attract both tourists and investment to the Valley.[28]

These measures had their effects. With the advent of the Automobile Age following World War I and the ensuing era of caravanning and car camping, the Valley proved to be one of the most popular areas in Virginia for tourists not only because of attractions such as Natural Bridge and the Valley's great limestone caverns, but also because its principal road, the Valley Turnpike, was deemed by some as the "best thoroughfare in the South."[29] The original Valley Road was so well constructed during the 1830s—ditched and crowned with an excellent macadam paving—and well-maintained thereafter that, a century later, the road stood out at a time when Virginia roads were elsewhere so miserable that the Automobile Association of America (AAA) warned its members to shun the state. But, when the AAA designated a "National Highway" to the famed 1607 Jamestown Exposition in 1907, it included the Valley Pike in the return route and maintained this designation in subsequent maps of America's best highways for automobiling. Unsurprisingly, the road became a key element of U.S. 11 after 1926, when the federal government designated the first system of national routes—north–south as well as east–west—across the nation. It was celebrated as the best route for driving from New York City to Atlanta or resorts in Florida.[30] The large number of travelers and tourists who took advantage of the road stimulated the development of a roadside landscape of restaurants, drive-ins, roadhouses, campgrounds, cabin camps, and a wide array of attractions from zoos to amusement parks. No wonder my mother wanted to drive the Valley in the family's Studebaker.

On that childhood trip we viewed the surface of things. I recall a blur of fences and fields, barns and houses, woodlands and pastures, towns and villages. Stops at picturesque roadside stands, a visit to Luray Caverns, glimpses of the great Shenandoah River, and an overnight in car cabins all punctuated our route with a variety of experiences. Though not yet a word in my vocabulary then, *landscape* was what drew us into my mother's romance with the place. She was so ardent in ogling its beauty and insisting that we share her pleasures that each exclamation of "Oh, look at that kids" brought waves of indignant giggling from the backseat.[31] But now, as a scholar, teacher, and student of the landscape, I see my mother's appreciation of natural and cultural beauty as anything but skin deep. Landscape may be the array of surface features visible to the eye, but, in the mind's eye, it represents the networks and webs of social relations, economic institutions, technological arrangements, political activities, and intellectual movements that seek expression on the ground. As J. B. Jackson, the founder of landscape studies in North America, professed, to read the landscape is to experience the deeper life of a people's culture.[32] For example, the majesty and grandeur of a great Pennsylvania bank barn in the Shenandoah Valley is but the visible manifestation of its varied technical functions as an agricultural machine for storing and processing grains, housing and feeding livestock, and keeping tools and tractors.[33] Even so, it is only one mechanism in the great manufactory of a farm that transforms the energy of the sun, fossil fuels, and human labor into a multitude of goods and foodstuffs to fulfill mankind's many needs. Think of the farm as a portal into the engines of human history.

Landscapes are layered. As each era channels the energy of the past into discrete expressions of landscape features, time and place succeed one another in a stratigraphy of cultural geography. Thus, great nineteenth-century stone taverns give way to urban hotels, themselves replaced by a succession of car camps and mom-and-pop motels, all leading to the ubiquity of anonymous franchise hotels today. Liveries yield to gas stations and then to mega service centers. Venerable old farms sprout a maze of subdivisions, shopping centers, and business parks. Knowing the patterns of succession provides keys to historic change. The present is only a roadcut in the past.

What Andrei Kushnir sees and paints, as displayed in this book, thus discloses a deep sense of place and history. The beauty of color and form, of light and shade in his work is a gloss to centuries of what men and women have done in life. Wittingly or not, these lives order a landscape. Its beauty—and Kushnir's ability to capture this beauty like lightning in a bottle—comes to us in our own connections to this order. This order has evolved, and we sense this evolution. Like the emergence of a species, we can describe it in a taxonomy of defining phases. For the Shenandoah Valley, its cultural history, and the multitude of meanings embedded in the compelling images Kushnir has herein recorded, three phases stand out as seminal in the origin of the landscape: (1) the era of high farming during the nineteenth century, (2) the age of republican travel at the end of the eighteenth century, and (3) the settlement period in which Europeans first encountered, claimed, and developed the Shenandoah Valley beginning at Opequon in the early 1730s.

The era of high farming, because it is the most recent and pervasive of the Valley's three eras, bears the greatest impact on how the Valley appears today. We sense and see it everywhere we travel. High farming entailed intensive land use, immense productivity, and a culture of prosperity. It peaked during the decades surrounding the Civil War, but it can be traced from the years before the American Revolution, when wheat and flour prices throughout the Atlantic world first rose high enough to make commercial grain farming feasible in the Shenandoah Valley, to post-World War II America, when a global era of chemically induced abundance rendered grain farming in the Valley redundant. That the Shenandoah Valley was the "breadbasket of the Confederacy" is now

*Spring, View of the South Fork from Mt. Airy, near Meems Bottom**
OIL ON CANVAS, 20" X 16," MARCH 24, 2010 (PAINTING #91).

I-House, near Hamburg (Shenandoah County)
OIL ON PANEL, 8" X 12," JULY 12, 2015 (PAINTING #243).

a truism which speaks to the plentitude of foodstuffs that Shenandoah Valley farmers produced during the nineteenth century. “The country has been alive with the industrious bands of cradlers, rakers, binders, and shockers,” the *Valley Farmer* observed in 1845. “Every farm—almost every golden-covered hill and valley—has been peopled by the harvesters in their white garments, securing the staple of our country, the wealth of the farmer, and the food of all classes.”[34]

Agricultural statistics for the nineteenth century bear out this imagery of abundance for the Valley. Using less than a tenth of the total improved acreage in Virginia in 1850, Valley farmers produced more than a fifth of the commonwealth’s wheat. At that time, farmers in many of the most productive grain-growing regions of the United States coaxed no more than six bushels of wheat from every one of their acres, whereas Valley farmers often realized yields of more than twenty bushels, and the most successful could cultivate wheat at the rate of forty bushels or more per acre. No wonder that nineteen of every twenty Valley farmers grew wheat. A trend toward increased productivity of wheat and flour—broken only momentarily by the Civil War—continued throughout the nineteenth century and was extended by World War I well into the 1920s. Fifty years later, wheat and flour production had plummeted by a factor of ten, as it was replaced by a hay and livestock system with local specialties in fruit and poultry. Climaxing just as the era of auto tourism dawned, the age of high farming endowed the affective landscape of tourists’ emotions with a rich stock of relic structures and vistas to wax nostalgic over or to preserve as regional heritage. This relic landscape is how we now best know the bygone era of high farming and its impact on the Shenandoah Valley.[35]

Many of the once-ubiquitous, dry-laid stone fences are gone—dismantled for the cold comfort of barbed wire—the stones removed and buried in house or barn foundations. Surviving fences, however, have often been relaid to bear again the cultural weight of time-honored field patterns. The dwellings that housed farm families in the former age of abundance have generally survived. Early in this age, the Shenandoah Valley was a center of *archigensis*, a process in which a new house type emerged as the domestic embodiment of agricultural success. For the past half century, geographers have called it an I-house (after the Midwestern “I” states of Iowa, Indiana, and Illinois, where it diffused, proliferated, and was first identified by scholars), a style characterized as a two-rooms-down and two-rooms-up structure with an entrance that is usually centered within balancing bays of windows.[36] When extended with wings and ells, these dwellings grew capacious enough for the ample families that agricultural prosperity spawned. The simplest I-houses were wood-framed, but the most enduring were built of stone or brick and, today, are lasting monuments to a time when abundance translated into large families, domestic felicity, and social competence.

Essential to this prosperity, of course, was the agricultural entourage of farm buildings. Lording over all was the Pennsylvania bank barn, with its ramped entrance to the threshing floor above and direct entry to stables and stalls for livestock below. Its magnitude depended upon a lucid geometry of architectural massing and an elegant system of timber framing that had evolved over centuries within a moral economy of architectural means.[37] Multiple dependencies in the form of granaries, cribs, sheds, stables, and, later, silos and garages bespoke the rational bureaucracy of farmstead management. Although the commanding elm and chestnut trees are now gone, victims of blight, majestic oaks and maples still enshroud these compounds in Acadian shadows. Interspersed along streams and rivers are the remnants of gristmills serving as reminders that irregular nature supplied the grid of power to drive the transformation of grain into flour throughout the age of high farming.

Other key components of the agricultural complex of high farming and the relic landscape that recalls it to us today include a hierarchy of hamlets, villages, and towns. To the farmer these settlements represented the commercial centers of trade and exchange without which their own economic competence and domestic comfort—to say nothing about the accumulation of wealth—were but a phantom prospect. To today's traveler to the Valley on, say, U.S. 11, 33, 50, 211, 340, 522, or any of their tributary roads, this hierarchy appears as a rhythm of town and country—streetscape and landscape—succeeding one another with the beat of visual diversity unknown on much of Interstate 81. The shops, stores, and manufactories in town, as much as the farmsteads and mills of the countryside, are reminders of the great age of high farming when all these elements hummed together in a vast system of agricultural productivity and prosperity.

The monuments of this era were what Kushnir most often encountered in his painting forays into the Valley. Some are derelict and decayed, others are beautifully maintained or restored, but all provoke responses to a presupposing age of high farming and natural abundance that probe much deeper into the psyche of our culture than simple nostalgia for a bygone era would betray. Kushnir leads us there. It is a world built upon grain, wheat, flour, and bread—foodstuffs, the stuff of life. It is a moral world, a world in which labor in the earth yields a profusion of nature's bounty—the good life. Washington Irving called the Valley a "veritable land of abundance."[38] Think "amber waves of grain," as in the famous anthem, "America, the Beautiful."

Thomas Jefferson famously linked the cultivation of wheat with republican virtue. Not long after a trip to the Shenandoah Valley during the early 1780s, Jefferson, in his *Notes on the State of Virginia*, compared tobacco—"a culture productive of infinite wretchedness"—with wheat: "Besides cloathing the earth with herbage, and preserving its fertility, it feeds the labourers plentifully, requires from them only a moderate toil, except in the season of harvest, raises great numbers of animals for food and service, and diffuses plenty and happiness among the whole."[39]

Jefferson's vision was profoundly and politically moral. "Those who labour in the earth are the chosen people of God, if ever he had a chosen people, whose breasts he has made his peculiar deposit for substantial and genuine virtue."[40] Feeding the people freed the farmer at the same time it fostered the public good. To Jefferson's generation, placing public interest above self-interest defined *virtue*. Thus, Kushnir's landscape is, indeed, a virtuous landscape that uplifts us, ennobles us, and makes us whole. And it returns us to an earlier age, a precedent for the era of high farming, to a time when the American republic was newborn. This is the second of our phases in the evolutionary landscape of the Shenandoah Valley: the age of republican travel.

Jefferson's paean to virtue was anything but light or transient. It evoked core principles of his era's political philosophy—principles which remain important to us, or this philosophy would not resonate so profoundly in today's politics. If virtue required devotion to the public good, then acting on behalf of the public—the republic—mandated freedom of the self from the controlling

High Farming on Headquarters Road, Shenandoah County
OIL ON CANVAS, 10" X 20," JULY 12, 2015 (PAINTING #242).

interests of others. In feudal or monarchical Europe, "others" meant the aristocracy, which governed the common people by expropriating the surplus value of their land in rents and obtained the means of political autonomy for themselves by impressing the people's labor. In Europe's industrial era, "others" meant proprietors and employers, or the controlling hand of commerce. The "casualties and caprice of customers. . . . begets subservience and venality," wrote Jefferson. This "suffocates the germ of virtue, and prepares fit tools for the designs of ambition."[41] In the republican era, landowning and freehold farming empowered virtue by ensuring economic independence—the competence of knowing that one's livelihood depended upon one's own or one's household's or one's slaves' labor on one's own land. The virtuous person was beholden to no one.

With its successful revolution against Great Britain and British autocracy, the young American republic proclaimed the possibility of a republican order so construed. Europeans wanted to see it, experience it, and understand what a people could achieve with freehold farming liberated from the manipulations of an ancient aristocracy. What celebrity the Shenandoah Valley had already achieved prompted travelers to view it as a model for republican society. Perhaps it was Spotswood and the milk-and-honey imagery of the Euphrates or the panache of the Knights of the Golden Horseshoe. More likely, George Washington's habit of recommending the Valley to his own soldiers and other acquaintances as the embodied promise of landowning in the new American West brought it to the attention of Europeans inspired by the American example of republican opportunity.[42] One of them, François Jean de Beauvoir, Marquis de Chastellux, Washington's principal liaison with his French allies during the American Revolution, made a point of traveling to the Valley when the fighting stopped. After arriving in Winchester, he extolled the "fine country around it." To this young aristocrat, destined to play a role in the affairs of Europe, "the scene is worth a voyage across the Atlantic."[43]

Thomas Jefferson's *Notes on the State of Virginia*, completed in 1781 and published first in Paris (1785) and then in London (1787), attracted the further attention of European travelers. One was François Alexandre, duc de la Rochefoucauld-Liancourt. "At last we reached the celebrated point, so much extolled by travelers, and the celebrity of which has been greatly increased by Mr. Jefferson's *Notes*," he wrote on arriving at the confluence of the Potomac and Shenandoah Rivers during the 1790s. "The view is beautiful and majestic. The Shenandoah sweeps in a south-east direction along the Blue Mountains. . . . The scene is grand; it deserves to be viewed, and is worthy of the admiration of travelers who delight in the magnificent operations of nature." My mother was evidently drawing on a much longer tradition of tourist fascination with the beauty of the Shenandoah Valley than she ever imagined. And Rochefoucauld made clear that it was not nature alone that imparted this beauty to the region. "The beautiful valley of Shenandoah," he continued, "is a fine country, inhabited by an industrious and active people; a country, formed by nature to be rich." It "deserves the praise of being the finest part of Virginia." The meadows "well furnished with timothy-grass and clover are interspersed with fields of wheat and Indian corn, and with orchards, which abound with apple-trees. . . . The fields are manured, and produce from fifteen to twenty-five bushels of wheat per acre. . . . The cows are very fine. . . . Pigs are bred here in great numbers," and so forth. Rochefoucauld had earlier tried to walk a fine line between royalty and revolution in France, making his sojourn in America as an exile in the 1790s.[44]

An earlier English tourist, Andrew Burnaby, gives insight into what Rochefoucauld might have meant in describing a "country, formed by nature to be rich." The people of the Valley were "ignorant of want, and acquainted with but few vices," he wrote when first encountering them in the 1760s. Here was *virtue* worthy of Jefferson, not the decadence of an aristocracy. "Their inexperience of the elegancies of life, precludes any regret that they possess not the means of enjoying them: but they possess what many princes would give half their dominions for, health, content, and tranquility of mind."[45]

Other republican travelers of this era made clear that landownership and freehold farming in the Valley embodied the human equality about which Jefferson had written in the Declaration of Independence. Isaac Weld, a child of the Enlightenment and namesake of Isaac Newton, commented on the "cultivated lands" that "are mostly parcelled out in small portions," during his visit in the mid-1790s. "There are no persons here, as on the other side of the mountains, possessing large farms; nor are there any eminently distinguished by their education or knowledge from the rest of their fellow citizens. Poverty also is as much unknown in this country as great wealth." It was in the Valley that Weld found a premise for a republican social order: "Each man owns the house he lives in and the land which he cultivates, and every one appears to be in a happy state of mediocrity."[46]

If the legacy of the era of high farming lay in the productivity of the Valley, then the lesson learned by republican travelers concerned the conjoining of abundance and beauty. It was the improvement worked into the land by an industrious and free population that, in the mind of these early tourists, created a landscape of virtue cultivated in the lives of the people. Rather than being subjects of a king, they thereby became citizens in a republic. Burnaby and Jefferson would have agreed about the springs of human happiness working deep beneath the surface of the land. So, I believe, would Andrei Kushnir. He has often commented to me that his days spent painting *en plein air* throughout the Valley were among the happiest of his career. We both understood that there is nothing clichéd about this happiness.

The landscape of Kushnir's Shenandoah Valley also cuts deep through the era of high farming and the age when republican travelers first visited the region to reveal the first phase of its evolution in the initiation of European settlement. That the Shenandoah Valley came to embody a republican social order—a landscape expressing the economic independence and political competence of the people—was due neither to an accident of nature nor the caprice of history. As a frontier in colonial Virginia, the Valley was an expression of imperial design; at the same time, however, it was a product of the people's own making—a self-made landscape. Thus, it was paradoxically the official ambition of empire that left this vernacular imprint upon the land. Otherwise, it would not have captivated the attention of travelers searching the new republic of America for what a people freed from aristocracy could accomplish on their own. Nor would the people have invested so much wealth and labor into improving the land when a market revolution later called forth the immense productivity of high farming during the nineteenth century. Returning to a point made at the beginning of this essay, it was a feeling for this vernacular imprint that drew me—and I suspect Kushnir—to the landscapes of the Shenandoah Valley.

During the early eighteenth century, the Valley was the frontier, first, of the British Empire in North America and, second, of its largest royal colony, Virginia. As the ragged edge of this Anglo-Virginia political order, it was a zone of conflict—another debatable ground. By the 1720s, the imperial bureaucracy in London and the colonial establishments in America were worried. In 1721, a report by the Board of Trade warned King George I that Virginia was "exposed in case of a rupture [war] on the one side to the Spaniards, on the other to the French, and surrounded by savages." The commissioners on the board could have added that planters living in Virginia's Tidewater communities, with a near-majority of African-American slaves, were also imperiled by the possibility of a rebellion by their own bondsmen. The desire of the enslaved to escape bondage and live free as maroons in Virginia's mountains would be realized within the decade. By then, Great Britain was already engaged in a war with slave maroons in the mountains of Jamaica. The internal threat posed by slavery thus compounded the external threats of other European imperial powers and native Indian tribes. Although the Appalachians might "serve at present for a very good frontier," the commissioners would not "propose them for the boundary of your Majesty's Empire in America." "On the contrary it were to be wished that the British settlements might be extended beyond them."[47]

It was no surprise that, within a decade, a Virginia governor issued land orders for hundreds of thousands of acres in the Shenandoah Valley—close to 400,000 between 1730 and 1732. Attached to these orders were requirements that recipients situate one family on this land for every 1,000 acres within two years.[48] This policy touched off one of the great migrations of American history. That most of those holding land orders came from southeastern and south-central Pennsylvania insured a flow of people to the marchlands of Virginia from the north and, in point of fact, originating from the marginal areas of Europe in the north of Ireland and the central Rhine River Valley. By the mid-1730s, several thousand Europeans were hacking farms out of what was, to them, an American wilderness.

This was all by design. As the governor boasted to his overlords: "most of these Petitioners are Germans and Swissers lately come into Pensilvania, where being disappointed of the quantity of land they expected . . . have chosen to fix their habitations in this uninhabited part of Virginia . . . for by this means a strong Barrier will be Settled between us and the French . . . and thereby so much weaken the Power of the French as to have little to fear from that Quarter hereafter." There was good reason for "encouraging more Foreigners to come Hither."[49] These Pennsylvanians, Germans, and Scots-Irish were farmers, not planters. They grew grains, primarily wheat, and raised livestock. When densely settled, they would form militias under the discipline of county governments, and, in defending their own freeholds, they would secure Virginia from its European and Indian enemies. By not replicating plantation settlements, furthermore, they would foil runaway slave maroons and stifle African-American discontent. It didn't matter that the majority were neither English nor Anglican, because they were all Protestants who would "immunize" the colony from the kind of French Catholic subversion that was at the same time making the English

Cyrus McCormick Farm (Walnut Grove), Steeles Tavern
OIL ON PANEL, 9" X 12," JULY 10, 2011 (PAINTING #23).

*Fields and Farms, Ottobine**
OIL ON LINEN, 18" X 24," MAY 23, 2011 (PAINTING #34).

occupiers of Acadia in Canada so nervous. The resulting ethnic and religious pluralism informs the landscape of the Valley to this day in ways embedded in so many of Andrei Kushnir's paintings.

The settlement of the Valley was no quiet push by European farmers simply looking for better land over the next hill. It was part of one of the great stories of imperial conflict during the eighteenth-century era of global warfare among European powers and their native allies—and enemies—in Asia, Africa, and the Americas. But these great forces of historical change had effects so profound and pervasive that they influenced the most seemingly mundane and minute activities in the lives of settlers on the ground of the Shenandoah Valley frontier. Consider, for example, one moment in the early 1750s. Abraham Van Meter and John Keywood are accompanying a surveyor who is fixing the boundary between their lands. At the "corner of the line wch [sic] was to divide between Keywood and Vanmeter," the surveyor called on the latter saying, "as you and Keywood has agreed the matter come and set the compass to run this land." Van Meter stepped up and "looking through the sight of the compass turned it a small matter, and raising himself up said 'I believe this will do.'"[50]

Small matter? Imagine William Rodgers. In his own words, "when he came up from Pensylvania [during the early 1730s] he was an intire Stranger to the methods . . . to take up tracts of Land." He made a "search to find such as he might think would do for him" and "pitched upon land he liked": 216 acres on a bend in the Shenandoah's North Fork. Only later did he find out that his land lay in the domain of Jost Hite, a German immigrant who lived about forty miles away along the banks of Opequon Creek and who had received one of the governor's land orders. "Happening to call at Mr. Hites," he "freely told . . . how he had proceeded and where his design lay." They soon had a bargain for ready money if Hite would "make him a title . . . or give him good Bonds."[51]

Fulfilling the injunction of the British crown to occupy the American backcountry was thereby left to these ordinary men and thousands of other men and women like them who found land in the Shenandoah Valley, negotiated boundaries with neighbors, surveyed it to their liking, and, in the process, converted wilderness into property as the first step in the evolution of a vernacular landscape. It was truly a landscape of their own making. As Hite himself said, "nothing but a preference to the choice lands, would tempt men to become adventurers" in this great migration. Thus, he "suffered the Purchasers to make their Surveys in what manner they thought best suited their Interests."[52] Seeking their own interests but always negotiating with neighbors, they created the "happy state of mediocrity" in which Isaac Weld found them. Several generations later, their descendants, still seeking their best interests and building upon the investments and improvements of their predecessors, transformed the Valley into one of the most bountiful farming regions in the United States.

Eventually, during the period following the American Revolution, these yeomen were joined in parts of the Valley—especially the eastern portions of the Lower Valley—by the scions of great planter families from Tidewater Virginia eager to capitalize on the salubrious air of the Valley and apply the strategies of plantation management, including African-American slavery, to the production of wheat.[53] They created a plantation landscape of large tracts of land where gangs of slaves cultivated wheat within the same mix of agricultural activities consuming the labor of farmers elsewhere in the Valley. But the economies of scale they achieved yielded a prosperity conducive to the great houses, fine furnishings, genteel manners, and cultured sociability that was tied to the plantation world of eastern Virginia. Their landscape, however, was no less expressive of the moral economy of producing wheat and flour as the breadstuff of the Valley.

Planter or farmer, it is that economy and its remnant landscapes that we revisit in this book and see again in the remarkable vision of Andrei Kushnir. We have here something much more than a rich collection of paintings. It is something that well exceeds a depiction, or even a celebration, of one of the great iconic regions of the United States and, indeed, the world. The notable phases over which this landscape evolved—imperial settlement, republican revolution, and high farming—and their broad historic importance in the development of America invest the images populating this book with varied but deeply entwined meanings. If the Valley became an iconic place by its numerous and dynamic representations in popular culture—the song, stories, battles, tourists, and family trips multiplied time and time again—then what made it iconic—the foundation of its fame—was anything but superficial or superfluous. My mother knew that a drive through the Shenandoah Valley was just as vital to the education of her children as visits to the great shrines of American life.

In *Oh, Shenandoah*, Andrei Kushnir takes us on an amazing journey into the deep and remarkable history of the Shenandoah Valley. He comprehends in his art the many encoded meanings of this legendary American landscape, which is known worldwide, even by those who have never seen it, and which inspired my mother and countless others over the centuries who were drawn to its amazing beauty. Earlier American artists were inspired to paint other American places that are now famous, among them Andrew Wyeth in the Brandywine Valley of Pennsylvania and Ashur B. Durand, Thomas Cole, and Frederick Church in the Hudson Valley of New York. In the process, they created world-renowned schools of regional art. So, too, has Andrei Kushnir been inspired to paint the scenic and historic Shenandoah Valley. His artistry may well inspire a new school of American painting.

Autumnal Sunset, Page Valley and the South Fork from the Skyline Drive
OIL ON PANEL, 6" X 8," NOVEMBER 14, 2011 (PAINTING #8).

*Natural Bridge**

OIL ON PANEL, 12" X 10," AUGUST 7, 2011 (PAINTING #92).

Andrei Kushnir's Vision of the Picturesque Virginia Landscape

William M. S. Rasmussen

Time and again I find myself surprised by the beauty and calm of the landscapes of Virginia's Shenandoah Valley and Blue Ridge Mountains and by the life-enhancement they provide. My reaction is not a new response. In the Valley in 1775, Philip Fithian, a colonial tutor and Presbyterian missionary, said much the same: "The Country at once surprizes me—Meadow Ground of the best Quality! It is exceedingly rich."[1] In 1864, the poet Walt Whitman, visiting wounded troops of the Union Army in the northern Piedmont at a time of much greater tumult than the subtler environmental crisis we face today, recorded his observation that, "Dilapidated, fenceless, and trodden with war as Virginia is, wherever I move across the surface, I find myself rous'd to surprise and admiration. What capacity for production, improvements, human life, nourishment and expansion."[2] Like today's casual traveler, those historical figures had not journeyed in search of beauty or with preconceptions; thus, their surprise. Many people in their eras, however, did approach the Valley with great anticipation of what they would see there, and at some sites the history of their responses remains with us.

The two most famous examples of the power of preconception are probably forever linked to our ability to look at Natural Bridge and Harpers Ferry with freshness of vision. Those old Virginia landmarks have become like Leonardo's "Mona Lisa." Thomas Jefferson famously boasted about them in his *Notes on the State of Virginia* (1785). Of Natural Bridge, he claimed it is the most sublime of nature's works: "It is impossible for the emotions arising from the sublime to be felt beyond what they are here."[3] We realize now that any sublimity in the Valley of Virginia is no match for the grandeur and scale of the Grand Canyon or many of the other great monuments of the American West. The idea of fearfully creeping to a parapet in order to look over it is what we actually do at the Grand Canyon but not at Natural Bridge. Jefferson had been reading Edmund Burke's *Philosophical Enquiry into the Origins of Our Ideas of the Sublime and the Beautiful* (1757), which led the future president to approach Natural Bridge with his own preconceptions.[4]

The British statesman-to-be Edmund Burke offered philosophies about the landscape that guided connoisseurs and artists in Europe and North America for more than a century. He wrote that the Beautiful has nothing to do with proportion, symmetry, or rules but is found in whatever "induce[s] in us a sense of affection and tenderness."[5] He found beauty in things that are small, smooth, varied in form, or delicate, like a rose or the bend of a swan's neck—elements that have little relevance for a landscape painter who works on a grand scale. Burke's greatest influence came from his explanation of the Sublime, which he defined as a sensation emanating from those forces of nature that threaten our self-preservation and make us aware of the futility of human arrangements—from tidal waves and cataracts to stillness, darkness, and death. In 1816, the American writer James Kirke Paulding, who also read Burke, further explained: There is no point in measuring dimensions to understand the effect of the Sublime, because what matters is the effect. At Natural Bridge, "my knees shook under me" when looking down, and from below "I was struck with a feeling of sublimity which no object I have ever seen had hitherto inspired."[6] At the bridge, he added, the effect is created by a combination of factors that are at play to create the effect—notably simplicity, name, and sense of duration.

The association of Natural Bridge with the Sublime made by Jefferson and Paulding was remembered by a number of those who followed them to Natural Bridge, but the responses of travelers would change dramatically with time. The minister Archibald Alexander wrote, in 1842, that he "never saw one . . . who did not view the object with considerable emotion," and he described his own "sudden" and "entirely new" response at the bridge as the "animal sensation which accompanied the genuine emotion of the sublime."[7] But, after the Civil War, the popularity of Natural Bridge and its visitation plummeted, in part because the more dramatic natural monuments of the American West had by then become famous. The bridge seemed almost an oddity to some of its post-war visitors. In 1870, Edward Pollard could suggest that it is both "sublime" and "pleasing and curious." In 1880, Mary Allan-Olney considered it "not frightful or stupendous" but instead "very wonderful as a freak of nature, and made a very pretty picture." In 1896, a traveler self-identified only as E.L.B., could claim to find "peace and calm" there: "It is one of those spots of earth that seem made for rest." Today, when I visit Natural Bridge, I am conflicted like Edward Pollard: I am struck by the impressive size of the structure, and I also find it "pleasing and curious." Perhaps some of those same feelings can be read in Andrei Kushnir's view of the bridge.[8]

The story surrounding the landscape of Harpers Ferry also starts at Thomas Jefferson's Monticello; it reached a less controversial conclusion because there Jefferson hedged his bets and offered alternative approaches to the landscape. Standing on high ground above the town, he imagined the confluence of the two rivers (Potomac and Shenandoah) breaking through the mountains in a stupendous collision, "a war between rivers and mountains, which must have shaken the earth itself to its center." The sight, he said, is "worth a voyage across the Atlantic [Ocean]."[9] Some observers, including Paulding, agreed: Its "lofty barriers of solid rock" are "both rugged, and of the full height of sublimity."[10] Others, however, were disappointed when they compared the reality of that landscape with Jefferson's description. In 1800, Isaac Weld complained that "it would be needless to go farther than Wales" to find "numberless scenes more stupendous."[11] In 1854, William Gilmore Simms, a leading literary figure of the Old South, rejected outright the idea of sublimity there: Jefferson is a "humbug" on this, because Harpers Ferry "in no place rises above the picturesque." The rivers,

Potomac River at Harpers Ferry, West Virginia
OIL ON CANVAS, 10" X 14," MAY 12, 2014 (PAINTING #199).

View of Three States from Hilltop House, Harpers Ferry
OIL ON PANEL, 8" X 12," MAY 19, 2014 (PAINTING #198).

he argued, "neither rive, nor rend, nor rage, nor roar among the rocks."[12] Today, we are inclined to agree with Simms, except, perhaps, when severe flooding follows major storms. In 1972, for example, Hurricane Agnes brought more than thirty-seven times the normal flow of water through the gap. In 1936, an earlier storm (unnamed and recorded only as the hurricane of September 18–19) brought fifty-two times more.

Jefferson had preceded Simms in using Harpers Ferry to introduce a third aesthetic for the landscape enthusiastic to consider: the Picturesque. The idea that a landscape was "like or suitable for a picture" would have lasting relevance in American art. Its origin lies with another author of the Enlightenment, the Reverend William Gilpin, who appreciated the wild and rugged mountain scenery of his native Cumbria in the far north of England and contemplated the aesthetics of landscape beauty. In his *Essay on Prints* (1768), Gilpin argued that a gentle scene with rough surfaces and irregular outlines can be as beautiful as those delicate forms in nature that Edmund Burke had identified, and he introduced the idea of "picturesque beauty," by which he meant "that kind of beauty which is agreeable in a picture."[13] Such a vision was akin to the landscapes that the famous seventeenth-century French landscapist Claude Lorrain had constructed on canvas. Several decades later, Uvedale Price, an English Baronet and amateur scholar with a strong interest in aesthetics, rejected the idea that the Picturesque is merely a subcategory of the Beautiful in his *Essay on the Picturesque* (1820). Price, who enjoyed a following in nineteenth-century America and whose writing rejuvenated interest in the subject, refined the term to mean like a picture with interesting elements that are well composed.[14]

Jefferson found "the distant finishing [at Harpers Ferry] . . . placid and delightful."[15] Few would disagree with that description. It beckoned Americans and foreigners alike to visit the site. Once the U.S. Congress decided, in 1790, to move the seat of the U.S. government from New York City to the Potomac River (though it would take ten years for Washington, D.C., to become the nation's permanent capital), visitation of the entire region increased. In 1797, Louis Philippe, the future king of France, endorsed Jefferson's enthusiasm for Harpers Ferry and added a comparative embellishment: "The banks of the river [there] are charming, and the whole region looks like Switzerland."[16] In 1835, William James Bennett used the medium of watercolor, in "Looking Across the Shenandoah Towards Harpers Ferry," to depict a bucolic and peaceful setting aglow with the tranquil light of late afternoon. Two decades later, William Gilmore Simms put Bennett's luminous vision into poetic language: "Beauty is here, and dignity, and the eye lingers with gratification upon the sweet pictures which are made of the scene, at the rising and the setting of the sun." Simms repeated the now oft-used terms "pleasing and picturesque" to describe Harpers Ferry; Samuel Mordecai, also in the 1850s, ranked the setting "the most singularly picturesque in America"; and, today, Andrei Kushnir shows us why high praise can still be bestowed on the region.[17]

Today, in the twenty-first century, few of us live on the land, so we need landscape art more than ever. For the past fifty years, our enjoyment of the land has been blocked by our uneasiness about its fragility. The Virginia landscape has been threatened by a series of changes—dramatic population increases, urban expansion (emanating out of Washington, D.C., and other major cities), and environmental contamination (particularly the dumping of the chemical insecticide kepone into the James River, the massive scale of the poultry-breeding industry in the Valley, and the now-present threat of rising sea levels along the Atlantic Coast). During the 1990s, landscape painters gave expression to our concern and melancholy. But, as nature writers predicted decades ago, we now seem ready to look again at Virginia's varied landscapes and learn what we can from them. As Annie Dillard wrote more that forty years ago, from her home in Roanoke, we can at least learn where we have been set down, even if we can't learn why. We can learn how we belong to this earth.[18]

And this prompts a few questions: Are we ready for nature worship like that of the nineteenth century? Do we believe what the English poet William Wordsworth preached, that "the passions of man are incorporated with the beautiful and permanent forms of nature," and "One impulse from a vernal wood / May teach you more of man, / Of moral evil and of good, / Than all the sages can"?[19] Do we, like the French Barbizon painters, believe that the moods of nature provide a means to help recover traditional values and a simpler rural past? Probably not. But we do seem poised to immerse ourselves in nature and find out what we may have been missing.

What path, then, should today's landscape painter follow? Some artists are intent to explore and record the environment in which they live—simply because it is what surrounds them. But if a painter wants his or her creation to elicit sensations of beauty and calm and life-enhancement in its viewers, the first consideration is to find an exceptionally picturesque setting. This should be obvious. The artist should search the countryside and critique each potential setting as if it were a work of art. If the landscape under consideration is not exceptional or revealing, the artist should keep looking.

Charles Joseph La Trobe (spelled "Latrobe" in his publications), an Englishman who visited America in 1835 fresh from mountaineering in the Alps, argued, in 1835, that, "taken as a whole," America is "far from possessing a fair proportion of . . . picturesque scenery. . . . The abrupt outlines of surface, so usual in the Old World . . . are of much rarer occurrence in the New." Writing at the conclusion of a very long American journey, where he had traveled in "every State [save one] and Territory in the Union," La Trobe was thinking primarily of the extensive "tracts of forest and prairie" that he encountered in the Midwest. But he also stated, "It is in vain to look for [the] common occurrence [of picturesque scenery] . . . between the Allegheny and the Atlantic." How did he fail to discover the Shangri-La of picturesque scenes in the Valley of Virginia that Andrei Kushnir shows us? La Trobe did manage to visit Harpers Ferry, which he ranked "one of the most striking scenes in the United States . . . [with] fine picturesque scenery . . . for the distance of a mile up both rivers." He planned a trip from Lynchburg to Natural Bridge and the Shenandoah Valley, but his travel there was prevented by "floods on all sides." As a result, La Trobe saw almost nothing of the Valley.[20]

Andrei Kushnir assures us that a plethora of scenes throughout the Shenandoah Valley remain remarkably undisturbed. With hindsight, we can wonder if its remoteness—which thwarted La Trobe—is not, in the end, an asset. In addition to the Arcadia of tidy farms and well-ordered fields, noted by travelers since the 1760 description by Andrew Burnaby of "the most delightful climate, and richest soil imaginable," today one can find parks in the Valley that the federal government and

Shenandoah Reflections along the South Fork, near Bentonville
OIL ON CANVAS, 5" X 7," AUGUST 27, 2007 (PAINTING #127).

private individuals have put into trust for future Americans.[21] These include Shenandoah National Park, a remarkable recycled landscape that has actually returned to wilderness after five decades of preservation, and Sky Meadows Park.

It should be no surprise that the Valley beckons to the landscape painter, because more than two centuries of travel literature have associated these areas with bountiful harvests, rainbows, ideal weather, and tranquility. When Thomas Jefferson jested in 1788, "Our own country . . . is made on an improved plan. Europe is a first idea, a crude production, before the maker knew his trade," he was thinking of these regions, which he knew well.[22] In 1854, William Gilmore Simms waxed at length about the picturesque nature of the Valley landscape as the "most perfect idea of Arcadia," with "charms . . . to inspire the most perfect idylls," where "the farmer may become the poet," and where "thought, enlivened by the picturesque, may rise to a constant enjoyment of imagination." Simms predicted fame for the Valley once it was more developed: "[A]s prosperity leads to leisure," the region will "be justly known, in all its charms and treasures," he wrote.[23] The Valley actually became famous a little earlier than Simms predicted, due to the Civil War, which brought Walt Whitman and many others there who recognized its beauty even in the midst of the turmoil of war. After the war, a spirit of renewal was often in evidence there. George Bagby wrote, in *Picturesque America* (1872), "From Harpers Ferry to the farthest southwest corner of the State there is literally a world of scenic beauties, ravishing to the artist, and inviting to even the dullest traveler or sight-seer."[24]

The experience of Russell Smith, an artist from Pennsylvania, along the western ridge of the Valley during the 1840s helps us to understand better the relevance of the Picturesque to the painter of the Virginia landscape. Accompanying a geological expedition led by William Barton Rogers of the University of Virginia, Smith sketched west of Harrisonburg (close to the present-day West Virginia line). He worked in the field with the linear precision of those earliest American artists who delineated, defined, and thereby hoped to understand an unsettled setting that was new to them. A linear, flat, reductive style seemed compatible with forthrightness, honesty, accuracy, and science. Bright light was valued, because it gives clarity of vision and freshness that makes distant features visible. When Smith returned to the studio to produce finished oil paintings developed from his drawings, however, he altered just about everything in order to transform his raw and honest landscape sketches into picturesque views—to make those images more "like pictures," to make the landscape softer and thus more comforting and appealing to the viewer.[25] The word "softer" is borrowed here from Henry Ruffner, the president of Washington College (now Washington and Lee University), who only a few years earlier, in 1839, had explained what in the landscape appealed to him and what also interests us today. Looking down from House Mountain outside of Lexington, "a thousand farms . . . were distinctly visible. . . . [T]he Blue Ridge mustered a hundred of his lofty heads. . . . [N]ear the base of my observatory, I was attracted by the softer beauties of the landscape. The woody hillocks and shady glens had lost every rough and disagreeable feature; the surface looked smooth and green like a meadow and wound its curvatures, dappled with shade and sunlight, so gracefully to the elevated eye that they seemed to realize our dreamy conceptions of fairy land."[26] This description calls to my mind a number of Andrei Kushnir's paintings. Looking down on a setting that is well lit, the viewer feels as if the artist has provided the viewer with

From the Top of Shenandoah Mountain
OIL ON CANVAS, 6" X 8," MAY 23, 2011 (PAINTING #39).

Evening, Shenandoah Sycamore along the South Fork (Study), Page County
OIL ON PANEL, 6" X 8," OCTOBER 24, 2010 (PAINTING #139).

what the art historian Kenneth Clark has called magic spectacles that enlarge our range of physical perceptions and thus heighten our sense of well being.[27] In the twentieth-first century, when the landscape has been photographed by satellites, we are well past the point of wanting topographical art. Increasingly, we seem to be in need of the restorative powers of *landscape*—at least as much as Henry Ruffner was when his outing allowed all "to return with gratified feelings to our college and our studies again."[28]

A second priority for today's landscape painter is to study the masters in order to learn the tricks of the trade. The painter must adopt devices that recreate, on a two-dimensional surface, an accumulation of sensations experienced in the field, because the artist has to incorporate into one image the total experience of being immersed in an actual setting. Andrei Kushnir's skillful utilization of such devices is evident throughout this book. In this way, he captures qualities of the Picturesque and makes a difficult task appear effortless.

This leads us back to Claude Lorrain, the French painter whose canvases everyone had in mind during the eighteenth and nineteenth centuries when the word "picturesque" was used—and who, for four centuries, artists have considered the master of that genre. Claude offered a vision of how nature can be laid out like a park for the enjoyment of man, and in the process he provided a model for European and American painters to follow. Many landscapists following Claude have revisited his wistful images of a better world. Many have concluded that a landscape is worthy of consideration only if it can be developed into a Claudian composition.

The Frenchman structured his canvases like a stage set that has coulisses on either side, which serve to lead the eye, gradually and gently, through planes of spaces. On one side is a large and dark tree; a shadow extends across the land and defines the foreground. The middle plane is established by a second coulisse on the opposite side—perhaps a group of trees. The eye is lured across water through two additional planes, the second of which is distant and luminous. Benjamin Henry Latrobe, the American architect and landscapist, in his *Essay on Landscape* (1798), wrote that Claude's canvases "live": "The spectator can travel in them. You almost feel the warmth of his Sun, or the coolness of his breeze, which appear to wave the vegetating foliage."[29] Latrobe routinely borrowed Claude's formula for his painting compositions. He would step back to establish a foreground, then reposition elements as he transformed the Virginia landscape into a picturesque vision.

It would be hard for me to understand the success of Andrei Kushnir's paintings without imagining how the example of Claude's mastery of space, light, and color underlie it. Landscape is, first and foremost, about space, and Claude's entire formula was designed to convey a sense of space. The viewer often stands either low or relatively low in the landscape, and trees serve to layer the progression of his vision inward. Kushnir does this as well. And Claude routinely introduced an expanse of water into his composition, as does Kushnir. Not only does the water serve to suggest the expanse of the setting, but water is welcome in a calming, picturesque landscape, because, as Annie Dillard argues, water is the element that is key to understanding nature. "If the day is fine, any walk will do; it all looks good . . . " she writes, "[b]ut I go to the water." In his canvases, Kushnir often takes us there.[30]

A different but equally effective mastery of space is found in the paintings of Paul Cézanne, the late-nineteenth-century French post-Impressionist who invented new ways to convey the vitality—with an almost gravitational pull—of objects that occupy space. His purpose was to suggest on canvas the sensation of viewing nature. Cézanne did this with still lifes that show fruit on a table top. And, with the landscape, he famously and repeatedly depicted Mont Sainte-Victoire in the background, with a tree branch dangling in the foreground, a technique which established the picture plane of the canvas and set into motion a push-and-pull between that plane and the illusion of a mountain far in the distance. Andrei Kushnir's mastery of this device is evident in several of the images in this book. This is one way that he is able to paint a landscape that is not just wide, but also deep.

Kenneth Clark has written that the landscape painter's greatest gift is an emotional response to light; it is through light that love of landscape is expressed.[31] In the paintings of Claude, it is the remarkable tonality of light that unites all of the elements and makes his poetic vision seem convincing. Clark adds that emotion is most convincingly conveyed in the poignant moment of twilight, when the landscape seems to give back the light it has absorbed all day. It does that at other times as well, and at any moment light can be made to play across a scene and bring objects and nature to life. This happens with passing clouds, as the English artist John Constable demonstrated. He famously wrote that the sky is the chief organ of sentiment and that the best lesson for the landscapist is that light and shade never stand still.

Kushnir's use of light and shade is noteworthy. But light, by itself, will not sufficiently convey the warmth of the sun, the coolness of the breeze, or the artist's love of the landscape, its beauty, its sense of calm and life-enhancement—all components of the picturesque landscape—without the introduction of warm, radiant color. In both Cézanne's still lifes and his landscapes, he strenuously avoided excessive modeling of form in order not to diminish the effect of both his color and his patterned and deep designs. Color is even more critical to the painter of the picturesque landscape. Without it, the beauty is lost, as is much of the calm. Kushnir demonstrates the importance of color in scenes where the viewer stands low in the landscape and is immersed in it. Color is a vital part of the experience. The feeling of atmosphere and moisture in the air, the tonality of changing outdoor light, the sense of nature's process of renewal, the artist's joy in the visible world—the illusion of all of this would be lost without a sensitive handling of color.

A component of Claude's poetic vision is a human presence on the land, to suggest the myth of Arcadia—the idea that a Golden Age of the past, marked by peaceful simplicity, was a part of a Western heritage that should be remembered and cherished. Claude often included elements from antiquity—notably architectural fragments that poignantly speak about ancient civilizations. Charles La Trobe, who complained about the dearth of picturesque sites in a monotonous American landscape ("where the forest still covers so large a portion of both mountain and plain"), placed part of the blame on the inhabitants: "What nature has to a certain degree denied, man has done but little to remedy," he quipped. "As to ancient architecture, it is not necessary to remind you that there is none."[32]

Two hundred years later, however, the American landscape has changed markedly. In painting the Valley today, an artist unavoidably encounters the architectural remains of multiple centuries of settlement. To local residents, at least, these human-made elements are to be valued, and they are

Canoe Launch on the South Fork, near Bentonville
OIL ON PANEL, 5" X 7," JULY 21, 2002 (PAINTING #21).

part of the entire nation's heritage. When so much of the architectural landscape of early America has been lost, as old buildings have been either destroyed or encroached upon by newer structures, the settings and lifestyles of earlier centuries can be seen as part of an American Golden Age when man had not intruded too much into the setting. From that viewpoint, Andrei Kushnir has worked intuitively to record, with a sense of respect and appreciation, the Valley's landscape as it appears today. As time passes, the landscapes in this book that picture architecture can only become increasingly valuable as that architecture disappears.

Today, of course, that future holds limited interest. Instead, we respond so intuitively and profoundly to the landscapes in this book because they affect us in the present. My wife's sister and her husband live near the town of Paris, along the Blue Ridge on top of a mountain that overlooks, far in the distance, Sky Meadows State Park. On a clear day, the view is expansive and spectacular. But only rarely can I enjoy that view and the life-enhancement it provides. As a memorable and inspirational substitute, I turn to beautiful and engaging paintings like those by Andrei Kushnir, who, with his book, presents us a valuable and enduring gift.

Rockfish Gap, Overlook 2 from the Skyline Drive
OIL ON CANVAS, 6" X 8," JULY 12, 2011 (PAINTING #115).

*The North Fork at Red Banks, Shenandoah County**

OIL ON CANVAS, 30" X 40," SEPTEMBER 22–OCTOBER 1, 2008 (PAINTING #130).

Plein-air-Painting:
An Interview with Andrei Kushnir

Andrei Kushnir has been asked many questions about his artistry at museum gatherings and exhibitions and other public venues and speaking engagements. Here are his answers to the questions most often asked of him.

What is plein-air painting? Can you convey where it started; that is, what are its known origins?

"Plein air" is a term normally used with landscape painting. It is a French expression that means painting "in the open air" or out-of-doors, and it is distinct from studio painting, which is performed in a more controlled environment. Plein air is the most direct form of painting, in that the artist attempts to capture a specific subject during a limited amount of time. Thus, plein air paintings tend to be more spontaneous and rely on the artist's knowledge of fleeting light, conventions of effective design, and quick execution of the painting in one session. Before photography, making a sketch on site, including color notes, was the only way an artist could, more or less, accurately capture a scene. Contemporary plein air paintings are often considered finished works, rather than studies.

It is known that the Chinese and ancient Greeks painted landscapes, though whether they relied on field studies is uncertain, as their works were often stylized and lacked perspective and scale. I would say the Dutch were the earliest Western artists who painted landscapes as we have come to know them, with large areas of the canvas depicting sky hovering over a low horizon and landscape filled with natural scenery such as fields, hills, and mountains and often featuring structures and sometimes bodies of water. While most of these Dutch paintings were produced in the studio, the natural phenomena depicted must have been sketched on site in order to preserve accurately the relationships of the various natural and cultural details of the scene.

Plein-air painting came of age during the nineteenth century. By then, watercolors had been around for a long time, and painting with them was easily done by applying water to hardened pigments and brushing the colors onto paper. The Germans, Italians, English, French, and others across Europe were expert in this medium. Regarding oils, tubes were introduced at this time, which made carrying paints into the field easier than powdered pigments or bladders containing pigments already mixed with linseed oil. The pochade box was invented about the same time, and an artist could cram all of the necessary materials into one easily transportable container. By the mid-nineteenth century, the practice of plein air watercolor and oil painting was known throughout Europe and the United States.

Who are some of the major artists who implemented plein-air painting? Which ones influenced you personally?

Foremost among early plein-air painters was Englishman John Constable (1776–1837), who not only created small works out-of-doors, but also made large studies (four by five feet, or more!) in preparation for finished studio paintings. These studies allowed him to express the feeling of a place with great clarity and resonance. Constable's works sparked the Barbizon movement in France, whose artists attempted to depict the natural world as it is, rather than as idealized scenes popularized by academic painting at the time. Theodore Rousseau (1812–1867), Jean-Françoise Millet (1814–1875), and Charles-François Daubigny (1817–1878) were some of the major artists in that movement, which was centered near the Forest of Fontainebleau outside Paris. These theories about landscape ultimately spread across Europe.

At the same time, in England, the influential art critic John Ruskin (1819–1900) further developed the idea that artists should rely on close observation of nature in his five-volume work, *Modern Painters* (1843–1860), which extolled the paintings of J. M. W. Turner (1775–1851), known for his watercolors, plein-air studies, and interest in the effects of light on a scene. Ruskin held that plein-air painting is the most direct way to achieve truth in nature with regard to depicting landscapes.

Ruskin's ideas had a great effect on landscape painters, art criticism, and collecting in the United States, and he was the touchstone for artists of the Hudson River School. These artists, based in New York City, where the market for their works centered, depicted picturesque, pastoral, and wilderness scenes surrounding the Hudson River and, later, other scenic locations in New England, the Mid-Atlantic, and eventually the American West and South America. Their intent was to express the romantic and often sublime sides of Nature in a naturalistic, convincing way. My favorite Hudson River School artists include Albert Bierstadt (1830–1902), Frederick E. Church (1826–1900), Thomas Cole (1801–1848), Sanford R. Gifford (1823–1880), John F. Kensett (1816–1872), Jervis McEntee (1828–1891), A. D. Shattuck (1832–1928), and T. Worthington Whittredge (1820–1910).

Beginning in 1874, the French Barbizon naturalist school began to give way to a group of Parisian painters, the French Impressionists, who regarded plein-air painting as central to their ideas of expressing ordinary, contemporary subjects in natural light by using broken, visible brushstrokes.

These influenced American artists, who flocked to Paris, and schools of American Impressionist painters soon developed in places such as Long Island, Cos Cob and Old Lyme, Connecticut, and California. After a period of relative neglect during the advent of modern and non-objective art movements in the twentieth century, plein-air painting today again enjoys a huge resurgence in popularity, with attendant magazines, festivals, competitions, and exhibitions.

I was first attracted to the idea of plein-air painting after being given, in the late 1970s, a five-volume set (1951–1964) of the artistic works of Ukrainian artist and poet, Taras Shevchenko (1814–1861). Several hundred of the images depicted watercolor paintings he did on site in various locations in Ukraine and central Asia, where he had been exiled. The paintings evocatively depicted the rivers, forests, deserts, settlements, and other elements of the landscapes he sketched on site. I was moved by the way they drew the viewer emotionally into the scene, creating "a sense of place." This has become an objective in my own work.

Another substantial influence was a book I found, also in the late 1970s, in the Washington, D.C., Public Library about the Hudson River School painters. I forget the title, but the thrust of this book was that these artists loved being out-of-doors and would just as much enjoy tromping in the woods and hunting and fishing as painting. It was their spirit of adventure and the memorable paintings they produced while engaged in roaming and enjoying the countryside that caught my interest. I thought to myself, "Now, that is what I want to do!"

Finally, while on vacation in New England in the early 1980s, I met the great-granddaughter of painter A. D. Shattuck and purchased from her one of his plein-air studies of a riverbend. I have enjoyed and studied that painting over many years and still learn from it.

When did you become entranced by plein-air painting, and how and where did you begin such work?

I always had an artistic bent, even since grade school, and in high school and college was a cartoonist for the school's newspapers. Afterwards, I experimented with colored chalks and acrylics, but the honesty of Shevchenko's watercolors and the Hudson River School painters' adventurous spirit drew me to landscape subjects, and the Shattuck painting inspired me to try to create something similarly precious.

My first oils were painted at the kitchen table during the early 1980s, after our daughter, Larissa, was born. I remember setting up a table-top easel and working from photographs while she slept nearby in her small crib. One fine day in the spring, I looked outside and thought, "This is nuts—I'm sitting here indoors, painting an outdoor scene, and not having much fun." So, after doing a little research, I mail-ordered an aluminum tripod and worked up an outdoor painting set-up, where I only had to carry the tripod and paint box, which held a loaded palette, brushes, a rag, panels on which to paint, and the tubes of every color on the palette. It was simple, light, and is essentially the same set-up I still use.

During the late 1980s, I took a few landscape painting classes with artist Michael Francis at the Alexandria (VA) Art League and started using his recommended palette colors. I worked on small canvasses and panels for about ten years, painting outdoors every chance I got. I liked the finished look of the Hudson River School artists, so I touched up my paintings afterwards, often making small adjustments, sometimes over many years. During the late 1990s, my art dealer in Washington, D.C., artist Michele Taylor, helped me transition to larger works, by advising me to use the same level of effort and care as on the smaller ones (and not just rely on bigger brushes and more paint!).

Painting *en plein air* forces the artist to work quickly, and the technique is unforgiving if you select a bad view: No matter what colors or how much bravura you might employ, your resulting design will result in a bad painting, though, of course, you can always move around the various elements in the painting. Often the best spot is under a shady tree, but more often it is not. So a hat, sunscreen, long pants, long-sleeved shirt, and boots are a must. I just hate getting sunburned and having insects crawling on my arms and legs. Nevertheless, one should be prepared to sweat profusely during summer or lose feeling in your toes from freezing temperatures in winter.

What is your a*pproach to selecting a place to paint, and what are the challenges and rewards of working outdoors?*

The location and scene to be painted are very important. If a site is on private property, permission should be obtained. You will rarely be refused, and often the owner or residents will help you out in some meaningful way. Sometimes, the location will be a scene I have painted before on a smaller scale, or where I love to be, or is visually stimulating for me. Many artists enjoy commissioned work, but I have undertaken that only when I felt a personal connection to the client and site.

Over the years, I have also developed a set-up that seems to work well when undertaking larger-scale paintings (24 x 30 inches or larger). If I have not painted a scene previously, I will do a smaller study (8 x 12 inches or so) to evaluate the design and suitability of the image for a larger-scale work. Once I decide on the necessary size and shape of the canvas, I affix one or two rods to the wooden stretcher back, for ease of carrying the canvas to the site. The trunk of the car is covered with plastic sheeting. A 30 x 40 inch painting will usually take about eight to ten sessions of four to five hours each, excluding the time of travel. Morning paintings need to be worked on only in the morning; the same holds true for afternoon paintings. Of course, the weather must be consistent.

The time limitations in this approach are actually beneficial, for they force the artist to keep on task; otherwise, the scene will change too much. Mosquitoes, tiny hornets, rain, wind, and an occasional goat or snarling dog can disturb you, but then you see shimmering rivers, spectacular skies, and landscapes and hear the trilling of songbirds and rustling of leaves in the treetops, making the field work so worthwhile.

How long does it take you to compose a plein-air painting? Do you always finish it on site, or are there occasions *when you finish or embellish it in the studio?*

Depending on the size of the painting, it might take twenty minutes to ten days or more to complete a plein-air painting. The smallest paintings in this book were quickly done and tightened up later that evening. For example, it was snowing while I quickly painted "Winter Twilight, Shenandoah Town Park (page 116), and, when I got to the motel, the painting was unrecognizable. With a few brushstrokes, however, it seemed miraculously to reconstitute itself! "Shenandoah River Skies" (page 106), on the other hand, was begun in earnest on the shore of the South Fork of the Shenandoah River, before the cloud in the painting actually rolled in and washed me out. It rained for almost the next two weeks that year, and, by the time I could go back, many of the leaves had fallen, and the scene had changed. I only completed the painting recently, using the studies made when I painted at the site, which are included in this book.

For those who may wish to paint en plein air *in the Shenandoah Valley, what advice might you give?*

The Shenandoah Valley is an extremely fertile source of subjects for plein-air painting. An artist could start with the views of the Valley from the Skyline Drive and Blue Ridge Parkway, which were among the sites of my earliest paintings. I love the long views of the fields and forests, with Massanutten Mountain and North Mountain in the background, a perfect foil for creating hazy Valley views and colorful sunsets.

After meeting Jeff Everett, my original perspective of painting the Shenandoah Valley changed. While I love the idea of painting from high up on a place called "Wildcat Ledge," Jeff, who grew up in the Valley, inflamed my plein-air passion by talking of Valley places with names like Meems Bottom, Orkney Springs, Red Banks, Rudes Hill, and Singers Glen. He enticed me further by describing the delightful meals one can sample at the Amherst Diner in Winchester, the Southern Kitchen restaurant in New Market, and Mrs. Rowe's in Staunton. After standing all day on a windy hill in the Blue Ridge Mountains, what could be better? If you decide to paint in the Valley, be sure to eat local—you will rarely be disappointed—and I am convinced your paintings will benefit. The Valley is lined with inexpensive motels and other lodging options, some of them first class (if you want to splurge!), which serve well as crash pads, if you should decide to stay overnight.

After more than 260 paintings of various sizes made in almost every corner of the Valley, I have still just scratched the surface of the Valley's cornucopia of visual treats. During my travels to capture specific views, I would pass many, many beckoning spots that are still begging for an artist with an easel. And any place depicted in this collection is an excellent candidate for views at another time of year or time of day. By all means, an artist should paint on site as often as possible. The Valley changes with every day and every season, and an artist can enjoy working within a noble tradition in one of the most beautiful and interesting places on Earth. As an artist I know once said, "Now, that is what I want to do!"

*Overlook 1, Shenandoah Valley from the Skyline Drive, near Front Royal**
OIL ON PANEL, 9" X 12," NOVEMBER 14, 2011 (PAINTING #142).

Overlook 2, Shenandoah Valley from the Skyline Drive, near Front Royal
OIL ON PANEL, 6" X 8," NOVEMBER 14, 2011 (PAINTING #124).

Painting the Shenandoah Valley: Three Portfolios by Andrei Kushnir

Although Andrei Kushnir's paintings are presented strategically throughout the entire book, the following three portfolios were created and sequenced in such a way that they represent traditional travel on three primary roadways in the Shenandoah Valley:

Portfolio I: From Harpers Ferry, West Virginia, at the confluence of the Shenandoah and Potomac Rivers, to Lexington, Virginia, along U.S. 340;

Portfolio II: From Williamsport, Maryland, a traditional crossing on the Potomac River, to Lexington, Virginia, along U.S. 11, known historically as the Valley Turnpike (Pike) or Valley Road;

Portfolio III: From Woodstock, Virginia, to Lexington, Virginia, along VA 42 and 252.

Beginning with the earliest Euro-American settlers during the seventeenth and eighteenth centuries, newcomers to the Shenandoah Valley experienced the Valley for the first time either by river or road. The three portfolios that follow thus allow the reader to experience the Valley historically in a similar way, discovering the Valley's rich cultural, natural, and urban landscapes along these three roads from both north-to-south and south-to-north directions.

Visitors to the Valley are also encouraged to explore the region by the many other roadways and riverways, including numerous scenic byways on land and on water. Perhaps they will follow along in the footsteps of Andrei Kushnir, bringing with them not only their cameras, but also, for some, an easel to conduct plein-air painting, rendering their experiences in a timeless and meaningful way.

PORTFOLIO I

Harpers Ferry to Lexington along U.S. 340

Detail, *White Post* (page 88)

Oh, Shenandoah,
I long to see you,
Away, you rolling river.
Oh, Shenandoah,
I long to hear you,
Away, we're bound away
'Cross the wide Missouri.

—First stanza of "Oh, Shenandoah" (1882)

*Harpers Ferry, West Virginia, from Sandy Hook Road, Maryland**
OIL ON PANEL, 7" X 12," MAY 10, 2010 (PAINTING #57).

Harpers Ferry, West Virginia, from Jefferson Rock (St. Peter's Catholic Church)
OIL ON CANVAS, 6" X 8," MAY 10, 2010 (PAINTING #56).

Shenandoah River from Under the U.S. 340 Bridge, Harpers Ferry
OIL ON CANVAS, 14" X 18," MAY 10, 2010 (PAINTING #40).

*Race Track, Charles Town, West Virginia**
OIL ON PANEL, 7" X 12," APRIL 21, 2015 (PAINTING #221).

Edge Hill Cemetery (Confederate Section), Charles Town, West Virginia
OIL ON PANEL, 6" X 12.5," APRIL 21, 2015 (PAINTING #232).

Rainbow Road Club, Rippon, West Virginia
OIL ON PANEL, 8" X 12," JUNE 5, 2011 (PAINTING #110).

Historic Post Office, Gaylord, Virginia
OIL ON PANEL, 4" X 6," JUNE 5, 2011 (PAINTING #58).

God and Country at Watermelon Park, near Berryville
OIL ON PANEL, 7" X 12," OCTOBER 12, 2010 (PAINTING #50).

Shenandoah River at Watermelon Park, near Berryville
OIL ON CANVAS, 18" X 24," OCTOBER 12, 2010 (PAINTING #131).

Private Property along the Shenandoah River at Watermelon Park, near Berryville
OIL ON CANVAS, 9" X 12," OCTOBER 11, 2010 (PAINTING #107).

Bears Den from the Rocks, Appalachian Trail, Clarke County
OIL ON CANVAS, 6" X 8," OCTOBER 12, 2010 (PAINTING #9).

Winter Evening, Shenandoah River, Clarke County
OIL ON PANEL, 7" X 12," MARCH 13, 2011 (PAINTING #177).

January, Shenandoah River at Hardin Island, Clarke and Warren Counties
OIL ON CANVAS, 9" X 12," JANUARY 16, 2011 (PAINTING #64).

January, Shenandoah River from the Top of Blue Ball, Clarke County
OIL ON LINEN, 16" X 20," JANUARY 16, 2011 (PAINTING #65).

Millwood in November
OIL ON PANEL, 8" X 12," NOVEMBER 5, 2012 (PAINTING #189).

Two Riders, Blandy Experimental Farm, near White Post
OIL ON PANEL, 6" X 8," MAY 10, 2011 (PAINTING #167).

Three Willows, Blandy Experimental Farm, near White Post
OIL ON CANVAS, 20" X 24," MAY 10, 2011 (PAINTING #161).

Side Entrance, Quarters Building, Blandy Experimental Farm, near White Post
OIL ON PANEL, 6" X 8," MAY 10, 2011 (PAINTING #146).

*The Quarters Building, Blandy Experimental Farm, near White Post**
OIL ON LINEN, 9" X 12," MAY 10, 2011 (PAINTING #108).

*White Post**

OIL ON PANEL, 8" X 12," OCTOBER 16, 2011 (PAINTING #174).

Dinosaur Land, Double Toll Gate

OIL ON ALUMINUM PANEL, 8"X 10," MARCH 24, 2015 (PAINTING #210).

[top] *Evening Landscape 1, Front Royal*
OIL ON PANEL, 4" X 8," SEPTEMBER 14, 2010 (PAINTING #45).

[bottom] *Evening Landscape 2, Front Royal*
OIL ON PANEL, 4" X 8," SEPTEMBER 14, 2010 (PAINTING #47).

Front Royal from Guard Hill Road
OIL ON PANEL, 10" X 16," SEPTEMBER 14, 2010 (PAINTING #44).

Campground, Front Royal
OIL ON PANEL, 8" X 12," AUGUST 15, 2010 (PAINTING #43).

The North Fork Joining the South Fork at Queens Highway in Riverton, Front Royal
OIL ON CANVAS, 6" X 8," JUNE 8, 2010 (PAINTING #46).

Boat Landing, Looking East, Front Royal
OIL ON CANVAS, 18" X 24," JUNE 8, 2010 (PAINTING #41).

Boat Landing, Looking West, Front Royal
oil on panel, 8" x 12," june 8, 2010 (painting #42).

Spelunker's, Front Royal
OIL ON PANEL, 5" X 7," SEPTEMBER 24, 2013 (PAINTING #197).

Warren County Courthouse, Front Royal
OIL ON PANEL, 8"X 12," APRIL 6, 2015 (PAINTING #220).

Pioneer Motel, Front Royal
OIL ON PANEL, 9" X 12," APRIL 6, 2015 (PAINTING #219).

*Detrick, Fort Valley**
OIL ON PANEL, 8" X 16," APRIL 4, 2011 (PAINTING #25).

Fort Valley Farm, near Dilbeck
OIL ON PANEL, 9" X 12," APRIL 4, 2011 (PAINTING #36).

Dry Run Christian Church, Fort Valley
OIL ON CANVAS, 9" X 12," APRIL 4, 2011 (PAINTING #26).

[top] *South Fork of the Shenandoah River (Study), Warren County*
OIL ON PANEL, 8" X 12," JULY 16, 2002 (PAINTING #135).

[bottom] *Riverbend on the South Fork, Warren County*
OIL ON CANVAS, 6" X 8," AUGUST 27, 2007 (PAINTING #27).

[top] *Oxbow on the South Fork, Warren County*
OIL ON CANVAS, 8" X 16," OCTOBER 1, 2004 (PAINTING #125).

[bottom] *Oxbow on the South Fork (Study), Warren County*
OIL ON PANEL, 4" X 8," SEPTEMBER 22, 2004 (PAINTING #126).

*South Fork of the Shenandoah River, Warren County**
OIL ON LINEN, 34" X 52," JULY–AUGUST 2002 (PAINTING #128).

*South Fork of the Shenandoah River from Wildcat Ledge, Warren County**
OIL ON CANVAS, 18" X 24," AUGUST 27, 2007 (PAINTING #132).

[top] *Big Sky over the South Fork, Andy Guest State Park**
OIL ON CANVAS, 30" X 48," SEPTEMBER 30–OCTOBER 1, 2004 (PAINTING #134).

[bottom] *The South Fork, Andy Guest State Park*
OIL ON LINEN, 16" X 24," SEPTEMBER 21, 2004 (PAINTING #133).

[top] *On the South Fork, Andy Guest State Park*
OIL ON PANEL, 8" X 12," SEPTEMBER 22, 2004 (PAINTING #99).

[bottom] *Twilight on the South Fork, Andy Guest State Park*
OIL ON PANEL, 6" X 8," SEPTEMBER 22, 2004 (PAINTING #166).

Autumn View along the South Fork, near Luray
OIL ON PANEL, 6" X 8," OCTOBER 26, 2010 (PAINTING #7).

River View along the South Fork, near Luray
OIL ON PANEL, 8" X 12," OCTOBER 26, 2010 (PAINTING #114).

[top] *The White House, near Luray*
OIL ON CANVAS, 18" X 24," OCTOBER 24, 2010 (PAINTING #172).

[bottom] *Shenandoah Sycamore along the South Fork, near the White House*
OIL ON PANEL, 9" X 12," OCTOBER 25, 2010 (PAINTING #140).

Valley along Kauffmans Mill Road, near the White House
OIL ON CANVAS, 12" X 16," OCTOBER 25, 2010 (PAINTING #69).

[top] *Drapery near Saracen's Tent, Luray Caverns*
OIL ON PANEL, 8" X 12," JUNE 17, 2013 (PAINTING #187).

[bottom] *Washington Column, Luray Caverns*
OIL ON PANEL, 6" X 7," JUNE 17, 2013 (PAINTING #188).

Dream Lake, Luray Caverns
OIL ON PANEL, 12" X 16," JUNE 17, 2013 (PAINTING #186).

[top] *Morning, Boat Ramp at Luray*
OIL ON PANEL, 6" X 8," OCTOBER 20, 2010 (PAINTING #87).

[bottom] *Afternoon, Boat Ramp at Luray*
OIL ON CANVAS, 12" X 24," OCTOBER 20, 2010 (PAINTING #2).

[top] *Moonrise over the South Fork, near Luray*
OIL ON PANEL, 8" X 12," OCTOBER 20, 2010 (PAINTING #83).

[bottom] *Evening, Boat Ramp at Luray*
OIL ON PANEL, 9" X 12," OCTOBER 20, 2010 (PAINTING #32).

Jewell Hollow, Overlook from the Skyline Drive, near Morning Star
OIL ON CANVAS, 10" X 14," AUGUST 8, 2011 (PAINTING #67).

Stevens Cottage, Shenandoah
OIL ON PANEL, 6" X 9," JULY 13, 2015 (PAINTING #249).

Winter Twilight along the South Fork, Shenandoah
OIL ON PANEL, 3" X 6.5," JANUARY 11, 2011 (PAINTING #179).

*Town of Shenandoah, South Fork**
OIL ON PANEL, 7" X 12," JANUARY 11, 2011 (PAINTING #165).

[top] *Ballfields in April, Elkton*
OIL ON PANEL, 7" X 12," APRIL 26, 2015 (PAINTING #222).

[bottom] *Downtown Elkton*
OIL ON PANEL, 6" X 9," JULY 13, 2015 (PAINTING #238).

Cemetery, Port Republic
OIL ON PANEL, 6" X 6.25," APRIL 26, 2015 (PAINTING #226).

The South Fork at Port Republic
OIL ON PANEL, 9" X 12," JANUARY 12, 2011 (PAINTING #113).

*The South River at Waynesboro**

OIL ON LINEN, 16" x 20," JANUARY 12, 2011 (PAINTING #151).

The Wayne Theater, Waynesboro
OIL ON PANEL, 8" X 12," APRIL 27, 2015 (PAINTING #231).

*Cowbane Prairie Preserve 1, near Stuarts Draft**
OIL ON PANEL, 8" X 16," NOVEMBER 11, 2012 (PAINTING #183).

Sam Houston Wayside, near Lexington
OIL ON PANEL, 6" X 8," APRIL 27, 2015 (PAINTING #228).

*Maple Hall, near Lexington**

OIL ON PANEL, 8" X 12," APRIL 27, 2015 (PAINTING #225).

PORTFOLIO II

Williamsport to Lexington along U.S. 11

Detail, *Apple Orchard* (page 136)

Oh, Shenandoah,
I love your daughter,
Away, you rolling river.
For her I'd cross
Your roaming waters,
Away, I'm bound away
'Cross the wide Missouri.

—Second stanza of "Oh, Shenandoah" (1882)

Williamsport, Maryland, from Riverview Cemetery
OIL ON PANEL, 8" X 12," JUNE 26, 2011 (PAINTING #175).

Woolen Mills, Martinsburg, West Virginia
OIL ON PANEL, 8" X 12," MAY 9, 2011 (PAINTING #76).

*Roundhouse, Martinsburg, West Virginia**
OIL ON CANVAS, 18" X 24," MAY 9, 2011 (PAINTING #75).

Apple Orchard, near Winchester, Virginia
OIL ON LINEN, 18" X 24," OCTOBER 10, 2011 (PAINTING #141).

Evening in the Apple Orchard, near Winchester
OIL ON CANVAS, 8"X 10," OCTOBER 10, 2011 (PAINTING #30).

*Springtime, Hopewell Friends Meeting, Clear Brook**
OIL ON PANEL, 8" X 12," APRIL 3, 2011 (PAINTING #62).

Daniel Morgan Statue, Winchester
OIL ON PANEL, 6" X 8," OCTOBER 13, 2014 (PAINTING #201).

Rainy Day, Gaunt's Drug Store, Winchester
OIL ON PANEL, 6" X 8," JUNE 18, 2013 (PAINTING #192).

Snow White Grill, Winchester
OIL ON PANEL, 8" X 6," APRIL 6, 2012 (PAINTING #149).

*Sarah's Glen, Shenandoah University, Winchester**
OIL ON PANEL, 8" X 12," OCTOBER 13, 2014 (PAINTING #202).

Spring-fed Racey Ponds, Shenandoah University, Winchester
OIL ON CANVAS, 20" X 24," JULY 5, 2011 (PAINTING #155).

Health and Life Sciences Building, Shenandoah University, Winchester
OIL ON PANEL, 7" X 12," OCTOBER 14, 2014 (PAINTING #203).

*John Handley High School, Winchester**
OIL ON PANEL, 8" X 12," OCTOBER 16, 2011 (PAINTING #68).

Triangle Diner under Renovation, Winchester
oil on panel, 8" x 12," june 18, 2013 (painting #195).

Amherst Diner, Winchester
OIL ON PANEL, 6" X 8," JUNE 18, 2013 (PAINTING #181).

April, Opequon Crossroads
OIL ON PANEL, 12" X 16," APRIL 3, 2011 (PAINTING #100).

Front View, Belle Grove Plantation, Cedar Creek Battlefield
OIL ON PANEL, 8" X 12," APRIL 3, 2011 (PAINTING #11).

Railroad Crossing and Signal Knob, Strasburg
OIL ON LINEN, 10" X 14," MARCH 24, 2015 (PAINTING #217).

*Railroad Depot, Strasburg**
OIL ON PANEL, 6" X 8," OCTOBER 14, 2014 (PAINTING #205).

Hotel Strasburg
OIL ON PANEL, 8" X 12," APRIL 6, 2015 (PAINTING #218).

Ice Cream Depot, Strasburg
OIL ON PANEL, 5" X 7," OCTOBER 14, 2014 (PAINTING #204).

[top] *October on the North Fork, near Strasburg*
oil on panel, 4" x 8," october 22, 2009 (painting #96).

[bottom] *Autumn on the North Fork, near Strasburg*
oil on canvas, 18" x 24," october 22, 2009 (painting #6).

The North Fork at Tumbling Run, near Fishers Hill
OIL ON CANVAS, 14" X 18," OCTOBER 21, 2008 (PAINTING #119).

Winter on the North Fork, near Tumbling Run, Shenandoah County
OIL ON PANEL, 9"X 12," FEBRUARY 1, 2010 (PAINTING #178).

Evening near Tumbling Run, Shenandoah County
OIL ON PANEL, 8" X 12," JANUARY 16, 2011 (PAINTING #31).

[top] *The North Fork at Narrow Passage, without the Swinging Bridge*
OIL ON CANVAS, 12" X 24," OCTOBER 2, 2008 (PAINTING #129).

[bottom] *Swinging Bridge at Narrow Passage**
OIL ON PANEL, 8" X 12," SEPTEMBER 30, 2008 (PAINTING #159).

From the Swinging Bridge at Narrow Passage, near Woodstock
OIL ON PANEL, 6" X 8," OCTOBER 20, 2008 (PAINTING #38).

[top] *Burnshire Dam on the North Fork, near Woodstock*
OIL ON CANVAS, 12" X 24," JANUARY 17, 2011 (PAINTING #20).

[bottom] *Winter at Narrow Passage, near Woodstock*
OIL ON PANEL, 3.75" X 7," FEBRUARY 1, 2010 (PAINTING #176).

Spring on the North Fork at Narrow Passage, near Woodstock
OIL ON CANVAS, 14" X 18," APRIL 4, 2011 (PAINTING #154).

Carnival Rides, Shenandoah County Fair, Woodstock
OIL ON PANEL, 8" X 12," SEPTEMBER 1, 2011 (PAINTING #121).

Midway, Shenandoah County Fair, Woodstock
OIL ON PANEL, 8" X 12," SEPTEMBER 1, 2011 (PAINTING #122).

Alms House and Farm, Shenandoah County

OIL ON PANEL, 6" X 9," JUNE 17, 2013 (PAINTING #193).

Bethel Lutheran Church, Hamburg (Shenandoah County)
OIL ON PANEL, 6" X 8," OCTOBER 23, 2011 (PAINTING #13).

[top] *Morning at Red Banks, Shenandoah County**
OIL ON CANVAS, 16" X 20," OCTOBER 1, 2008 (PAINTING #88).

[bottom] *Late Afternoon at Red Banks, Shenandoah County*
OIL ON PANEL, 5" X 7," SEPTEMBER 22, 2008 (SEPTEMBER #70).

Evening at Red Banks, Shenandoah County
OIL ON PANEL, 6" X 8," SEPTEMBER 30, 2008 (PAINTING #28).

The North Fork, near Mount Jackson
OIL ON PANEL, 7" X 7," AUGUST, 16, 2010 (PAINTING #93).

View from Rudes Hill at Meems Bottom, near New Market
OIL ON PANEL, 7" X 12," MARCH 24, 2010 (PAINTING #118).

[top] *Covered Bridge on the North Fork at Meems Bottom, near New Market*
OIL ON CANVAS, 9" X 12," SEPTEMBER 30, 2008 (PAINTING #22).

[bottom] *Meems Bottom from under the Covered Bridge*
OIL ON PANEL, 3" X 5," OCTOBER 1, 2008 (PAINTING #79).

[top] *Morning at Meems Bottom*
OIL ON PANEL, 8" X 12," SEPTEMBER 24, 2008 (PAINTING #84).

[bottom] *Geese along the Shore at VA 953, near New Market*
OIL ON PANEL, 5" X 7," AUGUST 16, 2010 (PAINTING #49).

Morning, Overlook of the North Fork from the New Market Battlefield
OIL ON PANEL, 7" X 12," AUGUST 17, 2010 (PAINTING #85).

*Home on the North Fork, Overlook at the New Market Battlefield**
OIL ON CANVAS, 15" X 30," AUGUST 17, 2010 (PAINTING #61).

*Southern Kitchen Restaurant, New Market**
OIL ON PANEL, 8" X 12," MAY 22, 2011 (PAINTING #152).

*Shenvalee Golf Resort, New Market**
OIL ON PANEL, 8" X 12," JULY 12, 2012 (PAINTING #144).

Shenandoah Sunset, Massanutten Peak from the Valley Pike, North of Harrisonburg
OIL ON CANVAS, 6" X 8," OCTOBER 24, 2011 (PAINTING #138).

*Rockingham County Courthouse and Spring House, Harrisonburg**
OIL ON PANEL, 8"X 12," MARCH 22, 2015 (PAINTING #212).

Arboretum, James Madison University, Harrisonburg
OIL ON PANEL, 6" X 8," JUNE 16, 2013 (PAINTING #185).

Wilson Hall, James Madison University, Harrisonburg
OIL ON PANEL, 8" X 12," JUNE 16, 2013 (PAINTING #184).

Buildings and the North River, Mount Crawford
OIL ON CANVAS, 9" X 12," JANUARY 17, 2011 (PAINTING #89).

Mount Sidney and Route 11
OIL ON PANEL, 8" X 12," MARCH 23, 2015 (PAINTING #213).

Stonewall Jackson Hotel, Staunton
OIL ON PANEL, 8" X 12," JULY 12, 2012 (PAINTING #158).

*Staunton from the Train Yard**
OIL ON PANEL, 8” X 12,” MARCH 14, 2011 (PAINTING #157).

[top] *American Shakespeare Center and Blackfriars Playhouse, Staunton*
OIL ON PANEL, 8" X 12," APRIL 28, 2015 (PAINTING #230).

[bottom] *Zynodoa Restaurant and New Performing Arts Center, Staunton*
OIL ON PANEL, 6" X 9," AUGUST 2, 2015 (PAINTING #262).

*Woodrow Wilson Birthplace and Library, Staunton**
OIL ON PANEL, 8" X 12," JULY 12, 2012 (PAINTING #180).

Dairy Barns, Virginia Museum of Frontier Culture, Staunton
OIL ON PANEL, 9" X 12," JULY 12, 2011 (PAINTING #24).

Augusta Farm Cooperative, Staunton
OIL ON PANEL, 6.5" X 16," MARCH 15, 2011 (PAINTING #4).

McCormick Gap, Overlook from the Skyline Drive
OIL ON CANVAS, 8" X 12," JULY 12, 2011 (PAINTING #78).

[top] *Pasture along Raphine Road, near Gibbs Falls*
OIL ON LINEN, 8" X 10," MARCH 14, 2011 (PAINTING #102).

[bottom] *Hull's Drive-In, Route 11, Lexington*
OIL ON PANEL, 5" X 7," AUGUST 4, 2015 (PAINTING #255).

*Old Main, Washington and Lee University, Lexington**
OIL ON PANEL, 7" X 12," JULY 11, 2011 (PAINTING #98).

*Barracks and Quad, Virginia Military Institute, Lexington**
OIL ON PANEL, 2" X 6," JULY 11, 2012 (PAINTING #234).

A. KUSHNIR

PORTFOLIO III

Woodstock to Lexington along VA 42 and 252

Detail, *Blue Hole* (page 217)

‘Tis seven years
Since last I’ve seen you,
Away, you rolling river.
‘Tis seven years
Since last I’ve seen you,
Away, we’re bound away
‘Cross the wide Missouri.

—Third stanza of “Oh, Shenandoah” (1882)

View from Oak Ridge, near Columbia Furnace
OIL ON PANEL, 4" X 10.5," APRIL 5, 2011 (PAINTING #168).

[top] *Lutheran Church, Jerome*
OIL ON PANEL, 4" X 5.5," APRIL 5, 2011 (PAINTING #81).

[bottom] *Jerome, at Alum Springs Road*
OIL ON PANEL, 8" X 16," APRIL 5, 2011 (PAINTING #66).

[top] *Shrine Mont at Orkney Springs*
OIL ON PANEL, 6" X 8," APRIL 5, 2011 (PAINTING #145).

[bottom] *Basye*
OIL ON PANEL, 6" X 6.75," MARCH 23, 2015 (PAINTING #208).

View to the East of Massanutten Mountain, near Timberville
OIL ON PANEL, 3" X 8," JULY 13, 2015 (PAINTING #246).

View to the West of the Allegheny Mountains, near Timberville
OIL ON PANEL, 3" X 8," JULY 13, 2015 (PAINTING #245).

[top] *Evening 1, along the North Fork, Timberville*
OIL ON PANEL, 3" X 5," OCTOBER 18, 2010 (PAINTING #163).

[bottom] *Evening 2, along the North Fork, Timberville*
OIL ON PANEL, 3" X 4," OCTOBER 18, 2010 (PAINTING #164).

Gretchen's Old Farm, Timberville
OIL ON PANEL, 7" X 12," OCTOBER 19, 2010 (PAINTING #55).

Bridge over the North Fork, Timberville
OIL ON CANVAS, 12" X 16," OCTOBER 18, 2010 (PAINTING #162).

Downtown Timberville

OIL ON PANEL, 9" X 12," JULY 9, 2015 (PAINTING #251).

*Evening in Broadway**
OIL ON LINEN, 9" X 12," MARCH 23, 2015 (PAINTING #209).

John Kline Home, Broadway
OIL ON PANEL, 6" X 8," OCTOBER 27, 2014 (PAINTING #207).

Evening, Brocks Gap, South of Fulks Run
OIL ON PANEL, 6"x 8," OCTOBER 19, 2010 (PAINTING #33).

The North Fork, near Fulks Run
OIL ON CANVAS, 16" X 20," OCTOBER 19, 2010 (PAINTING #123).

View from the Funk Store, Singers Glen
OIL ON PANEL, 8" X 12," MAY 12, 2011 (PAINTING #148).

Funk General Store, Singers Glen
OIL ON PANEL, 4" X 6," MAY 12, 2011 (PAINTING #48).

*Home of Joseph Funk, Singers Glen**

OIL ON LINEN, 18" X 24," MAY 12, 2011 (PAINTING #60).

Foursquare House in Harrisonburg, Original Office of the Center for American Places
OIL ON PANEL, 5" X 7," JULY 9, 2015 (PAINTING #239).

[top] *Soccer Practice, Eastern Mennonite Univeristy, Harrisonburg*
OIL ON PANEL, 6" X 8," JULY 9, 2015 (PAINTING #240).

[bottom] *Eastern Mennonite University, Harrisonburg*
OIL ON PANEL, 7" X 12," MARCH 22, 2015 (PAINTING #211).

*Shenandoah Valley Livestock Sales, Harrisonburg**
OIL ON PANEL, 6" X 16," JUNE 16, 2013 (PAINTING #194).

Dry River at Rawley Springs
OIL ON PANEL, 6" X 8," MAY 23, 2011 (PAINTING #109).

*Blue Hole, Rawley Springs**
OIL ON CANVAS, 16" X 20," MAY 23, 2011 (PAINTING #14).

*Buck Bowman Stadium, Clover Hill**
OIL ON PANEL, 7" X 12," JULY 10, 2011 (PAINTING #19).

Grandstand, Buck Bowman Stadium, Clover Hill
OIL ON PANEL, 12" X 16," JULY 10, 2011 (PAINTING #53).

Daniel Harrison House, Dayton
OIL ON PANEL, 6" X 8," JULY 10, 2015 (PAINTING #236).

Dayton Farmers Market
OIL ON PANEL, 8" X 12," JULY 10, 2015 (PAINTING #237).

[top] *After a Rain, Silver Lake in Dayton, from the Mill*
OIL ON PANEL, 8" X 12," JULY 10, 2015 (PAINTING #247).

[bottom] *Silver Lake Mill, Dayton*
OIL ON CANVAS, 11" X 14," JULY 10, 2015 (PAINTING #248).

*Pleasant View Mennonite Church, Dayton**

OIL ON PANEL, 8" X 12," JUNE 16, 2013 (PAINTING #191).

Ottobine Country Store
OIL ON PANEL, 8" X 12," MAY 23, 2011 (PAINTING #101).

Mennonite Country, Ottobine

OIL ON CANVAS, 12" X 24," MAY 22, 2011 (PAINTING #80).

Sunday at Bridgewater College
OIL ON CANVAS, 8" X 10," MAY 22, 2011 (PAINTING #15).

Edgebriar Park and the North River, Bridgewater
OIL ON PANEL, 12" X 16," MAY 22, 2011 (PAINTING #16).

Mossy Creek, Augusta County
OIL ON PANEL, 9" X 14," AUGUST 4, 2015 (PAINTING #259).

*Mossy Creek at the Bridge, Augusta County**
OIL ON PANEL, 6" X 8," AUGUST 4, 2015 (PAINTING #260).

*Henry Miller Farm, Augusta County**
OIL ON PANEL, 11" X 16," AUGUST 4, 2015 (PAINTING #254).

*Middle of March in Middlebrook**

OIL ON CANVAS, 18" X 24," MARCH 15, 2011 (PAINTING #82).

*Evening in Brownsburg**
OIL ON PANEL, 8" X 12," MARCH 14, 2011 (PAINTING #29).

Historic Brownsburg
OIL ON PANEL, 6" X 8," MARCH 14, 2011 (PAINTING #18).

Spring House, Rockbridge Alum Springs
OIL ON PANEL, 8" X 12," AUGUST 3, 2015 (PAINTING #261).

Waterfall at Jordan's Point Park, Maury River, Lexington
OIL ON PANEL, 6" X 9," AUGUST 3, 2015 (PAINTING #256).

Lee Chapel, Washington and Lee University, Lexington
OIL ON PANEL, 9" X 12," JULY 11, 2011 (PAINTING #73).

Quad and Barracks, Virginia Military Institute, Lexington
OIL ON CANVAS, 9" X 12," JULY 11, 2012 (PAINTING #169).

New Market Battlefield State Historical Park
OIL ON PANEL, 6" X 12.5," MARCH 23, 2015 (PAINTING #216).

Land and Life in the Shenandoah Valley

by Jeffrey C. Everett

> Think of the fields! There are the cotton fields of Alabama, the wheat fields of Kansas, the rolling grass fields of Vermont, and the orchard-covered hill-sides of New York State. They all cry aloud and clap their hands for joy. That painter would be immortal who could truly picture one of them. I have spent certain happy days in the fields of England; I have stood on the rolling fields of Alsace [-Lorraine], when the grain fields stretching away toward the Moselle seemed like the choicest lands of Paradise; but if I have a dis-passionate judgment left in me, I must still prefer the Shenandoah Valley and the banks of the Hudson . . .
>
> —Frank Albert Waugh, *The Landscape Beautiful* (1910)[1]

Known primarily for its associations with the American Civil War, a famous song, and as the setting for one of America's most popular national parks, the Shenandoah Valley is often perceived by the general populace as an unabashedly Southern locale and bucolic paradise that has largely escaped the incursion of urban sprawl. As is the case with many myths, there is some truth behind such generalizations, but the Valley's history is complicated, and that story has rarely been recounted holistically. The Shenandoah Valley also defies convenient categorization. It has elements of the Upland South, Lowland South, and Pennsylvania culture regions, yet the Valley does not fit comfortably into any of these groupings. It is, essentially, a region unto itself.

During the past several decades, pioneering studies of Virginia's colonial backcountry led by such notable scholars as Warren R. Hofstra, Kenneth Keller, Ann McCleary, Robert D. Mitchell, Karl Raitz, Pamela Simpson, and others have made readers aware of the vastly different patterns of culture and settlement that developed west of the Blue Ridge Mountains compared with eastern Virginia. Perhaps the Valley is not as outwardly distinctive in the way that Virginia's Tidewater or Southside regions are with their relatively homogenous landscapes, but borderlands—between east and west, north and south—such as the Shenandoah Valley are significant, because they tend to be both staging grounds for diffusion and innovation. The Valley is, by this measure, a quintessentially American landscape, where a diverse group of individuals, motivated by the opportunity to create better lives for themselves, carved communities out of the wilderness. The Valley was and still is a land where the middle class holds sway—an increasingly rare sight in contemporary American society and a place deserving of our attention.

To help demystify the Shenandoah Valley as one of America's most legendary places, it is important to look to the landscape for answers. Rather than relying solely on the usual assortment of tools utilized by the professional historian or geographer—journals, maps, letters, photographs, reports, and such—this book employs the skills of a modern plein-air painter, complemented by scholarly essays, to capture the Valley's multifaceted landscape legacy. In the absence of an art colony that developed in similarly scenic river valleys to the north such as the Brandywine, Delaware, and Hudson, Andrei Kushnir's *en plein air* painting tour of the Shenandoah Valley is an historic undertaking in its own right, documenting the Shenandoah River for the benefit of future generations.

To interpret how these landscapes collectively are representative of larger themes, I present nineteen vignettes about the land and life of the Shenandoah Valley. They are organized into two parts—the natural landscape and cultural landscape—with persons, places, and themes both familiar and unfamiliar to residents and visitors alike earnestly explored in the hope that the true essence of this iconic landscape is revealed.

Many of Andrei Kushnir's paintings depict resources listed on the National Register of Historic Places, Virginia Landmarks Register, West Virginia Historic Register, National Registry of Natural Landmarks, and Virginia Natural Heritage Inventory, due to their significance and integrity and ability to convey the themes and contexts being presented in this book. Contrary to popular perception, listing in these registers does not ensure the permanent protection of resources nor does the absence from a listing mean a resource is not eligible. In addition to tracing the Valley's landscape continuum through Kushnir's art, an early impetus for creating this book was to document many of those historic sites before they are lost forever. While many of the properties showcased in the book are publicly accessible, readers should keep in mind that some are private property, and, in keeping with the Valley's cultural dictates, permission should be sought from the landowner before attempting to enter.

With my roots in the Valley, I have incorporated local perspective into the narratives. Since the ever-pragmatic Valley folk rarely concern themselves with the aesthete, there was a concerted effort to include in this book utilitarian landscapes along with the scenic ones that typically fill books on the Shenandoah Valley. Alas, it is Andrei Kushnir's rare ability to execute any landscape before him—rural or urban, upland or riparian, agricultural or industrial—all the while working out in the elements *en plein air*, which separates him from the pack.

Like Warren R. Hofstra, I first discovered Andrei Kushnir upon seeing his catalog, *Painted History: The Landscapes of Valley View Farm* (2004), in which he uncannily captured through his plein-air paintings the countryside of Fauquier County. He has the distinction of being the only living artist accorded a one-person exhibition at the Virginia Historical Society in Richmond (2004) and only the second living artist after Mort Künstler—nationally known for his paintings of historical events, especially the Civil War—exhibited at the Museum of the Shenandoah Valley in Winchester (2016). After reading this book and viewing the artistry, I believe many will share the view that Andrei Kushnir has created a new Shenandoah School of Art where one did not previously exist.

*The South Fork at Elkton**

OIL ON PANEL, 16" X 12," JANUARY 11, 2011 (PAINTING #150).

*Winter at Red Banks, Shenandoah County**

OIL ON CANVAS, 14" X 18," FEBRUARY 1, 2010 (PAINTING #112).

PART I: THE NATURAL LANDSCAPE

In the history of nations, rivers and river valleys have stood out as objects of special significance. The Nile, the Tigris and Euphrates, the Po, the Danube, the Rhine, the Rhone, and other rivers in the 'old country' have been and still are widely known and each holds a foremost place in the history of the nation or nations thru which it flows, and of the world. Of like significance in the history of the United States are the Connecticut and Shenandoah, the Hudson, the Mohawk, and the Genesee, the Mississippi and its tributaries, the Columbia, the Colorado and the Rio Grande . . .

—Dr. John Lee Coulter,
Industrial History of the Valley of the Red River of the North (1910)[2]

While a combination of factors both natural and cultural have set the Shenandoah Valley apart as a distinct regional landscape, many of its constituent parts must be understood as belonging to a larger system. In terms of geomorphology, the Shenandoah Valley is part of the Great Valley, which is the widest and longest valley within the physiographic subdivision of the eastern United States known as the Ridge and Valley Province, which stretches from central Alabama to the Hudson River Valley in Upstate New York. The Shenandoah Valley is, in fact, one of many valleys within the Great Valley that take their names for the waterbodies that flow through them—for example, the Hudson, Lehigh, James, Roanoke, New, Holston, Tennessee, and Coosa. Other valleys are accorded place names such as the Kittatinny, Lebanon, Cumberland, and Hagerstown.

The Ridge and Valley Province, in turn, is a physiographic division of North America known as the Appalachian Highlands, which also consists of the adjacent Blue Ridge and Piedmont Provinces to the east, the adjacent Appalachian Plateaus to the west, and the Adirondacks, St. Lawrence River Valley, and New England to the north. The term "Appalachian Highlands" should not be confused with the term "Appalachia," which geographers more commonly use to describe only portions of the Blue Ridge, Ridge and Valley, and Appalachian Plateaus regions, particularly in their southern extensions. Instead, Appalachian Highlands refers to the ancient landmass, of which all seven of the previously named provinces are a part.[3]

A number of defining characteristics have been ascribed by geomorphologists for the Ridge and Valley's landscape, which includes, in part, the parallelism of ridges and valleys oriented in a northeast-to-southwest direction, trellis drainage patterns on the valley floor, major rivers such as the Potomac that flow transverse to the direction of the geologic structure, and the preponderance of wind gaps in the mountains through which streams previously flowed. The Valley's distinct topography—that of a broad, fairly level valley floor flanked by relatively narrow mountains running parallel to one another—is the result of the African continent colliding with North America during the Alleghenian Orogeny. The valley floor, which is underlain with less resistant rocks such as limestone and shale, subsequently eroded lower than the surrounding ridges, which are underlain by more resistant rocks such as sandstone and quartzite. The folding and faulting that took place gave rise to the Ridge and Valley Province being referred to as the Folded Appalachians.[4]

The alternating bands of weaker and stronger rocks has created a trellis drainage pattern in many parts of the valley floor where water bodies follow a longitudinal path and meet at right angles with its tributaries that follow a transverse path, the path being determined by how resistant the rock underneath is. The presence of the trellis pattern, at least in the Shenandoah Valley portion of the Great Valley, appears to be overemphasized in academic literature, since dendritic patterns are also frequently exhibited. Another distinctive fluvial process observed in the Valley is the meanders of the Shenandoah River and its tributaries. In the area known as the Seven Bends (of the North Fork of the Shenandoah) outside of Woodstock in Shenandoah County, the river is particularly sinuous. These so-called entrenched meanders have cut down to bedrock and the largest meanders tend to be associated with the relatively non-resistant shales of the Martinsburg Formation. While the Seven Bends has received most of the attention, similar meanders are visible along the South Fork of the Shenandoah River in Page Valley and along Middle River in Augusta County.[5]

The Shenandoah is a northward-flowing river system, giving rise to "Valleyspeak"—traveling south is considered going "up the Valley" and heading north is going "down the Valley"—which is somewhat awkward yet logical, since rivers flow from higher to lower elevations. Accordingly, the southern Valley has historically been known as the Upper Valley, with the northern Valley designated as the Lower Valley. Page Valley (also known as Luray Valley) is differentiated due to its isolated setting and is sometimes assigned to a "Middle Valley" division by scholars, while the other portion of the so-called Middle Valley, on the opposite (western) side of Massanutten Mountain, is often referred to as the "Main Valley" by locals. These divisions of the Valley are described in more detail in separate essays.

In hydrological terms, the Shenandoah Valley stretches from the South Fork of the Shenandoah River's headwaters near the Rockbridge-Augusta County line northward to Harpers Ferry, West Virginia, where the Main Stem of the Shenandoah River meets the Potomac River. In cultural terms, the Valley is nearly always extended into Rockbridge County and often into Botetourt County, even though these counties are predominantly drained by the James River; technically, a portion of Augusta County is also drained by the James, but it is always included in the Shenandoah Valley, and though most of Highland, Bath, and Alleghany Counties are likewise drained by the James, they are not generally associated with the Valley since they are west of the first ridges of the Alleghenies—Little North, Great North, and Shenandoah Mountains.

For the purposes of this book, taking into consideration both natural and cultural attributes, the Shenandoah Valley is defined as the counties of Berkeley, Jefferson, and the portion of Morgan County east of Cacapon Mountain in what is now West Virginia and the counties of Frederick, Clarke, Warren, Shenandoah, Page, Rockingham, Augusta, Rockbridge, and the portion of Botetourt

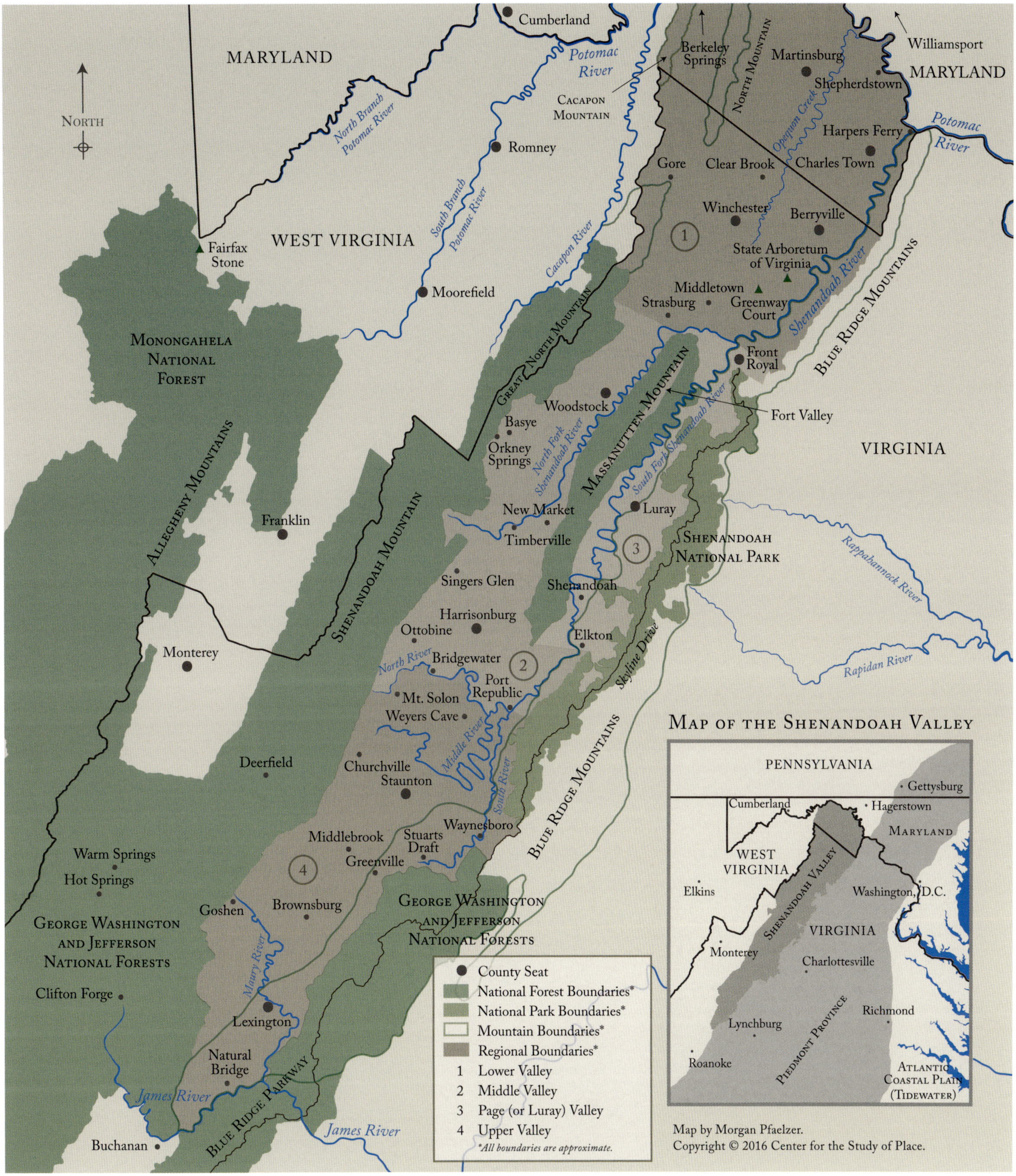
Map of the Shenandoah Valley
Cumberland
Maryland
North
North Branch Potomac River
Potomac River
Cacapon Mountain
Berkeley Springs
North Mountain
Martinsburg
Shepherdstown
Williamsport
Maryland
Harpers Ferry
Potomac River
Charles Town
Opequon Creek
Romney
Gore
Clear Brook
Winchester
Berryville
West Virginia
South Branch Potomac River
Fairfax Stone
Cacapon River
State Arboretum of Virginia
Middletown
Strasburg
Greenway Court
Shenandoah River
Blue Ridge Mountains
Moorefield
Great North Mountain
Monongahela National Forest
Front Royal
Massanutten Mountain
Woodstock
Fort Valley
Basye
Orkney Springs
North Fork Shenandoah River
South Fork Shenandoah River
Virginia
Allegheny Mountains
Shenandoah Mountain
Franklin
New Market
Timberville
Luray
Shenandoah National Park
Rappahannock River
Singers Glen
Shenandoah
Harrisonburg
Ottobine
Elkton
Monterey
North River
Bridgewater
Port Republic
Rapidan River
Skyline Drive
Mt. Solon
Weyers Cave
Middle River
Deerfield
Churchville
Staunton
South River
Blue Ridge Mountains
Waynesboro
Stuarts Draft
Middlebrook
Greenville
Warm Springs
Hot Springs
Goshen
Brownsburg
George Washington and Jefferson National Forests
George Washington and Jefferson National Forests
Maury River
Clifton Forge
Lexington
Natural Bridge
James River
Blue Ridge Parkway
James River
Buchanan
County Seat
National Forest Boundaries*
National Park Boundaries*
Mountain Boundaries*
Regional Boundaries*
1 Lower Valley
2 Middle Valley
3 Page (or Luray) Valley
4 Upper Valley
*All boundaries are approximate.
Pennsylvania
Gettysburg
Cumberland
Hagerstown
Maryland
West Virginia
Shenandoah Valley
Elkins
Washington, D.C.
Virginia
Monterey
Charlottesville
Piedmont Province
Richmond
Lynchburg
Roanoke
Atlantic Coastal Plain (Tidewater)
Map by Morgan Pfaelzer.
Copyright © 2016 Center for the Study of Place.

County north of the James River in Virginia. Most of this area is drained by the Shenandoah River and its tributaries, some is drained by the James River, and some by Opequon Creek, which empties directly into the Potomac; all, however, is bounded on the west by the Allegheny Mountains and on the east by the Blue Ridge Mountains, and all drainage ultimately flows into Chesapeake Bay. The portion of Botetourt County lying south of the James River shares some similar cultural and natural attributes to the Shenandoah Valley, yet the southern part of that county is drained by the Roanoke (Staunton) River, which ultimately empties into Albemarle Sound on North Carolina's Outer Banks rather than the Chesapeake Bay. With the marked constriction of the mountains and attendant narrowing of the Great Valley at Buchanan, geologists and geomorphologists have instead bestowed the name of Fincastle Valley to the part of Botetourt lying south of the James; thus, this portion of the county has not been included in the Shenandoah Valley for this study. The western portion of Morgan County has, likewise, been excluded, since it lies west of the first ridges of the Alleghenies and drains into the Cacapon River.[6]

While the Valley's landforms and natural resources are typical of the larger Ridge and Valley Province, the Valley's latitudinal position midway in the province results in it being the northern limits for some flora and fauna and the southern limit for others. Therefore, the theme of the Shenandoah constituting a borderland that is more fully discussed in the cultural landscape section of this book also applies to the natural landscape, with the Valley having more in common with other states in some instances than it does with other regions of Virginia.

Shenandoah River from the top of Blue Ball (Study), Clarke County
OIL ON PANEL, 8.5" X 10," JANUARY 16, 2011 (PAINTING #37).

Morning, Front Royal from Guard Hill Road
OIL ON PANEL, 9" X 12," SEPTEMBER 14, 2010 (PAINTING #86).

The Lower Valley

> At Harper's (sic) Ferry the Shenandoah and Potomac rivers unite their waters, forcing that remarkable and stupendous passage through the Blue Mountains which has been described by Thomas Jefferson, and is familiar to the thousands of Americans who have visited this famous spot. . . . All this portion of the country was the scene of many severe conflicts. To-day it is as peaceful, romantic, and picturesque, as if War had never shown his horrid front in the valley. Climbing to the top of the Blue Ridge Mountains at this point, the Shenandoah may be seen ranging the foot of the mountains for a hundred miles, seeking a passage to the sea. There is enough natural beauty in this section of country to engage an artist for a life-time.
>
> —*The Aldine* (1874)[7]

Oriented in a northeast-to-southwest direction, it is logical that the portion of the Shenandoah Valley closest to both Pennsylvania and the Chesapeake region, the two major source areas for Euro-American settlers, was settled the earliest. The term "Lower" serves as a double entendre—the elevation is lower in this portion of the Valley as compared with the Middle and Upper Valleys, and it is also the northernmost extent of the northward-flowing Shenandoah River.

Unequivocally bounded on the north by the Potomac River, the Lower Valley's southern boundary, for the purposes of this book, constitutes Cedar Creek and the North Fork of the Shenandoah River east of its junction with Cedar Creek in the vicinity of Strasburg and, in turn, the North Fork's junction with the South Fork of the Shenandoah River at Riverton (Front Royal) to form the Main Stem. In essence, the Lower Valley consists of the portion of the Valley between the Potomac River and Signal Knob (the northernmost promontory of Massanutten Mountain), from north to south and between the western slope of the Blue Ridge Mountains and front ranges of the Allegheny Mountains from east to west.

Bifurcating the Lower Valley for much of its length is Opequon Creek, which rises southwest of Winchester at the hamlet of the same name, eventually emptying into the Potomac southeast of Falling Waters. The Opequon effectively serves as a natural divide between the "uncouth set of people," as described by George Washington in his surveying expeditions, who hailed from the colonies to the north and predominated west of the Opequon, and the Cavalier stock from Virginia's Tidewater and Piedmont regions, who congregated east of the Opequon.[8]

The Main Stem of the Shenandoah River extends from Riverton (Front Royal) downriver (or north) through Warren, Clarke, and Jefferson (WV) Counties, where it finally joins the Potomac at Harpers Ferry. On John Warner's survey map of circa 1747, produced for Lord Fairfax, the North and South Forks are labeled the "North" and "South" Rivers, what is now Riverton is referred to as

"The Fork of Shannondoah," and the term "Shannondoah River" is applied to the Main Stem only. The Potomac River west of Harpers Ferry is depicted as "Cohongoronta," which is how the Five Nations Iroquois League (later, Six Nations) referred to it as. Ultimately, the name "Potomac" was applied to the entire length of the river (east and west of its junction with the Shenandoah), and it is always a curious matter what term is ultimately bestowed on rivers when two forks converge, such as the case with the Monongahela and Allegheny Rivers that form the Ohio in Pittsburgh; the Iroquois instead thought of the Allegheny and Ohio as one river.[9]

As mentioned in my introduction to "The Natural Landscape" but worth repeating here, one often confusing but revealing aspect of the Lower Valley involves elevation and directions. Because travel into the Shenandoah Valley, historically, was from lower elevations in the north (downriver) toward higher elevations in the south (upriver), one traveled "up" the Valley whether by foot, horse wagon, rivercraft, or rail. Thus, locals still refer to going "up" the Valley when they travel from Winchester to Lexington, even as most people in the Northern Hemisphere associate "down" with "south" and "up" with "north."

Another tell-tale sign of a "true" local is the exclusive and emphatic use of the singular in the word "cent," regardless of the amount of change one is due. Thus, if you hand a local merchant a dollar for a $.95 purchase, you may well hear, "Here's your five *cent*." As for native spelling convention, there are no apostrophes used for possessives such as Bears Den, Harpers Ferry, or Meems Bottom, the latter two named after prominent local citizens. On the other hand, for mercantile names without the possessive, such as the defunct Ben Franklin five-and-dime store in the Town of Woodstock (Shenandoah County), local convention dictates the use of an apostrophe, making it "Ben Franklin's."

Potomac River at Berkeley Springs, West Virginia
OIL ON CANVAS, 48" X 60," (FEBRUARY 2013) (PAINTING #233).

*Rainy Day, View of the Seven Bends of the North Fork from the Woodstock Fire Tower**
OIL ON PANEL, 8" X 12," OCTOBER 1, 2008 (PAINTING #111).

The Middle Valley

> This 39-mile section of the North Fork of the Shenandoah River (between Strasburg and Edinburg) is eligible for designation under the National Wild and Scenic Rivers Act. It is free-flowing and has outstandingly remarkable scenic, geologic, historic, and cultural values.
>
> —"Wild and Scenic Rivers Eligibility Determination Draft Environmental Impact Statement," George Washington National Forest (2011) [10]

The term "Middle Valley" appears in historical literature but is rarely used today among the local populace, who instead refer to it as the "Main Valley." For purposes of this book, the Middle Valley nomenclature is used to clarify the section of the Valley situated between the Lower and Upper Valleys and extending from the Allegheny Mountains in the west to Massanutten Mountain in the east, which divides the Valley in half for approximately fifty miles. The portion of the Valley of similar latitudes between Massanutten Mountain and the Blue Ridge Mountains situated east of Massanutten is instead referred to as Page (or Luray) Valley. In essence, the Middle Valley consists of the area south of Cedar Creek, which forms the boundary between Shenandoah and Frederick and Shenandoah and Warren Counties, respectively, and north of the North River in Rockingham County, which rises west of Bridgewater and joins with the South River at Port Republic to form the South Fork of the Shenandoah River.

The North Fork of the Shenandoah River is the predominate waterbody in this section of the Valley, rising in Little North Mountain at the first ranges of the Allegheny Mountains near the hamlet of Fulks Run in western Rockingham County, meandering through Shenandoah County and then bending around the northern end of Massanutten Mountain near Signal Knob to join the South Fork at Riverton, just north of Front Royal. While northern Rockingham County drains to the North Fork, the southern portion of the county drains to the South Fork's watershed, the headwaters of which are assigned to the Upper Valley for purposes of this book and the main stem of the South Fork being assigned to Page Valley.

The Middle Valley, in cultural terms, is a landscape dominated by the Virginia Germans, Shenandoah County having the largest percentage of residents of Germanic ancestry followed by Rockingham County. It is home to some of the most productive agricultural land east of the Appalachians, and the independent spirit that is characteristic of an agrarian society has consistently resisted government intervention, as evidenced by stalwart opposition to the listing of the North Fork as a Wild and Scenic River back when the Wild and Scenic Rivers Act was signed into law in 1968. Nevertheless, federal agencies have not given up the fight, as evidenced by repeated recommendations through the years calling for its designation.[11]

The White House (Study), near Luray
OIL ON PANEL, 7" X 12," OCTOBER 25, 2010 (PAINTING #173).

Page Valley

> From Front Royal station southward to Luray the [railroad] line passes through a region of wooded hills and deep ravines, the latter crossed upon some very high trestles. The river is often close beneath the track, and its course through these rocky highlands presents many views that excite our admiration. We are fairly among the foot-hills of the Blue Ridge here, though its central peaks are far enough away to show to good advantage. . . . Page valley is here several miles wide, and the surface is diversified by an endless series of knolls, ridges, and deeply imbedded streams . . .
>
> —Ernest Ingersoll, *Through the Shenandoah Valley: The Chronicle of a Leisurely Journey through the Uplands of Virginia* (1887)[12]

Page (or Luray) Valley is, arguably, the most scenic and most isolated of the four constituent sub-regions of the Shenandoah Valley, being wedged between Massanutten Mountain to the west and the Blue Ridge Mountains to the east without an interstate highway running through it. Its namesake, Page County, is located wholly within it, although Page Valley is sometimes referred to as Luray Valley after the county seat. The portion of Warren County south of Front Royal and northeastern Rockingham County between the towns of Elkton and Shenandoah can also be considered part of Page Valley, since they are located inside the northernmost and southernmost peaks of Massanutten Mountain—Signal Knob and Massanutten Peak, respectively.

The South Fork of the Shenandoah River dominates Page Valley, being wider and deeper than its counterpart that runs along the western slope of the Massanutten Mountains—the North Fork of the Shenandoah River—yet the latter is actually longer, due in large part to its sinuosity. The North Fork has twice as many dams as the South Fork; and, coupled with its depth and width and proximity to the tourist trade via the established tourist hubs of Front Royal and Luray and their attendant canoe liveries, the South Fork remains the more heavily trafficked of the two forks.[13]

Culturally, Page Valley, particularly in the vicinity of Luray, has a heavy Teutonic influence, and it was the location of one of the earliest Euro-American settlements in the Valley, the aptly named Massanutten Settlement, which included a number of Swiss-German Mennonites, skilled agriculturalists from Pennsylvania, most of whom relocated long ago to Rockingham County. Still, large portions of Page Valley retain their agrarian character to this day. Residing in Page Valley's numerous mountain hollows, the "holler folk," who, traditionally have lead a subsistence lifestyle that gives parts of Page Valley a more Southern Appalachian flavor than other locales in the Main Valley that more closely resemble the cultivated landscapes of southeastern Pennsylvania. Local lore abounds concerning "holler clans" using hound and gun, whether for hunting or as deterrents to trespassing.

*The South Fork at Port Republic**

OIL ON CANVAS, 10" X 14," JANUARY 12, 2011 (PAINTING #105).

The Upper Valley

> The soil is generally fertile, and well adapted to the purposes of agriculture. The country on the South River, on the Middle River, on Lewis' Creek, on Baker's Creek, on Christian's Creek, and on the other creeks and water-courses of the county, in richness of soil, is perhaps second to none in America . . . The water-shed of the Shenandoah or sources of that river are in Augusta; the thousand streams that form the head of the river are here, and consequently Augusta is better watered than counties lower down the Valley, where the creeks have collected into the main stream. Many of these sources are bold, perennial springs, capable of turning a mill or factory a stone's throw from their sources . . .
>
> —John Lewis Peyton, *History of Augusta County, Virginia* (1882)[14]

If the Lower Valley is that portion of the Shenandoah Valley north of Massanutten Mountain, and the Middle and Page Valleys occupy the western and eastern slopes of Massanutten Mountain, respectively, then the Upper Valley is that portion south of Massanutten Mountain. Specifically, it is the section of the Shenandoah Valley that contains the three major headwaters of the South Fork of the Shenandoah River: the North, Middle, and South Rivers in southern Rockingham and Augusta counties. The South Fork begins its journey adjacent to the Blue Ridge Mountains at the village of Port Republic, where the North and South Rivers converge, the confluence of the North River and Middle River occurring a few miles upstream between the communities of Weyers Cave and Grottoes.

Although a portion of the Upper Valley is drained by the James River rather than the Shenandoah River, local convention has always included the majority of this area within the boundaries of the Shenandoah Valley. Specifically, the Upper Valley stretches southward of the South Fork's watershed to the James River at Buchanan in Botetourt County, where the front ranges of the Alleghenies and the Blue Ridge noticeably constrict to a mile in width. In essence, while hydrologically it is more accurate to limit the Upper Valley to the South Fork of the Shenandoah River's drainage, it is more pragmatic to define the Shenandoah Valley as that territory between two of Virginia's most venerable rivers—the Potomac and the James.

Before the counties of Rockbridge and Botetourt were created, Augusta County encompassed the James River's watershed west of the Blue Ridge, the portion of the James west of its junction with the Rivanna River once being known as the Fluvanna River. Augusta County's northern limit, prior to the creation of Rockingham County, was the Fairfax Line, which separated not only Augusta and Frederick Counties, but also proprietary lands from lands owned by the British Crown. Thus, substantial portions of the Upper Valley were comprised of large land grants from the Crown through the Privy Council to speculators. These grants included the Borden Tract and Beverley Manor, and chief among its occupants were Scots-Irish Presbyterians, which is why Beverley Manor was referred to as the Irish Tract. Despite the Scots-Irish having a reputation as hardscrabble, backcountry herders, the Upper Valley was and still is a land of successful agriculturalists who established prosperous farms and towns and highly regarded institutions of higher learning.[15]

*Natural Chimneys, Augusta County**

OIL ON PANEL, 8" X 12," NOVEMBER 11, 2012 (PAINTING #190).

Caverns, Sinkholes, and Springs

> As the vernal season advances to the period, when it must resign its genial sway to the debilitating influences of summer, those persons in every section of our happy country, whose condition enables them to travel in pursuit of health or pleasure, will naturally turn their thoughts to the invigorating climate and medicinal waters of Western Virginia. Favored as our state is beyond all others, in the rich endowments of Providence, there is, perhaps, no advantage it enjoys more valuable than those mighty barriers which, at first sight, seem interposed by nature to the industry of man; as if she would say "Thus far shalt thou go and no farther." But the impartial-Dispenser of all gifts, has in this, as in every other favor, preserved that beautiful equilibrium so observable in all his works. If the west possesses not the expansive bays, navigable rivers, extensive cultivation, refined society, great wealth and greater luxury of Eastern Virginia, it enjoys blessings peculiar to itself, and adapted to the habits, comforts and happiness of its inhabitants. There nature appears in all her magnifi-cence. Behold those majestic mountains piercing the clouds!
>
> —Anonymous, "Virginia Springs," *Southern Literary Messenger* (1837)[16]

THE SHENANDOAH VALLEY is one of the nation's major karst areas. Karst is a term applied to areas where there is dissolution of carbonate rocks, particularly limestone and dolomite, due to acidic water and the attendant diversion of surface waters to underground routes. The Valley's many sinkholes are a visible indicator of subsurface drainage. Indeed, the paucity of surface waters is a defining physiographic feature of the Valley. Areas underlain by karst aquifers are vulnerable to groundwater contamination, which is why hydrofracking is of much concern in karst regions.[17]

Caverns are another karst feature, which is essentially a subterranean void formed in soluble carbonate rocks that are either dry or occupied by a stream. Caverns have been a major tourist attraction in the Valley for more than a century, and, in 1922, a scientific journal opined that "no one has adequately seen America who has not visited one or more of the caverns in the Shenandoah Valley." Today, half a million visitors a year visit Luray Caverns alone, with numerous other "show caves" in the Valley—Crystal, Endless, Grand, Shenandoah, Skyline, and Natural Bridge Caverns—open to visitation. Many more "wild" caves are present in the Valley and are frequented by speleologists and spelunkers.[18]

Known better as natural bridges, karst bridges are yet another prominent feature of karst topography, and Natural Bridge in namesake Rockbridge County—at 215 feet high with a span of ninety feet—is one of the best known in the world. Several theories abound for the factors responsible for its creation, but it is probably the result of subterranean stream piracy and the remaining roof of what was previously an underground tunnel. Natural Chimneys, a popular park near Mt. Solon in Augusta County, is another former cave that has succumbed to erosion.[19]

The Valley's carbonate geology is also responsible for a number of large springs found in the region. Springs mark the discharge point for groundwater to the surface, often at contact points between different rock formations. Springs have been used for public water supply in the Valley and also for medicinal purposes, and the Allegheny Mountains of the Virginias were once the epicenter of healing springs and attendant resorts for the Eastern Seaboard. The Homestead in Bath County and The Greenbrier in Greenbrier County, West Virginia, are two of the more renowned resorts, but the Shenandoah Valley proper had its fair share, including Orkney Springs in Shenandoah County and Rockbridge Alum Springs in Rockbridge County. The Southern gentry, looking to escape the heat and mosquitos of the Lowland South, would travel to these resorts and luxuriate in their waters, which were thought to have been endowed with healing properties that could cure various ailments.

There was a social hierarchy that prevailed at the Virginia springs that mimicked the plantation life that the gentry class was accustomed to, which was a marked departure from northern concerns such as Saratoga Springs in New York State. Maps produced as early as the antebellum period advertised these springs and the transportation routes that would carry travelers there. Many resorts such as Orkney Springs were aided by the railroad, the depot of the Manassas Gap Railroad being in nearby Mount Jackson. Whereas many of the old healing springs are no longer visible on the landscape, Orkney Springs is still teeming with visitors that come to hear the fifty-year old Shenandoah Valley Music Festival on summer nights, or attend conferences and retreats sponsored by the Episcopal Diocese of Virginia, which has owned the hotel and grounds since 1979 and built the outdoor cathedral of Shrine Mont in 1925.[20]

Mineral springs were not only soaked in, but bottled for consumption. In fact, the bottled water industry is a not a recent phenomenon in America but dates back to the first quarter of the nineteenth-century at the aforementioned Saratoga Springs. Near Elkton in the Shenandoah Valley, the Bear Lithia Water Company (later changed to Bear Lithia Springs of Rockingham County) was chartered in 1889 and bottled mineral water for sale, maintaining offices and a warehouse in New York City. Bear Lithia would transport its mineral water in glass-lined tank cars via railroad and bottle it in New York for sale to the urban market.

The bottled water tradition continues today, with national and even international notoriety being bestowed on Shenandoah Valley waters. In 2012, two bottled water producers—Almost Heaven (bottling Berkeley Springs, West Virginia, water) and Virginia's Best Natural Artesian Water (a product of Wholesome Foods in Edinburg) took home third- and second-place honors, respectively, in world competition held, appropriately, in Berkeley Springs in eastern Morgan County.[21]

*Berkeley Springs, West Virginia**
OIL ON PANEL, 12" X 9," OCTOBER 27, 2014 (PAINTING #206).

Cowbane Prairie Preserve 2, near Stuarts Draft
oil on panel, 4" x 8," November 11, 2012 (painting #182).

Land Cover

> Every few years our large mountains are fired, I think, by parties who put cattle into pasture, or by persons hired by them. Penalties against setting fires do not amount to much, as persons can hardly ever caught at it.
>
> —Jacob Crisler, Liberty Furnace, Shenandoah County (ca. 1882)[22]

Presently, the Shenandoah Valley's floor is largely cleared for agriculture or for residential, commercial, industrial, or institutional uses, with the surrounding mountains predominantly forested—a ratio of approximately thirty-four percent open land to fifty-six percent woodland. Land cover during the colonial period is not as easily quantified and has been an ongoing debate for years. A number of nineteenth- and early-twentieth-century historians described the Valley as a vast prairie, while modern historians have generally refuted this appraisal.

Historians have traditionally relied on accounts of travelers, surveyors, and settlers to attempt to answer this question, but each source has inherent flaws. Travelers typically kept to well-traveled thoroughfares and, for the most part, were not trained naturalists. Land surveying at the time was largely a rudimentary affair, with surveyors typically choosing trees as corners, since they were durable monuments and their use did not necessitate making and carrying stakes into the field. Because they were establishing boundaries rather than retracing them, the process did not have to be exact, and what was most convenient for surveyors working in difficult conditions held sway. Hence, it is problematic to glean the density of a forest from calculating the ratio of witness trees to stakes in early metes-and-bounds surveys. Further complicating matters is the misidentification of tree species and a surveyor's bias in selecting certain witness trees over others. These discrepancies characterized early surveys in the Eastern states but most especially in the Mid-Atlantic and South. The journals and diaries of surveyors and settlers, while often a valuable resource for assessing the condition of the land at the time of settlement, cannot exclusively be relied upon to gauge forest cover accurately prior to European possession, since the Valley had been unoccupied by permanent American Indian settlements for probably a century or more. Even if the Valley were predominantly an open landscape during Indian tenure, the forests would have been substantially regenerated by the settlement period.[23]

The accounts of early explorers, which predate settlement by sixty or so years, perhaps provide more insight into the native landscape. If augmented with modern research that incorporates ecology, botany, and forestry, a more accurate picture of pre-European forest density may be reconstructed. In the area of the United States roughly east of the 100th meridian, the pre-contact landscape was dominated by forests. Nevertheless, open areas did exist. Most contemporary scholars accept the fact that American Indians burned the understory of forests to perpetuate wildlife habitat, improve hunting, ease travel, and facilitate agriculture, although the extent of fire usage is still contested. A number of scholars, from the late-nineteenth century to the present, have mentioned the Shenandoah Valley, in particular, as having been extensively burned by aboriginals. Burning may have been most pronounced in riparian areas, where American Indian occupation tended to be concentrated as part of a system of swidden agriculture, yet upland areas where fire was used to drive game likewise show evidence of fire history; fire-scar chronologies and charcoal and pollen analyses, coupled with archaeological evidence of Indian occupation, help to reinforce claims of Indian burning. Since the onset of the Holocene epoch, oak forests began to predominate in the East due to fire disturbance as well as climate change. The dominance of oak prior to European occupation has been affirmed by studies of old-growth forests, and its continued presence on the landscape after European settlement is confirmed by land survey records. Specifically, *Quercus alba L.* (white oak) is the species most frequently documented in witness-tree references from early surveys in the Shenandoah Valley.[24]

Indians were not the only cultural group burning the forests, as colonists likewise contributed to the fire regime for many of the same reasons, especially for farming and hunting. Burning was not confined to the settlement period, as cattlemen set fires in the mountains as late as the turn of the twentieth century to improve forage for ranging cattle. Suppression of forest fires, seen as an elixir to the degradation of the forested landscape, characterized the policy of the newly created U.S. Forest Service during the early twentieth century. Oak, a very fire-tolerant yet shade-intolerant species—attributes that allowed it to prosper during periodic burning—began to be supplanted by more fire-intolerant and shade-tolerant species such as red maple during the era of fire suppression.

Early explorers' accounts of "savannas" in the Appalachian Highlands appear to have been accurate, as modern botanists and ecologists conjecture that oak savannas, more typically associated with the Midwest, likely constituted significant acreage on the valley floor before European settlement. That savannas occupy a position midway between prairie and forestland is an important distinction to make, for they contain more tree cover than prairies yet possess less tree cover than forests. In other words, tree canopy cover is, in order of lowest to highest percentage, is prairie, savanna, woodland, and forestland.[25]

In addition to savannas, early explorers in the Valley accurately described the presence of "barrens." Both barrens and glades were historically used by early settlers to denote relatively open tracts of land, but their meanings have gone through several iterations and are terms not used consistently by modern scholars either, their nomenclature varying on a regional basis. Barrens, as they are known in the Ridge and Valley Province of the Virginias, occur on both limestone and shale. Shale barrens occur on steep, southwest-facing hillsides, which are hotter and drier than other slope orientations—conditions that are responsible for the paucity of vegetation. Limestone and dolomite barrens are similarly developed on shallow soils but are, instead, dominated by perennial, warm-season prairie grasses. Some scholars refer to perennial grass-dominated limestone barrens as xeric limestone prairies, which have been verified to be the same natural community described in historical accounts of the Great Plains area of Penns Valley in Centre County, Pennsylvania, which is located in the Ridge and Valley Province along with the Shenandoah Valley. Likewise, glades are associated with limestone but are, instead, characterized by significant exposure of bedrock as well as sparse vegetation consisting of annual grasses. In addition to xeric (dry) prairies, other grasslands historically known in the Shenandoah Valley include mesic (moderate moisture)/wet-mesic prairies, such as that found along Abrams Creek in Frederick County, and wet prairies/prairie fens, such as that found at Cowbane Prairie in Augusta County.[26]

Indeed, the landscape at Cowbane Prairie, conserved in perpetuity by the Virginia Department of Conservation and Recreation and The Nature Conservancy, provides a unique glimpse into grasslands that co-existed alongside forests in the Deciduous Forest Biome. Considering the valley floor and adjacent ridges as well as anthropogenic (created by humans), geological, edaphic (related to soil), and hydrological sources, the Valley was probably a mosaic of prairies, savannas, open woodland, and closed-canopy forests.

While true tallgrass prairies are located in the Midwest and Great Plains, "prairie-like" areas definitely existed in the Shenandoah Valley, which is consistent with one conjectured Iroquoian naming convention for Shenandoah—"great meadow" or "great plain(s)." Unfortunately, agriculture, development, and invasive species over the years have diminished these unique ecological communities that are home to a number of rare plants. But, in a unique turn of events, non-profit conservation groups and government land managers are burning grasslands and woodlands once again in the vein of the Indians in order to perpetuate ecological health. Whether or not this positively impacts biodiversity is a matter of ongoing research and debate, but, to many, an even greater challenge than maintaining biodiversity is preventing the Valley's rural landscape from being converted into suburban and urban uses that replicate homogenous American places elsewhere, including the wide swath of northern Virginia near Washington, D.C.[27]

Rockfish Gap, Overlook 1 from the Skyline Drive
OIL ON LINEN, 18" X 24," JULY 12, 2011 (PAINTING #116).

The Blue Ridge Mountains and National Parks

> A peculiarity of the Blue Ridge may be noticed here, and it is a royal one. It is the change of its robes, and especially of those gorgeous ones which it puts on at evening. All mountains seen afar are blue—distance lends this enchantment to the view—but this particular range of mountains in Virginia has a depth, a variety and a wealth of different shades of blue that are strikingly peculiar, and so much so that the color has given them their name. It is a blue of infinite richness, of a strange misty depth that baffles analysis, and as variable as the sunset sky that joins with it. Now mist-gilded, again light as the heaven's arch, again purplish, again indescribable as a mixture of blue and red, and all these phenomena taking place, perhaps, in half an hour's span of the sun, the garments of the mountain changed, swift as the weaver's shuttle that makes them in the light woven of earth and sky. The writer has repeatedly, while traveling near these mountains and struck by effects of color, found himself reflecting that if these effects were transferred to canvas, how art-critics would exclaim that they were fictitious and impossible!
>
> —Edward A. Pollard, *The Virginia Tourist* (1870) [28]

The Blue Ridge Mountains are synonymous with the Shenandoah Valley, their beauty lauded by residents and visitors alike. Their range, however, extends well beyond Virginia's borders, from Pennsylvania to Georgia, and constitutes its own physiographic province—aptly named the Blue Ridge Province—that is situated between the Ridge and Valley Province (of which the Shenandoah Valley is a part) and the Piedmont Province. The Blue Ridge Mountains are so named for the bluish haze that hangs over them, especially in late spring and summer, which is thought to be caused by a hydrocarbon called isoprene being emitted by trees to help mitigate hot temperatures.[29]

The Blue Ridge Mountains are bisected with numerous mountain gaps known as wind gaps, which include McCormick Gap and Rockfish Gap. Several theories abound for the natural phenomenon that produced these features. One theory, which has been championed for more than a century, postulates that these wind gaps were former water gaps through which streams previously flowed unfettered until they were captured or "pirated" by the more-dominant Shenandoah River and its master river, the Potomac. The pirating essentially "beheaded" the stream into two sections, causing each to flow opposite one another on either side of the Blue Ridge. Another theory, nearly as old as the previous, offers a more simplistic explanation—the gaps were caused by two streams flowing in opposite directions on either side of the mountain that retreated and carved a notch in the process. These gaps, regardless of causation, are a distinctive feature on the landscape, and they provided a natural crossing for settlers from eastern Virginia who migrated westward into the

Shenandoah Valley on what, today, would be WV 9, VA 7, U.S. 50, U.S. 522, U.S. 211, U.S. 33, U.S. 250, VA 56, U.S. 60, U.S. 501/VA 130, and VA 43. Indeed, the Blue Ridge Mountains have served as both a natural and cultural barrier between eastern and western Virginia since the eighteenth century.[30]

During the second quarter of the twentieth century, there was a groundswell of interest in protecting the scenic beauty of the Blue Ridge, which led to the establishment of Shenandoah National Park, Skyline Drive, Blue Ridge Parkway, and, although not confined to the Blue Ridge, the Appalachian Trail, all of which are currently administered by the National Park Service, of the U.S. Department of the Interior. While treasured by the American public, the creation of these large conservation areas was not without controversy.

Shenandoah National Park, established in 1936, became the first national park established east of the Mississippi River after what is now known as Acadia National Park in Maine. Unlike many of the national parks in the American West, the lands that became Shenandoah National Park were home to substantial numbers of full-time residents, many of whom had lineage in the area dating back to the mid-eighteenth century. The National Park Service decided that it would not accept title to the lands that would comprise the park until all residents were removed. To facilitate removal, the Commonwealth of Virginia passed the Public Park Condemnation Act in 1928, which provided enabling legislation for eminent domain to be utilized. To bring the park to fruition, Virginia bore not only the responsibility of evicting residents, but also all land acquisition costs. Only after these actions were completed would the federal government take title to the land via a deed conveyance from the Commonwealth.

The process was further delayed by reluctant landowners, who, in some instances, had to be evicted by the county sheriff's department, and others, who filed lawsuits protesting the taking of their land. These cases were eventually dismissed, and approximately 465 families were removed—an estimated total of 2,317 people. Resettlement communities known as Shenandoah Homesteads were established for 340 families in seven separate locations in the Valley and Piedmont by state and federal agencies, but these mountaineers never became fully acclimated into mainstream society. As a testament to the flawed removal policies of state and federal government, only a few families remained in their "subsistence homesteads"—an artificial replication of the lifestyle the mountaineers lost—by the last quarter of the twentieth century.[31]

Although viewed by many as a success story in the conservation of natural resources, the creation of Shenandoah National Park is seen by many locals as a dark chapter in the Valley's history. The removal of families from their land, when the resources they owned were coveted, is a twentieth-century iteration of what had been occurring since the seventeenth century with American Indians in Virginia. Seemingly justifying removal at the behest of state and federal government agencies and a view no doubt encouraged by promoters of the park was the notion that mountaineers led a submarginal existence and would lead a better life in the resettlement communities. Audrey Horning, in her archeological study of several of the mountain hollows that were included within the park, refutes the notion that the mountaineers were destitute, as evidenced by the discovery of various and sundry mass-produced consumer goods. Another myth accepted as truth was that the land had been severely abused by the mountaineers. Reed Engle, a former Cultural Resources Specialist for Shenandoah National Park, suggests that resource exploitation was more likely caused by absentee landowners and corporate entities who owned ninety percent of the parcels that would comprise the park's boundaries. Ironically, the creation of Skyline Drive and Blue Ridge Parkway may have done as much or more damage to the environment than a scant number of mountaineers.[32]

Despite limited population density, the Civilian Conservation Corps (CCC) was requested to remove all vestiges of human occupation in the national park in order to perpetuate a natural setting. In actuality, the land was never untouched by man in recent history, as it had been managed as a game preserve by American Indians long before European settlement. In fact, it is likely that no area within immediate view of Skyline Drive could be considered "natural" due to the heavy hand of the CCC. Despite all of these efforts to "restore" the scene to pre-Columbian times, editors of *National Geographic* magazine opined, at the time of the park's creation, that "the mountaineers, not the scenery, were the real tourist attraction." This philosophy was perpetuated on the Blue Ridge Parkway—the cultural landscape was thought to enhance the motoring experience—but, apparently, the existing vernacular landscape was deemed not worthy enough, so a contrived one was created in its stead.[33]

The reverberations of past government land-use policies can still be felt to this day, as Valley residents are inherently contemptuous of regulation. Alas, if both the natural and cultural resources of the Shenandoah Valley are to be sustained well into the future, a more carefully designed and holistic paradigm must be employed in lieu of a heavy-handed, top-down approach that alienates locals instead of incorporating them into decision-making.

Nonetheless, the creation of Shenandoah National Park, Skyline Drive, Blue Ridge Parkway, and the Appalachian Trail are huge draws, as millions of people each year come to experience the wonders of the Blue Ridge Mountains and Shenandoah Valley. More than 123,000,000 have visited the park since its founding in 1936, making it among the most visited places in the national park system. Peak visitation was in 1976–1977 (2,448,600 and 2,789,100, respectively) during America's bicentennial celebration, compared with 694,098 in 1936 and 1,255,321 in 2014. According to the National Park Service, a peer-reviewed spending analysis of visitors to Shenandoah National Park reveals an economic benefit to the Valley of $104,700,000 during 2014 alone, with visitation supporting an estimated 1,100 local jobs.[34]

The North Fork and Signal Knob, near Strasburg
oil on panel, 8" x 12," september 23, 2008 (painting #147).

Massanutten Mountain

> To the million and a half young men and war veterans who have been or are today enrolled in the Civilian Conservation Corps camps, I extend greetings on this third anniversary of the establishment of the first CCC camp. Idled through no fault of your own, you were enrolled from city and rural homes and offered an opportunity to engage in healthful, outdoor work on forest, park and soil conservation projects of definite practical value to all the people of the Nation. The promptness with which you seized the opportunity to engage in honest work, the willingness with which you have performed your daily tasks, and the fine spirit you have shown in winning the respect of the communities in which your camps have been located merit the admiration of the entire country. You and the men who guided and supervised your efforts have caused to be proud of the record the CCC has made in the development of sturdy manhood and in the initiation and prosecution of a conservation program of unprecedented proportions.
>
> —Franklin D. Roosevelt (April 17, 1936)[35]

Situated between the Allegheny Mountains to the west and Blue Ridge Mountains to the east, Massanutten Mountain effectively divides the Valley in half for roughly fifty miles. The northern terminus of Massanutten between Strasburg and Waterlick is known as Signal Knob, which both Confederate and Union armies used during the Civil War as an observation and signal station. The southern terminus between Harrisonburg and Elkton is known as Massanutten Peak, which developed into a healing springs resort named Rockingham Springs after the Civil War and a four-season resort aptly named Massanutten Resort beginning in the early 1970s. Massanutten Mountain is known not only nationally, but also internationally by military historians and combat instructors who have studied the tactics of Confederate General Thomas J. "Stonewall" Jackson during his 1862 Valley Campaign, who used the mountain deftly to shield his maneuvers from the Union Army. In addition, geologists and geomorphologists have extensively studied its unique physiographic form and structure.[36]

Much of the mountain land is under federal ownership as part of George Washington National Forest. As with the Allegheny Mountains, nearly all of Massanutten's high-grade timber was clear-cut during the nineteenth century to support the various iron furnaces that operated nearby. Further, its forest health had been compromised due to repeated forest fires before it came under federal ownership in 1918. In 1933, it was on Massanutten Mountain that Camp Roosevelt, the first Civilian Conservation Corps (CCC) camp, was established as an outgrowth of President Franklin D. Roosevelt's New Deal. Comprised of young men, primarily city dwellers, the CCC worked to improve the forests on Massanutten Mountain and in other CCC camps by planting trees as well as constructing campgrounds and trails. It operated until the U.S. Congress discontinued the program in 1942. Additional federal presence on Massanutten was contemplated when it was being promoted as the site of Shenandoah National Park by a local businessman's association known as Shenandoah Valley, Inc. that was formed to stimulate tourism. Ultimately, it was decided that Massanutten could not compete with the Blue Ridge Mountains in terms of views, remoteness, and quality of trout streams. Despite the opinions rendered on Massanutten's worthiness as a national park, it remains one of the more distinctive natural features of the Shenandoah Valley.[37]

Wedged between Massanutten's ridges is one of the more isolated and scenic locales in the region—Fort Valley. It is a valley within a mountain within a valley; technically, it is a U-shaped, downfolded syncline. Because Massanutten Mountain is comprised of quartzarenite of Silurian age known as Massanutten Sandstone, it did not erode when the Great Valley was formed like the less-resistant limestone and shale belts in the valleys east and west. According to local lore, Fort Valley was a place of last refuge for George Washington's troops, had the American Revolution not ended as it did. Although this legend remains unsubstantiated, Washington would have had gained knowledge of the area while working as a land surveyor for Lord Fairfax.[38]

Fort Valley is, essentially, the Shenandoah Valley in miniature, with forestland occupying the ridges and agriculture predominating in the valley floor. Without a major thoroughfare running through it, much of Fort Valley looks like it did a century or more ago. Local pride is pervasive, although the closure of some businesses and schools over the years have forced residents to travel either to the Main Valley to the west or Page Valley to the east for goods and services.

*At the Foot of Massanutten Mountain near Tumbling Run, Shenandoah County**
OIL ON CANVAS, 12" X 24," OCTOBER 20, 2008 (PAINTING #3).

Autumn, Massanutten Mountain and Shenandoah Valley from the Skyline Drive
OIL ON PANEL, 7" X 11," NOVEMBER 14, 2011 (PAINTING #77).

The Allegheny Mountains
and National Forests

> The Alleghaney (sic) being the great ridge which divides the waters of the Atlantic from those of the Missisipi (sic), its summit is doubtless more elevated above the ocean than that of any other mountain. But its relative height, compared with the base on which it stands, is not so great as that of some others, the country rising behind the successive ridges like the steps of stairs . . .
>
> —Thomas Jefferson, *Notes on the State of Virginia* (1782)[39]

The Allegheny Mountains extend from northern Pennsylvania to central West Virginia and continue southward through Kentucky to Tennessee as the Cumberland Mountains. The Allegheny Front is a steep escarpment that divides the Appalachian Plateaus Province to the west (Ohio River drainage) from the Ridge and Valley Province to the east (Chesapeake Bay drainage). The Shenandoah Valley, located at the eastern end of the Ridge and Valley Province, contains the first ridges of the Alleghenies, which include Little North Mountain (elevations that range from 1,033 to 2,693 feet), Great North Mountain (elevations that range from 1,365 to 4,455 feet), and Shenandoah Mountain (elevation 3,051 feet). That certain counties west of these ridges remained in Virginia—Alleghany, Bath, and Highland—while others similarly situated were included in the State of West Virginia—Pendleton, Hardy, and Hampshire—is a testament to the divisiveness created by the Civil War.[40]

Much of the Alleghenies within the Virginias are included in the National Forest System administered by the U.S. Forest Service. Collectively, about acres 2,700,000 acres of national forest land is located in the two states, but some of that acreage is within the Cumberland Mountains rather than the Alleghenies. The Shenandoah Valley proper contains roughly 508,000 acres of national forest land. The northernmost section of national forest lands in the Shenandoah Valley was originally called Shenandoah National Forest, when it was created in 1918, before being renamed George Washington National Forest in 1932. Likewise, Natural Bridge National Forest, located along the Blue Ridge instead of the Alleghenies, was created in 1918 before being transferred to George Washington in 1933. Jefferson National Forest, which was adjacent to George Washington and extended from Rockbridge County southward, was created in 1936 and administratively merged with George Washington in 1995. Unlike condemnation through eminent domain that was used to acquire lands that became Shenandoah National Park, in most instances the Forest Service purchased lands for national forests in the East from willing sellers.[41]

Virginia's pig iron industry was centered in the Allegheny Mountains, which, in addition to abundant deposits of iron ore, had abundant timber needed to produce charcoal used during the smelting process. Numerous hamlets, particularly in Shenandoah County, took their names from the furnaces that developed there: Columbia Furnace, Elizabeth Furnace, Liberty Furnace, and Van Buren Furnace. These furnaces were critical to producing munitions for the Confederacy, since the South's industrial economy was not as highly developed as that in the North. Unfortunately, forest health was severely compromised by the clear cutting of timber to produce charcoal, which was representative of national forests in the East at the time of their acquisition. Tanneries also depleted forests, as trees were clear-cut for their bark, which produced tannic acid that was used in the leather-tanning process before the advent of chemical tanning. Stewardship of forest resources has greatly improved over the years, and logging with horses, which was once commonplace in Valley, is again making inroads, as a number of loggers seek to increase a dialogue of sustainability.[42]

While a large portion of the Alleghenies in the Shenandoah Valley has been historically characterized by oak-hickory forest (it may have been predominantly oak-chestnut before the massive chestnut blight of the early twentieth century), the higher elevations in the Alleghenies contain some spruce-fir forest (balsam fir and red spruce) as well as northern hardwoods (beech-birch-maple), which distinguish this region of Virginia from the oak-pine and pine forests (shortleaf, loblolly, and Virginia pine) that are found east of the Blue Ridge Mountains. More often identified with New England and Upstate New York, Virginia has a number of commercial maple syrup producers who are centered in Highland County, located just west of the Shenandoah Valley but sometimes associated with it.[43]

Aside from the forest resources of the Alleghenies, its mineral resources deserve mention. In addition to the aforementioned iron-ore deposits, a valuable Devonian age shale formation—Marcellus Shale—is found in the western Shenandoah Valley and, especially, in much of West Virginia, Pennsylvania, eastern Ohio, and the Southern Tier counties of New York State. Its potential for supplying natural gas appears to be tremendous but so, too, are the environmental impacts associated with drilling it. Hydraulic fracturing, known as hydrofracking or simply "fracking," is the process by which large amounts of water, sand, and chemicals are injected at high pressure during the drilling process to fracture the shale beneath in order to release the natural gas imbedded within, at times and in certain conditions causing groundwater contamination. Also, transporting the natural gas to refineries and markets from such rural locations requires a new infrastructure, including proposals for new pipelines such as the controversial 594-mile-long Atlantic Coast Pipeline whose current alignment from West Virginia to North Carolina will traverse portions of the Blue Ridge Parkway, George Washington National Forest, and historically significant and environmentally sensitive areas of Augusta County. Time will tell what the future of this industry may hold in the Shenandoah Valley and beyond.[44]

Henrietta Furnace, Shenandoah Alum Springs
OIL ON PANEL, 6" X 8," JULY 12, 2015 (PAINTING #241).

*Thomas Hudson House and Environs, Hudson Crossroads**
oil on panel, 7" x 12," july 12, 2015 (painting #250).

PART II: THE CULTURAL LANDSCAPE

> On this occasion three of the passengers were discussing the claims of several of the States to the "Garden Spot of America," while others listened or slept. One of the three presented the claim of Lancaster county, Pennsylvania, in its then highly cultivated condition; its rich limestone soil, its beautiful rolling surface, its never failing harvests, its immense barns, etc. The second, in elegant terms, portrayed the region round about Frankfort, Kentucky, for beauty and climate, and for fertility of soil and elegant improvements, as the "Garden Spot." And the third gentleman presented and urged the claim of the Shenandoah Valley, of Virginia, surrounded by the mountains and watered by ten thousand never failing springs gushing from the mountains; its golden harvests of grains and luscious fruits, and its blooded flocks upon a thousand hills . . .
>
> —Unidentified newspaper article (ca. 1821)[45]

Distinct from natural landscapes, cultural landscapes are aptly defined by the World Heritage Committee as those that "represent the combined works of nature and of man [and] are illustrative of the evolution of human society and settlement over time, under the influence of the physical constraints and/or opportunities presented by their natural environment and of successive social, economic and cultural forces, both external and internal." With an economy historically based on agriculture and, to a lesser extent, on forestry and mineral extraction, residents have utilized the natural resources of the Shenandoah Valley for centuries. Even before European settlers cleared extensive wooded tracts for farming, Indians in the Valley manipulated forestland and grassland by burning in order to perpetuate agriculture, improve wildlife habitat, and facilitate travel. The term "Indian Old Fields" or simply "Old Fields," used in the Colonial era to denote such areas, survives to the present, as evidenced by the hamlet of Old Fields north of Moorefield (WV) in the South Branch Valley of the Potomac River.[46]

This section of the book is organized into the more common types of human activity that have influenced the Valley's cultural landscape and are illustrative of its unique cultural heritage. The groupings are based loosely on the National Register of Historic Places Criteria for Evaluation pertaining to Areas of (Historic) Significance. Whereas the National Register in its infancy focused on individual buildings and structures, in recent decades we have seen the application of historic significance to landscapes that provide context for these buildings and structures. Where cohesive landscapes of national significance exist, the U.S. Congress has designated National Heritage Areas. The Shenandoah Valley Battlefields National Historic District is one of forty-eight such areas designated, although the district includes a non-Shenandoah Valley county (Highland) and precludes two Valley counties (Jefferson and Berkeley) that are in West Virginia. While the primary focus of this National Heritage Area is the Civil War, the Shenandoah Valley should be considered a nationally significant historic landscape exclusive of that watershed event, as the following vignettes in this section reveal.[47]

Although this section presents the Valley's cultural landscape in ten vignettes, it is important to remember that, in conjunction with the natural landscape, people and land are interconnected. Therefore, our understanding of the uniqueness of the Shenandoah Valley must encompass its historic buildings, both high-style and vernacular, and its cultivated fields, managed woodlots, and transportation network that have been adapted to fit the topography.

The Valley's variegated landscape, however, has been increasingly imprinted by urbanization and its attendant homogeneity that has been spurred on by Interstates 81, 66, and 64 and the fact that approximately seventy percent of America's population east of the Mississippi River now resides within an eight-hour drive of the Shenandoah Valley. Thus, even as one can appreciate the local, it is hard to escape the pressures of the global, even in a landscape as beautiful and historic as is the Valley's.

Truck Stop at Exit 200 on I-81, Fairfield
OIL ON PANEL, 8" X 12," APRIL 28, 2015 (PAINTING #223).

The South Fork and Page Valley from the Skyline Drive
OIL ON PANEL, 7" X 11," NOVEMBER 14, 2011 (PAINTING #196).

Boundaries, Settlements, and Urbanization

> To my mind nothing is clearer, than that Congress never did undertake to give its consent to the transfer of Berkeley and Jefferson counties to the State of West Virginia until March 2, 1866. If so, the consent came too late, because the legislature of Virginia had, on the fifth day of December, 1865, withdrawn its assent to the proposed cession of these two counties. This withdrawal was in ample time, as it was before the proposal of the State had become operative as a concluded compact, and the bill (in my judgment) shows that Virginia had sufficient reasons for recalling its proposition to part with the territory embraced within these counties . . .
>
> —Associate Justice David Davis, of the U.S. Supreme Court Dissenting Opinion in *Virginia v. West Virginia* (1870)[48]

Although synonymous with natural beauty, humans have had a strong hand in shaping the Shenandoah Valley's landscape according to their cultural dictates. Boundary disputes, settlement policies, and wars have all imprinted the land in different ways, and, with a careful eye, the contemporary traveler can still discern these nuances. The Valley is, in essence, the Alsace-Lorraine of Virginia, a cultural borderland that has had contested ownership claims by various entities over hundreds of years. Indeed, the Valley was settled by a fair number of Alsatians and much resembles the Rhine River Valley—a broad valley floor with a legendary river running through it and flanked by mountains. The Town of Strasburg in Shenandoah County bears witness to these Rhenish roots, named after Strasbourg, the capital and cultural hub of Alsace.[49]

At the time of contact with European settlers, the Shenandoah Valley was generally devoid of permanent aboriginal villages and had been for nearly a century. A number of American Indian peoples of Algonquian linguistic stock living in and adjacent to this region in the Late Woodland Period appear to have migrated to the Atlantic Coastal Plain and banded together to form fortified villages. Their movements may have been prompted by threats from tribes of Iroquoian linguistic stock living to the north and west. Specifically, evidence suggests that these Algonquian peoples were dominated by the Susquehannocks after that tribe migrated to the lower Susquehanna River Valley of Pennsylvania between 1550 and 1575. Several archeological sites associated with the Susquehannocks have been found in the South Branch Valley of the Potomac River, confirming their presence near the Shenandoah Valley. To be sure, indigenous groups used the region as hunting grounds and as a thoroughfare for conducting trade and making war. In particular, the Great Valley was used by the Five Nations Iroquois League (which later became the Six Nations) in present-day New York State as an avenue to attack the Catawbas and Cherokees to the south in the present-day Carolinas.[50]

Desirous of buffering older Virginia settlements east of the Blue Ridge Mountains from the French and Indians to the west, Virginia's Lieutenant Governor Sir William Gooch offered various incentives to land-hungry settlers from the northern colonies to compel them to migrate southward. By the second quarter of the eighteenth century, land was becoming expensive in Pennsylvania, and settlers began looking elsewhere for opportunities. Because the lords proprietor of Maryland and Pennsylvania—the Calverts (Lords Baltimore) and Penns, respectively—were engaged in a boundary dispute, many settlers initially bypassed Maryland for the more southerly Shenandoah Valley, where, theoretically, they could obtain clear title to land. The situation north of the Potomac River would not be resolved until 1767, when Charles Mason and Jeremiah Dixon, two English surveyors, finished drawing the famous Mason and Dixon line demarcating the borders of Delaware, Maryland, Pennsylvania, and what is now West Virginia.[51]

The Pennsylvanians arrived in the Shenandoah Valley mainly by way of the Great Philadelphia Wagon Road, which began in Philadelphia and ran southwestward through Maryland, Virginia, and into the Carolinas. From the Susquehanna River to the Potomac River, it generally followed an old Indian trail known as the Monocacy Path, although an extension of the Wagon Road that passed through the Cumberland and Hagerstown Valleys and by what is now Williamsport en route to the Shenandoah Valley followed another Indian trail aptly named the Virginia Path, which purportedly was the easternmost trail that the Six Nations Iroquois used to strike their enemies to the south. Since the Valley notably lacked permanent Indian villages, settlement proceeded relatively peaceably. In addition, some historians credit the influence of the British Quakers and Germanic sectarians—both pacifists—for setting the stage for peaceful relations.[52]

Nevertheless, as the region became more populated, tensions arose between settlers and natives concerning the use of the Valley as a highway for Indian travel. At a treaty conference in Albany, New York, in 1722 between Pennsylvania, Maryland, Virginia, and the Iroquois, an attempt was made to set a line of separation between Indian movements and white settlement. While the Iroquois thought the line was located at the Blue Ridge Mountains, the Virginians thought it to be farther west along the Alleghenies. The situation still was unresolved by the time of the 1744 treaty conference in Lancaster, Pennsylvania, where the Iroquois again asserted their claims to the Shenandoah Valley. In essence, they believed the Virginians to be trespassing on lands they claimed through right of conquest of the Susquehannocks. To satisfy the matter, the Iroquois were finally compensated for these lands, which they deeded over to the Virginians. As a result, the Iroquois agreed to move the Great Warriors Path farther west into the Allegheny Mountains.[53]

Settlers in the Virginia backcountry, whatever their cultural background, shared the common goal of obtaining decent land at reasonable prices. Although they neither had to contend with Indian claims to the same extent that caused a delay in the settlement of western Pennsylvania nor concern themselves with the well-known boundary dispute between the Penn and Calvert families, they, instead, found themselves in the middle of another controversy concerning land claims. Like the Calvert and Penn family lands in Maryland and Pennsylvania, the lands in the Shenandoah Valley were part of a vast, private estate known as the Northern Neck Proprietary, which was owned by the Fairfax family rather than the Colony of Virginia. King Charles II had originally

Ferry Hill Plantation above the Potomac River, Sharpsburg, Maryland
OIL ON PANEL, 6" X 8," JUNE 26, 2011 (PAINTING #35).

*Greenway Court, near White Post**

OIL ON PANEL, 8" X 12," FEBRUARY 6, 2012 (PAINTING #54).

granted all the land between the Potomac and Rappahannock Rivers, from their headwaters to Chesapeake Bay, to seven individuals in 1649 as a reward for faithful services rendered. Among these patentees were two members of the Culpeper family, whose interests passed to the Fairfax family through marriage. Eventually, Thomas, the 6th Lord Fairfax, would come to Virginia to assert his claim over the proprietary, as its geographic boundaries were being challenged by the Colony of Virginia, and he was not profiting from the land grants being awarded in the Valley. In essence, Virginia disputed the location of the Potomac's headwaters, stating they ended at the Blue Ridge rather than the Alleghenies, thereby giving the colony control over the Shenandoah lands—a strikingly similar strategy used to negate the land claims of the Five Nations Iroquois League. After hearing the evidence and examining the extensive surveys that were made, the Committee of Trade and Plantations in London, England, decided in favor of Fairfax in 1745, thereby confirming his ownership of the lands in the Shenandoah Valley and South Branch Valley of the Potomac; the aptly named Fairfax Stone was placed to mark the western limit of the (North Branch of the) Potomac River and of Lord Fairfax's domain.[54]

The aptly named village of White Post grew up around a wooden signpost that marked the way to Greenway Court, the seat of Lord Fairfax, the 6th Baron of Cameron. Lord Fairfax, a lifelong bachelor, appears to have had relative comfort in his backcountry environment, as evidenced by a woodcut of Greenway Court, which burned and was replaced by a more modest brick dwelling that is still standing. Fortunately, the original Land Office is still extant and is currently located on private property. Two famous Virginians were employed by Lord Fairfax in administering the duties of the Proprietary Land Office—Robert "King" Carter as a land agent and George Washington as a land surveyor.

Because there were no requirements imposed for establishing towns, the Valley, during its initial period of settlement, was characterized by dispersed settlement patterns, as settlers sought out individual land grants. A number of geographers and historians refer to this pattern among the Valley's numerous Pennsilfaanisch Deitsch (Pennsylvania Dutch) settlements as the "Einzelhof"—German for "isolated farmstead"—that was widespread in what is now Germany and may have been brought to Pennsylvania and thence to the Valley. This pattern is conjectured to have developed during the Middle Ages, as forestland was cleared and farmers gradually moved away from nucleated villages and associated communal land holdings. Other scholars suggest the isolated farmstead was known in other parts of Europe, including Wales, western England, and Ulster. Whatever its antecedents, the economic system that first developed in the Valley reinforced the dispersed farmstead pattern, with the majority of goods being consumed at home and surplus generally bartered with neighbors who shared a similar cultural affiliation. The clustering of cultural groups in specific areas of the Shenandoah Valley may have been indicative of the communal goals of these settlers. As stated succinctly by historian James Henretta, "linguistic and religious ties extended beyond settlement patterns to encompass economic relationships." In essence, economic gain was still important to these settlers but was not as important as the yearly subsistence and long-term financial security of the family unit and greater community.[55]

Warren R. Hofstra and Robert D. Mitchell, two of the most accomplished scholars of the Valley's colonial history, have eloquently argued and persistently reinforced the notion that, as subsistence farming transitioned to specialized agricultural production—endemic of a capitalist economy—hamlets, villages, and towns were developed to serve as centers of trade for the output of the dispersed farmsteads. Opequon in Frederick County, Millwood in Clarke County, and Singers Glen in Rockingham County are three such enclaves that served the needs of surrounding farm communities, subscribing to the "irregular village" model of town planning, with its unordered system of roads jutting in and out. Other hamlets and villages such as Middlebrook and Brownsburg (in Augusta and Rockbridge Counties, respectively) were arranged as "linear villages" that tightly hugged the old turnpike that passed through them.[56]

In addition to Hofstra and Mitchell, other outstanding scholars have studied the Shenandoah Valley and its cultural source areas in great detail, including Richard Pillsbury and Wilbur Zelinksy, the latter including the Lower Valley in a study of Pennsylvania town morphology. Zelinsky opined that towns located in the so-called Pennsylvania Culture Region were characterized by their compactness, density, lack of green space, preference for a mixture of building materials (in addition to brick) such as stone and log, and predominance of row houses or duplexes. Zelinsky surmised that the Pennsylvania Culture Region's robust agricultural and industrial economies and its prime location resulted in its early urbanization. Indeed, traveling across the Middle Valley and Lower Valley and adjacent parts of Maryland and Pennsylvania today, one seems to encounter a substantial town every few miles. The most-heavily Germanic county in the Valley—Shenandoah—perhaps most resembled the German-settled areas of Pennsylvania in its copious amount of towns, villages, and hamlets. Pennsylvania and Virginia Germans were known as having a fair number of artisans among its populace, who maintained shops in these enclaves. Furniture produced by Valley maker Johannes Spitler today commands record prices at antique auctions.[57]

While Pennsylvania was a source area for many Valley settlers and the Pennsylvania-like traits that are evident in the Valley's landscape are a recurring theme throughout this book, one must not ignore eastern Virginia's contributions to the Valley's landscape. Clarke County, with nary a town of substance save for the county seat of Berryville, is typical of the settlement patterns found east of the Blue Ridge, where the self-sufficient plantation economy that revolved around the production of a staple crop—tobacco—obviated the need for towns. Towns, where they existed in the Lowland South and its extensions, were the antithesis of the Pennsylvania town; they were not as compact with fewer rowhouses and duplexes, the building material was predominantly brick, and a plethora of non-farm rural residences dotted the countryside. While it would be convenient to argue that various counties in the Valley subscribed either to Pennsylvania or Tidewater/Piedmont Virginia settlement phenomenon, the truth lies somewhere in the middle. While not as rural as eastern Virginia, the Valley certainly did not have the population densities that a more fully developed manufacturing state like Pennsylvania had.[58]

While the forces that developed during the colonial and federal eras greatly influenced patterns in the Valley's landscape, so, too, did the antebellum period and subsequent Civil War era. After Abraham Lincoln was elected President in 1860, the states of the Deep South, fearing that Lincoln would abolish slavery, passed ordinances of secession from the Union to form the Confederate States of America. Virginia, in the Upper South, was not so quick to secede and even took the lead in calling together a convention of all the states to discuss the state of affairs of the nation. At a

*Long Branch Plantation, Clarke County**
OIL ON PANEL, 12" X 16," FEBRUARY 6, 2012 (PAINTING #74).

subsequent state convention in April 1861, Virginians voted overwhelmingly against secession. That changed when President Lincoln issued a call for 75,000 volunteers from the remaining states in the Union after the South Carolinians' attack on Fort Sumter, and Virginia promptly reversed its course and voted for secession. Although a sizable number of Virginians still desired to remain in the Union, mostly in the counties west of the Allegheny Mountains, the secessionists saw Lincoln's call for troops as a heinous act that pitted Virginia against her sister states to the South.[59]

The ordinance of secession adopted by Virginia did not sit well with its western counties, many of whose delegates walked out of the convention and called for a pro-Union convention that first met in Wheeling (then, still a part of Virginia) in May and again in June. In October, western Virginians voted for statehood to establish the new state of West Virginia, which included forty-eight counties formerly within the Old Dominion. But it would be June 1863 before the new state was formally created. While this was the culminating event that severed ties between the two regions of the state, relations had been strained for many years prior. Essentially, western Virginians felt like their concerns were not being addressed in Richmond, which was dominated by delegates from east of the Alleghenies. The talk of the secession of western Virginia from the rest of the state was actually considered before, after a state convention met in 1829. In essence, there was always a substantial geographical, cultural, political, and economic divide between the sections of Virginia east and west of the front ranges of the Alleghenies.[60]

While West Virginia generally included those counties west of the Alleghenies (in the Appalachian Plateaus Physiographic Province), the border was not geographically consistent; several counties in southwestern Virginia, located in the Appalachian Plateaus Province, were not made part of the new state, while some counties in the Ridge and Valley Province ended up in West Virginia with others remaining in Virginia. In the Shenandoah Valley portion of the Ridge and Valley, Morgan, Berkeley, Jefferson, and Frederick Counties were not originally included in the new state, although the Constitution of West Virginia provided them with the choice of being included, should elections decide there was ample sentiment among their respective residents. When the citizenry of Jefferson and Berkeley Counties later voted on the issue, the results appeared to be overwhelmingly in favor of including these counties in West Virginia. But the Union Army controlled these counties and opened only several polling places, where they intimidated and harassed potential voters. In addition, many Confederate sympathizers were under house arrest and disallowed to cast their vote. Despite the desire of the majority of residents to remain in Virginia, particularly in Jefferson County, the counties were nevertheless appended to the new state. There was too much at stake for these counties to remain in the Old Dominion, particularly since the Baltimore and Ohio Railroad ran through this region now known as the Eastern Panhandle, and the federal government wanted to insure that its tracks lay within states loyal to the Union.[61]

After the Civil War, Virginia sued West Virginia to recover Berkeley and Jefferson Counties, and the case eventually made it to the U.S. Supreme Court in 1870. With justices undoubtedly unsympathetic to Virginia and its role in the Civil War, the high court awarded these counties to West Virginia. Many residents, particularly in Jefferson County, have ever since been bitter about this decision, and, according to local lore, it was a practice some years ago to place the word

"West" in parentheses when addressing an envelope. In 2011, 146 years removed from the end of the "War between the States," a state senator from Berkeley County introduced a bill that would give residents the opportunity to vote as to whether Berkeley, Jefferson, and Morgan Counties should secede from West Virginia and return to the Old Dominion.[62]

The portion of the Valley that became part of West Virginia has been influenced by specific state laws that differed from those in nearby Virginia. As to manufacturing, unions were a part of the woolen-mill landscape in Martinsburg, whereas Virginia has been a Right-to-Work state; strikes broke out in Martinsburg during the mid-twentieth century between management and workers, and the mills eventually shut down, some say as a result of organized labor. Commercial casinos are permitted in West Virginia but not in Virginia, as the casino adjacent to the Charles Town Races attests to, and a plethora of gentlemen's clubs dot the Eastern Panhandle's landscape, a testament to West Virginia's more relaxed laws regarding strip clubs. Finally, zoning regulations are less restrictive in these counties, as evidenced by the tremendous amount of land development that has occurred in this area during the past several decades, though crossing the Virginia state line does not exactly serve as a panacea to urban sprawl.[63]

The Shenandoah Valley's population currently sits at approximately 727,000 people, having increased by more than a quarter-million from 1982 to 2007 alone. The counties with the highest rate of growth, not surprisingly, are located in the Lower Valley within the Washington-Baltimore-Arlington Metropolitan Statistical Area (MSA), which is part of the greater Northeast Megalopolis region, with Harrisonburg-Staunton-Waynesboro comprising its own fast-growing MSA and Botetourt included within the Roanoke MSA. It is not population growth per se that has altered the rural landscape, but the consumptive manner in which land has been used. During the same twenty-five year period, between 1982 and 2007, urban land uses increased more than fifty-five percent. Despite being a marked departure from the extensive urbanization that characterizes the nearby Northern Virginia suburbs of Washington, D.C., like most areas of the nation, a sharp demarcation between town and country has been shunned in the Valley in favor of large, suburban-style lots that are, in land conservationists' lexicon, "too small to farm and too large to mow."

Farmers, who by necessity need to increase their holdings in order to compete in today's global agricultural economy, have found it difficult to afford increasingly expensive land whose "highest and best use" is deemed not as farmland but as residential subdivisions. As is too often the case, the very people who find views of farmland a major draw in purchasing a building lot in a particular subdivision are those who start complaining the minute the farmer spreads manure to fertilize his fields or hauls his slow-moving equipment down back roads. Thus, the perception of open land as parkland clashes with the reality of farmland and the harvesting of timber being part of the working landscape. With the passing of traditional livelihoods also comes the passing of rural culture, which is as much part of the landscape as the land itself. In its seminal study, *Farming on the Edge* (2015), the American Farmland Trust, a national farmland preservation non-profit, delineated much of the Valley as containing high-quality farmland with high development pressure, with threatened forestland possessing high economic value identified by the Virginia Department of Conservation and Recreation and Virginia Department of Forestry.[64]

Sprawl has not only had a deleterious effect on the rural landscape, but has affected the plethora of small towns in the region. Sprawl's bedfellows are the ubiquitous chain stores that conspire to render obsolete owners of independent small-town businesses. Nearly every town along the Old Valley Pike (U.S. 11) had hardware and grocery stores at one time, but small-town concerns have largely given way to regional shopping clusters that offer little in the way of community character. The unique and prideful downtowns along the Valley Pike have had to reinvent themselves, often in the form of specialty shops that must offer something different than the chain stores in order to survive. Unfortunately, the provision of useful goods and services are too frequently discarded in favor of esoteric offerings that cater to the leisure class who fan out from Northern Virginia each weekend in search of respite from suburban life and are attracted to the Valley's historic townscapes.

As the Valley's major urban enclaves—Martinsburg, Winchester, Harrisonburg, and the Staunton-Waynesboro corridor—expand their proverbial britches into the countryside vis-à-vis expansive new commercial and residential development, competition between city and county governments over annexation leads to tension over land-use planning, public services, transportation, water supply, and economic development. With a governmental structure almost unique in America, thirty-eight of the nation's independent cities are located in Virginia. The City of Staunton, in 1908, pioneered modern-day government when it hired its first city manager, the first such hire in American history. Cooperation is always the more positive approach to resolving issues as diverse as the location and maintenance of courts and courthouses, the sharing of emergency 911 access, and civil defense, but the political divide is often reinforced at the ballot box, where the rural county vote trends heavily (sometimes greater than seventy percent) toward the Republican party, regardless of its configuration, while the city vote is often evenly split or a slight lean toward the Democratic party, as was evidenced when voters in Winchester, Harrisonburg, Staunton, and Lexington preferred President Barack Obama in the presidential elections of 2008 and 2012.[65]

U.S. 33 at Harrisonburg
OIL ON PANEL, 8" X 12," OCTOBER 23, 2011 (PAINTING #117).

Potomac River from the Bavarian Inn, Shepherdstown, West Virginia
OIL ON CANVAS, 6" X 8," JUNE 26, 2011 (PAINTING #106).

Transportation

> No one can dispute that the valley pike has played a big part in the farming development of the four Virginia counties it traverses, and in view of the country-wide interest in good-roads building, a few words concerning this superb highway's history should be pertinent. . . . It is said that since 1837 there has never been a serious dispute about the management and economical administration of the pike, and of all the farmers I met in the valley, not one had a complaint to utter. . . . Yes, the valley pike is a great road to haul grain and apples on, probably as fine a farmers' highway as there is in the world . . .
>
> —Barton W. Currie, "Along the Shenandoah Valley Pike," *The Country Gentleman* (1913) [66]

The earliest routes through the Shenandoah Valley were Indian paths that were improved for use by Euro-Americans. The most celebrated of these was the Philadelphia Wagon Road, also known as the Great Wagon Road, which had two branches—one that crossed the Potomac River at Williams Ferry near what is now Williamsport, Maryland, and an easterly branch that crossed at Pack Horse Ford near present-day Shepherdstown. Taking advantage of the broad valley plain in the Cumberland, Hagerstown, and Shenandoah Valleys, respectively, the westernmost branch of the Wagon Road was a natural conduit for settlers migrating from Pennsylvania. Similarly using topography to advantage, settlers from Virginia's Piedmont and Tidewater regions entered the Valley through the multitude of wind gaps in the Blue Ridge, through which various roads extended from the port towns of Alexandria (on the Potomac), Falmouth (on the Rappahannock), and Richmond (on the James). Modern roads generally follow these colonial routes: the easternmost branch of the Wagon Road is now WV 480/Jefferson County Route 1, while the westernmost branch became the Valley Turnpike (also called the Valley Road) and eventually U.S. 11; WV 9 through Key(e)s Gap (originally Vestals Gap, elevation 906 feet), and VA 7 through Snickers Gap (originally Williams Gap, elevation 1,056 feet) converge before reaching Alexandria, albeit at a more westerly junction today than shown on the 1751 Fry-Jefferson Map of Virginia; U.S. 17 begins at the foot of Ashby Gap (elevation 1,027 feet) near Paris en route to Falmouth; the old Three Chopt (also known as Three Notch'd) Road ran from Staunton to Richmond through Jarmans Gap (originally Woods Gap, elevation 2,172 feet) generally along what is now U.S. 250, which parallels Interstate 64.[67]

Not surprisingly, many of the Valley's towns and cities developed where the north-south roads crossed the east-west routes. To complement the north-south orientation of the Valley Turnpike, which originally ran from Winchester to Staunton but now traverses the entire length of the Main Valley, U.S. 340 passes through Harpers Ferry (WV) and Charles Town (WV) from Frederick,

Maryland (originally, the Frederick and Harpers Ferry Turnpike and Smithfield, Charlestown, and Harpers Ferry Turnpike, respectively) and stays within sight of the Blue Ridge Mountains as it continues to Berryville and Front Royal and through the Page Valley to Waynesboro, where it begins to head westward to its junction with U.S. 11 near Greenville in Augusta County. The northern portion of U.S. 340 that extended only from Frederick to U.S. 50 at Boyce in Clarke County is shown on the first highway map published in 1926 by the Bureau of Public Roads, quartered in the U.S. Department of Agriculture before being transferred to the Public Roads Administration within the Federal Works Agency and finally to the Federal Highway Administration within the U.S. Department of Transportation. Along with U.S. 50, U.S. 60, U.S. 11, and U.S. 211, U.S. 340 is among only a handful of U.S. primary highways located in the Valley when the first highway map was published. By 1933, U.S. 340 began to take on more of the appearance of today's route with its Page Valley and Upper Valley extensions.[68]

In comparison to Page Valley, the Main Valley—local parlance for the Middle Valley on the opposite side of Massanutten Mountain—is wider and not confined to one major north-south route. In addition to the Valley Turnpike, two other significant historical north-to-south routes are the Middle Road and Back Road, likely named because of their geographic relation to the Valley Turnpike, which were in existence prior to the Civil War. Today, VA 42 partially follows the course of both of these old roads, following the Back Road in Shenandoah County along the foot of Little North Mountain from Columbia Furnace through Conicville and Hudson Crossroads, turning eastward at Getz Corner, and linking up with the Middle Road at Forestville en route to Timberville and Broadway in Rockingham County and, eventually, to Harrisonburg, Dayton, Bridgewater, Churchville, and beyond. In the Upper Valley, the Staunton-Lexington Turnpike, currently identified as VA 252, was a major road that linked the county seats of Augusta and Rockbridge Counties through the villages of Middlebrook and Brownsburg, albeit westerly of the Valley Turnpike that eventually was extended to connect Staunton and Lexington.[69]

Virginia has had a long history of excellent roads. A standard bearer of the Valley's tradition of fiscal conservatism, former Governor and U.S. Senator Harry F. Byrd Sr., of Berryville, developed the "pay-as-you-go" mantra to road building instead of issuing bonds to finance them—a stance that Byrd's biographer opined hurt capital projects down the road because of unfavorable bond ratings due to insufficient credit. Byrd had cut his teeth on road operations while president of the Valley Turnpike during the early twentieth century, and he was responsible for making it the best road in the Commonwealth and one of the best in the nation at that time.[70]

Aside from the development of roads, the Shenandoah River was a key means of transportation during the eighteenth and nineteenth centuries. While not as deep as the tidal rivers in Tidewater Virginia and impeded in places with significant rapids, serious attempts at navigation of the Shenandoah River were being considered at least as early 1784, when George Washington made an entry into his diary to that effect. The Virginia General Assembly subsequently made a number of appropriations to improve navigation on the river, and some sections were even declared to be a public highway, according to Dr. John Wayland, an esteemed Valley historian of the early twentieth century. Port Republic was aptly named for its role in river navigation, which was

Valley Pike, with Bethlehem Stone Church, Tenth Legion
OIL ON PANEL, 8" X 12," JULY 13, 2015 (PAINTING #252).

accomplished by a shallow-drafted boat known as a gundalow, aided on its journey to Harpers Ferry by the Shenandoah Canal, which bypassed the rapids at Virginius Island before meeting the Potomac River at Harpers Ferry. Navigation on the Potomac was aided by the Patowmack Canal (on the Virginia shore of the Potomac) and, later, the Chesapeake and Ohio (C&O) Canal (on the Maryland shore of the Potomac), which had endeavored to link the District of Columbia downriver with Pittsburgh, Pennsylvania, on the Ohio River but only reached Cumberland, Maryland. At the opposite end of the Valley was the James River and Kanawha Canal, which was envisioned to link Richmond on the James with Point Pleasant on the Ohio River, then Virginia's westernmost boundary, but it was never fully realized, having terminated in Buchanan, about 11.5 miles south of Natural Bridge. Lack of funding, floods, and competition from more efficient means of conveyance—namely railroads—served as the death knell for river and canal traffic.[71]

A number of railroads helped to stimulate industrial growth in the Valley during the antebellum period: the Manassas Gap Railroad that ran from Manassas Junction (now the City of Manassas) to Mount Jackson; the Virginia Central Railroad that ran from Richmond past Staunton and westward to Jackson's River Station (now Clifton Forge); the Baltimore and Ohio (B&O) that ran from Baltimore, Maryland, through Harpers Ferry and Martinsburg westward to Wheeling, (West) Virginia; and the Winchester and Potomac that connected Winchester with the B&O at Harpers Ferry. All told, antebellum railroads traversed eight of the Valley's twelve counties.[72]

Although the roundhouse and shops at Martinsburg were not constructed until a year after the Civil War ended, replacing an earlier group of structures destroyed by Confederate General Thomas J. "Stonewall" Jackson, they are significant as the oldest covered roundhouse extant in the country and are symbolic of the historical importance of the B&O Railroad, including its role in the severing of the counties of Morgan, Berkeley, and Jefferson from Virginia and inclusion in West Virginia so the railroad would remain within Union territory. After the war, the B&O was continued beyond Winchester to link up with the old Manassas Gap Railroad at Strasburg, extending beyond the Manassas Gap's terminus at Mount Jackson to Staunton, where it connected with the Chesapeake and Ohio Railroad (formerly the Virginia Central). Another north-south branch was completed post-war, notably, the Shenandoah Valley Railroad that ran from Hagerstown, Maryland, to Roanoke via Page Valley. Since 1890, this line has been part of the Norfolk & Western system, while the Shenandoah Valley Railroad today refers to a short-line railroad that runs small freight between Staunton and Harrisonburg. As for passenger service, the Valley is linked to AMTRAK at Staunton, with service from New York City to Chicago via Washington, D.C., Cincinnati, and Indianapolis. AMTRAK also connects through Harpers Ferry and Martinsburg from Washington, D.C., to Chicago via Pittsburgh and Cleveland.[73]

Just as river traffic was supplanted by railroads, so, too, have railroads been supplanted by highways as the primary means of conveyance. Interstates 81, 64, and 66 were proposed on the first Interstate Highway map published by the Public Roads Administration in 1947, north-south being denoted by odd numbers and east-west routes by even numbers. Construction on the stretch of Interstate 81 that traverses the Valley did not commence, however, until 1957 and lasted until 1966. The Valley's portion of Interstate 66—not to be confused with the historic Route 66 that ran from

Chicago, Illinois, to Santa Monica, California, by way of Oklahoma and the Southwest—was not completed until 1971, but, in concert with I-81, it has drastically changed the Valley's landscape. Throngs of commuters travel these highways to work in the edge cities of Washington, D.C., each day, spurring on increased residential and commercial development in the Lower and Middle valleys. Commuter rail service via the Maryland Area Regional Commuter (MARC) Train using the old B & O line (and current AMTRAK route) in the Valley from Martinsburg, Duffields, and Harpers Ferry is available, although the Virginia Railway Express (VRE) near the route of the old Manassas Gap line does not extend out to the Valley.

Perhaps old technology will come back in vogue again to alleviate the congestion inherent to the Northern Virginia cities and suburbs and, increasingly, the I-81 corridor, with plans "in the works" for more than two decades to widen that major north-south artery with its ever-increasing car and truck traffic. Since 1975, traffic volume on the Virginia portion of I-81 has tripled, and, today, more than 10,000 cars and trucks traverse I-81 daily, with holiday traffic notoriously problematic. Indeed, increasing rail service is one of many concepts on the planning table, which has precedent in one of the world's other great mountain chains—the Alps—when Switzerland's citizens voted to amend the Swiss Constitution in 1994 to transition truck traffic moving goods through the country to rail in an effort called the Alpine Initiative. Alas, effective transportation planning and the aesthetization of unsightly entrance corridors is prudent along roads such as U.S. 33 east of Harrisonburg, which belie the charm of the Valley's traditional towns and scenic beauty.[74]

The Valley is also connected to the larger world by way of Shenandoah Valley Regional Airport in Weyers Cave, which has served for years as a connection for United Airlines and its hub at Dulles International Airport in Chantilly, west of Washington, D.C. Increasingly, corporate jets—related to nearby corporations such as Merck and MillerCoors Brewing in Elkton and leisure travel to the area's many resorts by the well-to-do—are a part of the Valley's aviation scene. The other regional airports located just outside of the Shenandoah Valley in nearby Charlottesville and Roanoke are served by multiple commercial carriers, with numerous direct flights not only to Dulles and Washington, D.C., but also Atlanta, Chicago, and New York City.

Mauck's Meeting House, Hamburg (Page County)
OIL ON PANEL, 5" x 7," JULY 13, 2015 (PAINTING #244).

Indian Inheritance, Ethnicity, and Religion

> Whatever may be the imaginary, the greater portion of the real denizens of this part of the country are mere matter-of-fact Germans; four square, solid, and deliberative smokers, as e'er put pipe in mouth, or carried a tin tobacco-box. They are of the genuine useful class of people, who make two dozen ruddy blades of clover grow where never a one grew before—who save all they make—work harder and harder, the richer they grow; speak well of the government, except when the taxing-man pays a visit, and pay their trifle of assessment with as bad a grace as any people you will see in a summer's day. It is singular, what a difference there is between these and the Tuckahoe. The latter is a gallant, high-spirited, lofty, lazy sort of being, much more likely to spend money than earn it, and who, however he may consume, is not very likely to add much to the fruits of the earth. People are very apt to judge of themselves by a comparison with others, and the Tuckahoe, feeling himself so greatly superior to his slaves, is inclined to hold every body else equally his inferior . . .
>
> —James Kirke Paulding, *Letters from the South by a Northern Man* (1817)[75]

American Indian names abound in the Valley— Allegheny, Massanutten, Opequon, Potomac, and, of course, Shenandoah—as a testament to the region's original occupants. There are nearly as many theories for the origins of the word "Shenandoah" as there are spellings of it. The favorite translation that emerged over time is "Daughter of the Stars," which has been in use for at least a century, though its provenance in uncertain. As is the case with many aspects of the Shenandoah Valley's lore, popular perception may be more rooted in myth than fact.

John Heckewelder, a missionary to the Lenni Lenapes (Delawares), translated Shenandoah as meaning "the sprucy stream—a stream flowing past spruce-pines." But this was probably in reference to what is now Schuylkill County, Pennsylvania, where there is both a creek and a borough by the same name and where hemlocks ("spruce-pine" was the eighteenth-century word for "hemlock") may have been more commonly found than in the more southerly and lower-elevation Shenandoah Valley of Virginia, where an oak-hickory forest predominated during the Colonial era as it does now. In fact, Heckewelder spent more time in Pennsylvania than he did in Virginia.[76]

Another translation for Shenandoah is "great meadow" or "great plain," which supports the long-held belief among some historians that the Valley of Virginia contained sizable prairie habitat at the time of contact with Europeans. In fact, the area between New Market and Timberville was named "The Plains" by European settlers. But this translation may, instead, refer to the Indian settlement of Shenendehowa that was in Saratoga County, New York, and is now the Town of Clifton Park and thought to be a word of Mohawk (one of the Six Nations Iroquois) derivation. Nevertheless, one anthropologist conjectured long ago that Shenandoah was to the Iroquois what Wyoming was to the Lenni Lenapes—a word that translates to "great plains" and is applied to not one but many locales that exhibited this characteristic.[77]

There is also a theory that the Virginia Valley was named for Oneida Chief Skenandoah, who was an ally of the colonists during the Revolutionary War and ensured that rations were delivered to Washington's starving troops at Valley Forge. Because of his support, it has been theorized that Washington named the Valley in his honor, but this is unlikely, since maps showing derivations of the word "Shenandoah" were in existence well before this time. Chief Skenandoah, however, was an adopted Susquehannock (Conestoga), so there may be a connection between the chief and the Valley, since the Susquehannocks likely controlled that part of Virginia before it was claimed by the Six Nations through right of conquest. Chief Skenandoah was born around the same time that this word began to appear on maps of the Valley, perhaps strengthening this argument. When I queried the Oneida Nation for this vignette, I was informed that Chief Skenandoah's name translates to *Skanu·tó*, which means "the deer," and it may be that the Iroquois' use of the Valley as a large hunting reserve resulted in it being named after its most important food source rather than in honor of their leader—a theory that should resonate with modern-day hunters in the region.[78]

While it is not definitive whether Shenandoah, in the context of the Valley of Virginia, means "sprucy stream," "great plains," or "(place of) the deer," the word is probably of Six Nations origin, for they came to control the entire area from the Hudson Valley down through the Schuylkill Valley and into the Shenandoah Valley. Rather than confined only to the Six Nations (who call themselves Haudenosaunee, meaning "people of the longhouse"), it may be part of the vocabulary of various Iroquoian speakers as a possible derivative of the word "Shenandoah"; the word *skenogg* exists among the Huron (later called the Wyandot or Wendat), where it likewise means "deer." Indeed, deer is a common clan name that exists among the Haudenosaunee and the Huron.[79]

A different version of the word may exist among yet another Iroquoian-speaking tribe: the Massawomecks. Little seems to be known about them and whether they are one and the same as the Haudenosaunee or, perhaps, a separate tribe. According to John Lederer's map of 1672, they lived in a location west of the Blue Ridge, although it is difficult to ascertain if this is meant to depict the Shenandoah Valley or another location to the northwest. Several scholars suggest either a Potomac headwaters or western Pennsylvania homeland, but, given their proximity to the Shenandoah, the Massawomecks were undoubtedly familiar with it. A pair of brothers who were early fur traders in the region, Henry and Edward Fleet, stayed among the Massawomeck and spoke of their four villages governed by kings of possibly the same name, one of which—Shaunetowa—bears a striking resemblance to the word Shenandoah. Shaunetowa, according to several scholars, may mean "deer," further reinforcing the likeliest translation of the name for the famous Virginia Valley given the available evidence.[80]

Aside from Iroquoian speakers, Eastern Siouan speakers known as the Monocans likely had territory that extended westward into the Shenandoah Valley from their base in Amherst County. Their oral tradition credits the Great Creator for supplying the Natural Bridge in their time of need, when their warriors were trying to escape pursuit by their enemies. Not surprisingly, Natural Bridge is sacred to the Monocan people, who, through perseverance, have survived incursions on their land and discrimination through hundreds of years. The passage of the Racial Integrity Act of 1924 by the Virginia General Assembly, whereby many Virginia Indians were classified as black, nearly ensured that their lineage was forever lost. The law also made miscegenation illegal, which was struck down as unconstitutional in the U.S. Supreme Court case *Loving v. Virginia* (1967).[81]

The primary author of the Racial Integrity Act was Walter Plecker, a native of Augusta County who served as longtime State Registrar of the Virginia Bureau of Vital Statistics. He had a personal vendetta against the Monocans, who resisted attempts aimed at dissolving their culture. Plecker's connections to the Nazi eugenics movement and his campaign to detribalize Virginia Indians is a dark chapter in Virginia history. In 1989, the Monocans were at last recognized as a state tribe. Until 2015, when the Pamunkey Indians of King William County in the Tidewater region became the Commonwealth's first federally recognized tribe, no federally recognized tribes existed in Virginia, precluding them from gaining access to many federal benefits such as health care, housing, and economic development. But, arguably, the most publicized benefit of federal recognition is the ability to conduct legalized gaming (namely, casinos) on sovereign land, and it is fair to wonder if the Commonwealth's anti-casino stance is a major impediment to Virginia tribes seeking recognition. Contemporary politics aside, the Racial Integrity Act still casts a dark shadow over Virginia's Indians, since birth, marriage, and death records are vital for extending federal recognition.[82]

Compared to Tidewater Virginia, European settlement of the Shenandoah Valley was relatively peaceful due not only to the paucity of permanent Indian villages, but also to the ethnicity of settlers. William Penn's policies were generally respectful towards the Indians, and Quakers who migrated to the Valley from Pennsylvania seem to have carried this ethos with them. Unlike the settlers who were drawn to Jamestown in lure of imagined riches that the New World offered, many of the Shenandoah Valley's earliest European inhabitants immigrated to the American colonies in search of religious freedom. In addition to the Quakers who were of English, Welsh, Anglo-Irish, and even Scots-Irish extraction, Swiss-German Mennonites, French Huguenots, and Scots-Irish Presbyterians initially found refuge in Pennsylvania, drawn to Penn's Holy Experiment. Within a generation, however, competition for land and attendant high prices drove these groups southward to the Shenandoah Valley. Some would continue southward to the Carolinas and westward to Tennessee, Kentucky, the Ohio Country and beyond, but many would stay and make the Shenandoah Valley their permanent home. Their farms were generally modest-sized, diversified operations that were worked with family labor in contrast to the single-crop system of plantation agriculture that prevailed in the Piedmont and Tidewater regions. Not befitting the nostalgic image of "Old Virginia"—a genteel land of white-columned mansions—the Shenandoah Valley was an ethnically and religiously diverse region whose populace had more in common with the Middle Colonies than the Lowland South.[83]

Near the hamlet of Fort Defiance in Augusta County sits one of the oldest churches west of the Blue Ridge Moutains known as Augusta Stone Church. Constructed by Scots-Irish Presbyterians in 1749, it also is credited as being the oldest Presbyterian Church in Virginia in continuous use. The Scots-Irish originally were Lowland Scots who were utilized by Queen Elizabeth and,

*Augusta Stone Presbyterian Church, Fort Defiance**
OIL ON PANEL, 8" X 12," OCTOBER 24, 2011 (PAINTING #5).

later, King James I (James VI of Scotland) to colonize Northern Ireland during the seventeenth century, only to see their religious freedom diminished by the Anglicans. Accordingly, they set sail for the New World and settled in significant numbers in southeastern Pennsylvania, particularly in the Cumberland Valley. The enticement of affordable land soon lured them to the Shenandoah Valley, where their population soon became concentrated in what are now Augusta and Rockbridge Counties, particularly on the Beverley Manor land grant, aptly named the "Irish Tract" as well as the more southerly Borden Tract.[84]

Whereas the Upper Valley was the stronghold of the Scots-Irish, the Middle Valley counties of Rockingham, Page, and Shenandoah were the Teutonic heartland, comprised mainly of Lutherans and German Reformed. Collectively called the Pennsylvania Dutch but known in the Shenandoah Valley as the Valley Dutch (a corruption of Deutsche, the word for "German"), these Germanic settlers hailed from the Rhineland-Palatinate region of what became Germany, the adjacent Alsace region now in France, and the northern cantons of Switzerland, although some Netherlanders and French Huguenots came to be associated with the Germanic settlers. Also among this population were the Mennonites, an Anabaptist sect founded in Zürich, Switzerland, during the Protestant Reformation and subsequently named for Menno Simons, a Catholic priest from the Netherlands. The word "Anabaptist" means to "rebaptize," and adult rather than infant baptism was central among the tenets of this religious movement. Amish, Hutterites, and German Baptist Brethren (known as Dunkers) were also counted among the Anabaptist groups, but only the Mennonites and Brethren were present in significant numbers in the Shenandoah Valley. Title disputes with Lord Fairfax, Proprietor of the Northern Neck, pushed Mennonites south of the Fairfax Line from Shenandoah (originally Dunmore County) into Rockingham County, which has, for some time, held the largest Mennonite community in Virginia and one of the largest east of the Appalachians.[85]

Mennonite landscapes have historically been distinguished by intensive agricultural production worked with family labor. The distinctive landscape around Dayton and Ottobine in Rockingham County is Old Order Mennonite, as evidenced by the frequent horse-and-buggy traffic in the area. While few Mennonites remain in Page and Shenandoah Counties, a number of their dwellings survive there such as White House at the base of Massanutten Mountain between Luray and New Market. Located in one of the oldest Germanic settlements in the Valley aptly named Massanutten, this dwelling exhibits Pennsylvania German architectural features, including a characteristic internal chimney with direct outside entry into the hearth room (kitchen), with a stove room directly behind the kitchen on the opposite side of the chimney. The pragmatic Pennsylvania and Virginia Germans found that houses could be heated more efficiently with stoves rather than open fireplaces; and, so as not to waste even the smoke exiting from the chimney, smoking chambers for curing meats were often located in the attic. Cooling cellars for keeping perishables were usually located in the cellar, with some houses constructed over springs, obviating the need for a separate springhouse. Concentrated in the Pennsylvania Culture Region, which was heavily settled by Germans and Swiss-Germans, this building form represents an amalgam of European and American building traditions. Nearby, the White House (known locally as White House) is Mauck's Meeting House, which is a rare, eighteenth-century Mennonite log meetinghouse in the Valley, later used by Baptists after the Mennonites migrated out of the area, likely to Rockingham County. Both denominations are known for erecting and utilizing meetinghouses that are free from ostentation, and Mauck's austere form is nearly indistinguishable from a dwelling, which both the Mennonites and Baptists often met in in the absence of a church building.[86]

The British groups predominated in the Lower Valley counties of Berkeley, Jefferson, Frederick, Clarke, and Warren. North of Winchester, near the hamlet of Clearbrook (the original spelling before the words were separated), sits one of the oldest religious structures west of the Blue Ridge and the oldest Quaker meeting house in the Commonwealth of Virginia. Constructed in 1759, Hopewell Friends Meeting House was established by Anglo-Irish Quakers who had migrated to the Shenandoah Valley from the Delaware Valley beginning in the second quarter of the eighteenth century. Originally part of the Philadelphia Yearly Meeting, Hopewell, along with Centre Friends Meeting in Old Town Winchester, is now part of the Baltimore Yearly Meeting. The Society of Friends were successful farmers who, like the Mennonites, were generally adverse to slavery and the attendant, cash-crop system of tobacco that prevailed until the Civil War east of the Blue Ridge. These Virginia sectarians, who undoubtedly continued a dialogue with their brethren who had remained in southeastern Pennsylvania, emphasized meat and grain production that distinguished them from the tobacco planters of eastern Virginia.[87]

The eastern portion of Frederick County, which would, in 1836, become the new County of Clarke, was more analogous to Virginia culture east of the Blue Ridge Mountains than it was to its neighboring counties in the Valley. Robert "King" Carter, land agent for Lord Fairfax and one of the wealthiest planters in Virginia, helped to influence the population of this county by eastern Virginians by conveying tracts of land to his many offspring. As members of the landed gentry, the Carters and other leading families of Tidewater Virginia were members of the established Anglican Church. Eighteenth-century Anglican churches are rare in the Valley, and Old Chapel near Millwood is an even rarer example, since it has been little altered subsequent to its construction date in 1793. Its architecturally restrained form executed in native limestone is similar to the dissenters' houses of worship constructed in the Valley during the eighteenth century. Manor houses constructed by the gentry class are found in significant numbers in the Lower Valley, including Belle Grove near Middletown in adjacent Frederick County and The Tuleyries between the villages of White Post and Millwood in an area known as Waterloo, the sizable and architecturally refined slave quarters for The Tulyeries being located on the nearby property of the Blandy Experimental Farm/State Arboretum of Virginia and the mansion house on an adjacent, privately owned property.[88]

African-Americans, whether enslaved or free, were primarily comprised of the Igbo people from what is now Nigeria, Virginia having one of the largest Igbo populations in the New World. On the eve of the Civil War, Frederick County ranked in the top ten of all Virginia counties (including those that were later included in the State of West Virginia) in their free-black population as a percentage of the total black population, with Page and Shenandoah Counties likewise having sizable percentages of free blacks. Methodism, which had by far the most church buildings in the Valley in 1860, included many African-Africans among its congregants. Historically, the largest African-American populations in the Valley were centered in the Lower Valley's counties that had

[top] *Old Chapel, Millwood*
OIL ON PANEL, 6" X 8," OCTOBER 16, 2011 (PAINTING #97).

[bottom] *Temple House of Israel, Staunton**
OIL ON LINEN, 6" X 8," JULY 11, 2012 (PAINTING #160).

the highest percentage of slave ownership in the region. These counties remain the most racially diverse in the twenty-first century.[89]

The Valley has historically been an overwhelmingly Protestant region, with modest numbers of Catholics and Jews among its population. Irish Catholics began to arrive during the mid-nineteenth century, and many were employed in the construction of railroads in the region. St. Peter's Catholic Church in Harpers Ferry is, not surprisingly, one of the oldest Catholic churches in the Valley, having been completed in 1833 on the Virginia side of the Potomac River directly across from Maryland, which was founded as a haven for English Catholics. Jews, predominantly from southern Germany, likewise arrived during the mid-nineteenth century and subsequently established synagogues in Harrisonburg and Staunton in the third quarter of the nineteenth century, both of which remain small but active. Some were Confederate veterans, including Major Alexander Hart, one of the highest-ranking Jews in the Confederate Army and one of the progenitors of Temple House of Israel, a very rare Moorish Revival synagogue built in Staunton in 1925. It was designed by Staunton's most prominent architectural firm, T. J. Collins and Sons, which designed more than 200 structures in the area—an architectural heritage that has made Staunton one of Virginia's—and the nation's—most popular and aesthetically pleasing small cities. Recent accolades from *Smithsonian* magazine ("One of the best small towns in America"), *Travel + Leisure* magazine ("one of America's greatest main streets"), and *Southern Living* ("one of the prettiest and most progressive [towns] in the South") speak volumes to Staunton's growing reputation.[90]

Compared with the more industrialized Northern states, immigration from eastern and southern Europe during the first half of the twentieth century was limited in both the Valley and Virginia as a whole, although there was some diversity in the Valley's agricultural sector. A number of agricultural commodities produced in the Shenandoah Valley are labor intensive, and a sufficient labor force has been a concern for years. Temporary workers from the Bahamas and Jamaica began to replace American-born migrant workers after World War II in the Valley's apple orchards, who, in turn, were supplanted by workers from Mexico during the early 1990s. Whereas the early native migrant workers and seasonal guest workers stayed in labor camps for a few months of the year, the Latino presence has been more permanent, with Mexican stores and restaurants being added to the cultural landscape. Many of the year-round residents are employed in the poultry industry, although Latino labor has branched out to encompass work in the construction business and other trades.[91]

Regardless of ethnicity or religion, Valley residents have always been hard-working folk. The Valley has historically been a bastion of the yeomanry, and it is not surprising that, as of the most recent U.S. Census, the Valley's median income is nearly identical to that of the United States as a whole. Independent thinkers and self-reliant by nature, the Valley's citizenry defies convenient categorization. Perhaps most illustrative of the Shenandoah's dichotomous persona is the vote for the Ordinance of Secession in 1861, when Virginia was contemplating secession from the Union. Two votes were taken—one on April 4, when Virginia counties voted nearly two-to-one against secession, and one on April 17, two days after President Abraham Lincoln called for 75,000 volunteers to suppress the rebellion in the Deep South, which ultimately led to Virginia voting to secede from the Union. In both instances, Clarke County, although holding the highest percentage of slaves in the Valley, voted against secession, while Shenandoah County, with the lowest percentage of slaves, voted for it.[92]

Once a Democratic stronghold, the Valley has, by and large, remained staunchly Republican for the past sixty years. A duality, however, currently exists between the Valley's rural county voters, who vote Republican, sometimes by a seventy percent or more majority, and city voters, who trended ever so slightly Democratic in the 2008 and 2012 federal elections compared with the 2000 and 2004 elections, when the Valley's cities more closely mirrored the vote of the surrounding counties. This phenomenon is attributable, in part, to the influx of non-natives—young professionals, retirees, and immigrants—to the Valley's cities, where the vast majority of its colleges and universities are located, which historically have been associated with a more progressive brand of politics.

Picnic in the Apple Orchard, near Winchester
OIL ON CANVAS, 10" X 14," OCTOBER 17, 2011 (PAINTING #104).

Agriculture

> Further northward, separated by long spurs of the Cumberland Plateau, lie the three great limestone basins, the Nashville Basin, the Kentucky Bluegrass, and the Great Valley of which the Shenandoah is a part. Here in rich soils diversified farming has reached its southern zenith. In grass, grain and dairying, fine horses, fine cattle and fine folks these regions excel . . .
>
> —Dr. Rupert B. Vance, *Human Geography of the South* (1932)[93]

The Shenandoah Valley's reputation as a prosperous agricultural region is of almost mythic proportions. Before the opening up of the frontier west of the Appalachians to settlement, the Valley was one of the nation's premier farming regions, earning it the moniker "Granary of the Confederacy." Part of its legendary status may emanate from the limestone soils that abound here. One early twentieth-century agronomist aptly described the nexus between limestone soils and agricultural productivity when opining that, "It does not follow that every farm in such limestone valleys as the Shenandoah, Cumberland, and Lebanon, or in the great corn belt having a naturally calcareous soil, is prosperous, or that a multitude of owners of such lime-deficient areas as the belt in a portion of southern New York and northern Pennsylvania, or the sandstone and shale regions of many states, have not overmatched natural conditions with fine skill. We treat only of averages when saying that a 'lime country' shows prosperity in its farm buildings and general appearance that does not come naturally and easily to any lime-deficient territory." Whereas the soils of Virginia, like much of the South, were generally acidic and low in fertility, the Valley's productive limestone soils were rich in calcium, phosphorous, and magnesium—important minerals for bone growth in large animals such as cattle and horses, which thrived on the Valley's rich pastures. When referring to Berkeley County, George Washington stated that, "in point of fertility, (it) is without doubt, the richest county in the State." Nevertheless, there is more to prosperity than soil quality, with farming systems and cultural traditions of farmers likewise being of significance.[94]

The original economy of Virginia was built on tobacco culture, and its attendant system of plantation slavery was utilized to cultivate this labor-intensive staple crop. Tobacco notoriously robs soil of its nutrients, and successive years of planting had depleted the soil in the Tidewater region such that planters had to seek new lands in the Piedmont region in order to perpetuate their livelihood; these planters had rejected the notion of fertilizing with manure in the belief that it gave the tobacco an unpleasant taste. Eventually, the Piedmont's lands became exhausted as well, and visitors and residents alike remarked on the deplorable conditions in agriculture that existed in much of Virginia. Sir William Strickland, an English traveler, observed, "The country in general is very unhealthy, infested with fever and ague, and bilious complaints, as may be expected from such a surface, in such a climate; and is much worn out, having been long settled, and the chief produce tobacco."[95]

While the plantation system did exist in the Valley, particularly in the eastern portions of Frederick and Berkeley Counties (which later became Clarke and Jefferson Counties, respectively), the Valley was generally a region of diversified agriculture that had much more in common with the Southeastern Pennsylvania region than Virginia's Tidewater or Piedmont regions. The Valley has long been known for its innovation in agriculture, beginning in the eighteenth century with Quaker, Mennonite, and Brethren farmers. Geographer James Lemon astutely observed that the sectarians were probably more affluent farmers than other groups, because their values and religious structure favored discipline and cooperation. He suggested that this affluence may have contributed to agricultural innovation, as they could afford to risk some capital while experimenting with newer methods. The sectarians generally shunned slave labor and reliance on tobacco as a staple crop and, instead, favored a diversified system of meat and grain production that utilized crop rotation and soil amendments to preserve the soil's fertility. This "Pennsylvania" system of farming eventually shifted to the lands east of the Blue Ridge, as Washington, Jefferson, Madison, and other gentlemen planters began promoting agricultural reform in the period after the Revolutionary War, extolling the virtues of wheat over tobacco.[96]

Wheat production was long a mainstay of the Valley's economy, once being one of the most important wheat-producing regions in the nation. Agricultural geographer, Oliver E. Baker, in his seminal study, "Agricultural Regions of North America," (1926–1933), placed the Shenandoah Valley within a region he called the Corn and Winter Wheat Belt, which was wedged between the Corn Belt to the north and the Cotton Belt to the south. Baker aptly noted that this region "is a transition zone between northern and southern agriculture, the crops and systems of farming being much the same as in the North, but the people and the social traditions, except in Kansas, similar to those in the South." As the nineteenth century progressed, wheat production marched steadily westward, where large acreage and lower costs of production offered stiff competition for the older wheat-producing districts such as the Shenandoah Valley. Production in the Valley and other selected regions of the East did persist well into the twentieth century but often in areas underlain by limestone.[97]

Cyrus McCormick, who is often credited with producing the first mechanical reaper that revolutionized the harvesting of grain during the second quarter of the nineteenth century, exemplified the Valley's tradition of agricultural innovation. Born and raised in Rockbridge County near Steeles Tavern, his farmhouse and workshop where his reapers were first produced are still extant, and the farm has been owned since 1956 by Virginia Polytechnic Institute and State University (Virginia Tech) for use as an agricultural research and experimentation station—fitting of its historical roots.[98]

The Civil War devastated the Valley's agricultural economy, but, compared to other regions of Virginia and the South, its diversified agricultural system of small farms worked primarily with free rather than slave labor led to a quicker economic recovery during the Reconstruction Era. Nevertheless, agricultural specialization began to increase during the period. The apple industry began in earnest during this time, with the Valley eventually developing into of the most important fruit-growing districts in the nation. Former Governor and U.S. Senator Harry Byrd, Sr., infamously known for his efforts to block the racial integration of Virginia's public schools, was an accomplished orchardist from Berryville who was the self-proclaimed "Apple King" of America, a claim bolstered by his net worth of $1,000,000 and his ownership of the single-largest orchard in the world. By the mid-twentieth century, the Valley had also become one of the leading counties in the nation for poultry, as the two large turkey statues at both ends of Rockingham County along U.S. 11 attest to. The trend of agricultural specialization in a region that was heretofore diversified continued with the expansion of the dairy industry into the Valley. The Washington, D.C., milkshed was originally concentrated in the Piedmont regions of Virginia and Maryland, but, as suburbanization increased in those regions, the milkshed moved westward to the Great Valley.[99]

Some agricultural commodities have been produced in the Valley of Virginia since the colonial era. The Valley has always been known as a major beef cattle producer, as drovers would raise cattle locally and then drive them to market to Alexandria, Baltimore, or even as far as Philadelphia. Some historians credit Ulstermen from Northern Ireland for bringing this tradition to the Valley as a continuance of their Celtic traditions in the New World, while others credit the Pennsylvania Germans. Remarkably, cattle driving continued until the mid-twentieth century, albeit becoming increasingly shorter in duration. Whereas cattle were once driven and sold either at Virginia markets or to professional drovers who sold them well beyond Virginia's borders, the more modern cattle drives involved driving them to the surrounding mountains during planting season and driving them back down to the valley floor after the crops were harvested, letting the animals graze on the remnants in the field.[100]

Horses are another holdover from colonial days. Virginians have always had an affinity for horses, which is a cultural tradition emanating from England. Pennsylvania and Virginia Germans typically used horses for work, whereas the Virginia nobility utilized them for sport, particularly for racing and foxhunting. These sporting traditions continue into the present, particularly in the Lower Valley counties of Jefferson and Clarke, where the influence of eastern Virginia is most pronounced. Whereas privately owned Commonwealth Park—logically located in the horse-centric Piedmont (Culpeper County)—was once the premier horse facility in Virginia, that distinction arguably shifted to the Virginia Horse Center, located near Lexington in Rockbridge County. Opened in 1986 with the assistance of state funds, the facility is now owned by the Virginia Horse Foundation.[101]

The Shenandoah Valley is still the leading agricultural region in Virginia, with four of the top five counties in agricultural sales, according to the most recent agricultural census. Rockingham County, the leading agricultural county in the Commonwealth, ranked first in poultry, dairy, and beef cattle. At the northern end of Virginia's portion of the Valley, Frederick County leads the Commonwealth in apple production, with adjacent Berkeley County leading the State of West Virginia. Meanwhile, Jefferson County leads West Virginia in dairy production and equine operations, with neighboring Clarke County being among the top-five equine counties in Virginia.[102]

While the Valley continues to produce traditional commodities, value-added agricultural ventures are gaining a foothold. There has been an explosion in viticulture in recent years, with Virginia ranked fifth in the nation (behind California, Washington, Oregon, and New York) in number of wineries and eighth in grape production. And positive national and international press coverage appearing in such publications as *Food & Wine* magazine, *The New York Times*, *The Wall Street*

Journal, and *Wine Enthusiast* magazine and in broadcasts on National Public Radio have helped expand Virginia's reputation for wine. While the Northern Piedmont along the Blue Ridge Mountains leads the Commonwealth in the number of wineries and tons of grapes harvested, the Valley is home to several wineries that took home prestigious gold medals in the 2015 Governor's Cup: Barren Ridge (Augusta County), Bluestone (Augusta County), Cross Keys (Rockingham County). Muse Vineyards (Shenandoah County), and Rockbridge Vineyards (Rockbridge County). Muse Vineyards took home the Governor's Cup as the highest scoring wine in the Commonwealth in 2015, with Rockbridge included with Muse among the twelve best wines that comprise the Governor's Cup case. Meanwhile, Jeff White, Glen Manor's (Warren County) owner and winemaker, has received national attention for the quality of his wines and was named the Virginia Association's Grape Grower of the Year in 2014.[103]

While Virginia's viticulturists have worked hard to overcome the humid climate that prevails east of the 100th meridian, which causes various fungi on grapes, so, too, has Virginia's hops growers have had to contend with fungi and diseases, as they strive to provide products to the up-and-coming craft brewery movement. Originally centered in Upstate New York before migrating to Wisconsin and finally to the semi-arid climate of eastern Washington, eastern Oregon, and western Idaho, hops are returning to the East Coast, with Virginia's hops growers producing more than 8,000 pounds of wet hops in 2014.[104]

In terms of material culture, the many historic agricultural buildings found on the Valley's landscape attest to its diversified agricultural heritage and include apple-packing sheds, dairy barns, horse stables, pig pens, and poultry houses, among others. But the agricultural building that has come to symbolize the Valley's agricultural prosperity is the so-called "Pennsylvania Barn," due to its initial American development in the Southeastern Pennsylvania region. This barn type spread to other parts of North America, and thus it is useful to cultural geographers in identifying areas of the Upland South and Midwest settled by Pennsylvanians, particularly Pennsylvania Germans.

The distinguishing feature of this barn type is a projecting "forebay" in front, while its rear is sited into an embankment. The banked siting provides access to the upper level of the barn, which was traditionally used to process and store grain and hay. The lower level was used to shelter various kinds of livestock, which the projecting forebay protected during inclement weather. This bi-level arrangement saved considerable time in performing farm chores, since it allowed feed to be thrown down to the stabling area from the upper level. Furthermore, the forebay allowed stable doors on the lower level to swing unobstructed when hay and straw were thrown into the barnyard from above. Although bank barns are known in England, the cantilevered forebay, the most distinctive feature of the Pennsylvania Barn, most likely originated in Switzerland. So practical and innovative was this feature that many English and Scots-Irish settlers incorporated the forebay into their bank barns.[105]

The barn at Lick Run Plantation near Bedington in Berkeley County was built by Peter Lichte (Anglicized to Light), who was of Pennsylvania German ancestry, having migrated to the Valley from Caernarvon Township in Lancaster County. Not surprisingly, the barn resembles those found in eastern Lancaster County and, especially, in neighboring Chester County, conforming

[top] *Pennsylvania Bank Barn, Bushong Farm, New Market Battlefield*
OIL ON PANEL, 7" X 12," JULY 9, 2015 (PAINTING #235).

[bottom] *Bedington Barn, Berkeley County, West Virginia*
OIL ON PANEL, 8" X 12," FEBRUARY 7, 2012 (PAINTING #10).

Edinburg Mill
OIL ON PANEL, 8" X 10," JULY 30, 2012 (PAINTING #143).

to the barn typology that Robert Ensminger, distinguished scholar of the Pennsylvania Barn, calls the Stone-Posted-Forebay Barn. Although this barn type contains a forebay, it is supported for its entire length by stone posts rather than relying only on cantilevered beams to carry the weight. In essence, the forebay is independent of the rest of the structure, functioning essentially as an addition that enlarges the structure for increased storage as well as improved functionality relative to protecting the barn doors on the ground level. Without the forebay, it resembles the English bank barns of the Lake District, which employed pent roofs rather than forebays to protect the first-floor stabling area from the elements. The addition of a forebay likely represents an incorporation of Germanic elements into English building practices. Indeed, this barn type is seen in Pennsylvania where areas of predominantly Anglo settlement interfaced with heavy Teutonic influence. This multi-ethnic settlement dynamic also existed in Berkeley County, although this barn type is a rare survivor south of the Potomac, particularly one that is executed in limestone.[106]

It is difficult judging which barn typologies where common in the Shenandoah Valley prior to the Civil War, thanks to the "total war" policy—one that did not just involve armies but also citizens—employed by Ulysses S. Grant, General-in-Chief of the Union Army, and his subordinates and sanctioned by President Lincoln (whose family, incidentally, once farmed in Rockingham County). Known as "The Burning," the Union high command in 1864 desired to lay waste to the Valley's agricultural infrastructure that supported the Confederate Army, which included setting fire to barns and mills, destroying crops, and driving off livestock. In its adoption of this scorched-earth paradigm, the federal government was seemingly oblivious to the fact that many unionists and pacifists lived in the Valley, whose barns and mills met the same fate as Southern sympathizers. Such was the fate of Rife's Mill (once referred to as Dayton Roller Mills and now referred to as Silver Lake Mill) near Dayton, whose owners were congregants of the Brethren Church and loyal to the Union. It was rebuilt by 1866 and stands to this day. An extant example of an antebellum mill that was spared destruction was the old Grandstaff Mill in Edinburg. Local legend contends that the mill was set fire but saved by the pleading of local women to Union officers, which is corroborated by the presence of charred timbers inside. It is noteworthy that several of the Union generals who executed The Burning—among them Philip H. Sheridan and George Armstrong Custer—carried the total-war concept to the West during the subsequent Indian Wars, where Custer ultimately perished at the hands of Sitting Bull and Crazy Horse at the Battle of Little Bighorn.[107]

Whereas the Pennsylvania Barn is symbolic of the diversified agriculture that held sway in the Valley during the eighteenth and nineteenth centuries, a barn type that is identified with the agricultural specialization that developed during the twentieth century is the Wisconsin Dairy Barn. The Valley evolved into the most important dairying region of Virginia, with the twin barns now on the grounds of the Frontier Culture Museum in Staunton being tangible reminders of the region's dairying prominence. Their design incorporates innovations in agricultural engineering that were promulgated by the U.S. Department of Agriculture and land-grant institutions such as the University of Wisconsin-Madison. As the dairy industry grew during the latter half of the nineteenth century, new barn designs were being promoted to increase efficiency and productivity. Agricultural reformers were constantly urging farmers to save time and money by erecting large, centralized barns to replace the plethora of smaller outbuildings. Dairy-barn design was further defined when the milk produced in these buildings was expected to meet certain government health standards. As a result, the land-grant colleges as well as the federal government disseminated information to farmers in order to assist them in the design and construction process.[108]

In particular, the design of roofs on dairy barns reflected the improvements in agricultural engineering that were being advocated. The first innovative roof design was the gambrel roof, which began to appear on dairy barns in the last quarter of the nineteenth century as an improvement in loft capacity over the gable roof. Similarly, the semi-rounded gothic roof was an improvement on the gambrel roof. Finally, the rainbow roof, the ultimate form of the round roof, provided slightly more storage than even the gothic roof. The construction of these complicated roof forms was made possible by the introduction of wire nails and dimension lumber, which was lighter and stronger than the old timber framing. All of these barn types can be found in the Valley.[109]

Other than the roof, dairy barns contained other features that reflected innovations in agricultural engineering. Often the top section of a dairy barn was constructed of frame and sheathed in either horizontal or vertical board siding, while the first story was constructed in concrete block. The first-story floor was also of concrete construction, as were the mangers and manure gutters. Essentially, concrete was a durable material that was also easy to keep clean. The second-story interior floor was also influenced by sanitary requirements, as many barns contained narrow, tongue-and-groove floorboards that eliminated fodder from falling through cracks in the floor, which was frowned upon by milk inspectors.[110]

Another design feature that reflected improved sanitation was the proliferation of windows on the first story of dairy barns, as the penetration of sunlight was believed to destroy bacteria. The windows themselves were often single sash instead of double, so they can be dropped at the top, which lessens the chance for draft directly on the cows when opened for air circulation. Air circulation was an important component of good dairy-barn construction, which is visible in the large ventilators seen atop the roof ridge of barns. In fact, most dairy barns utilized the "King system" of ventilation, which was designed by Professor F. H. King, of the University of Wisconsin-Madison. Essentially, the system was designed to remove foul air form the interior of the barn while simultaneously providing for the entrance of fresh air.[111]

Other than specific architectural features, the location and layout of dairy barns was purposeful. Many dairy barns had a north-south orientation that allowed the maximum amount of light to penetrate the interior during the day. In addition, many barns located the silo so it was connected to the feed room in order to centralize the feeding operations as well as prevent silage odors from entering the milking area. Furthermore, the calf/bull pens were located under the same roof as the milking operation for convenience. Finally, the milkhouse was located near the barn but connected by a closed passageway for sanitary considerations. Like the dairy barn, it was advocated that the milkhouse be constructed of concrete for ease of cleaning and that sufficient light and ventilation be provided by way of numerous windows.[112]

The dairy barns at the Frontier Culture Museum, with their gothic roofs and matching milkhouses, possess nearly all of the aforementioned architectural features and are a tangible representation of the innovative practices in agriculture and barn building that has characterized the Valley since the eighteenth century. Many Valley farmers, however, could not afford to build such elaborate specialty barns, ingeniously retrofitting the area beneath the forebay of their all-purpose Pennsylvania Barn for use as a milking parlor. Indeed, many older farmers interviewed over the years have complained of the intrusion of government and universities into dairying (as well as agriculture in general), as all of the expensive upgrades sent a clear message to the small farmers that it was either "get big or get out" of the business. The trend continues to the present, with more and more cows being milked on fewer and fewer farms.

The tradition of agricultural innovation and disdain for governmental intervention that has characterized the Valley for several centuries is perpetuated in the present day by such visionaries as Joel Salatin, owner of Polyface Farms in Swoope who was featured in two acclaimed documentary films, *Food, Inc.* (2008) and *Polyfaces: The Film* (2015), and in Michael Pollan's noteworthy book, *The Omnivore's Dilemma* (2006), a *New York Times* Best Seller. Polyface's "localvore" approach—non-industrial agriculture that produces food consumed locally—is being sought out by more and more Americans fed up with the status-quo factory farming system that has dominated the agricultural industry for more than half a century. Consumers can purchase products directly from Polyface on the farm or enjoy them by eating at a number of restaurants that utilize local purveyors, as Polyface refuses to sell to supermarkets or ship their product long distance.[113]

Route 11 Potato Chip Factory, Mount Jackson
OIL ON PANEL, 4" X 8," SEPTEMBER 7, 2015 (PAINTING #264).

Industry

> The men at the plant were a close knit bunch of people, always helping out one another, in sickness or in health, even helping out at the houses if needed. They stayed together, most of them drank together, some gamble together, even at times a little tussle, but they were a group of hard nosed skilled working men, who knew there (sic) jobs well, and working in hazardous conditions. Some couldn't read or write, but that did not keep him from knowing his job. Somewhere along the way, the good Lord had to be looking out for these men, I can remember the hard labor and low pay, and drinking heavily on weekends, but Monday morning, back down the hill to there (sic) jobs. Somewhere even today the Lord is still watching them, and if he would ever need hard working skilled men, he surely would know where to find them . . .
>
> —James L. "Dixie" Wiltshire, Former Standard Lime and Stone Company Worker (1998)[114]

Though predominantly agrarian in nature, the Shenandoah Valley possesses an important industrial history that is often overlooked. Historians rightfully argue that natural resources and access to transportation influence the predominance of manufacturing in certain locales, but the cultural disposition of their residents should not be neglected. The Valley has, historically, had the largest number of manufacturing establishments of any rural region in Virginia. At the time of the 1820 Census, it is the only region of the Commonwealth with contiguous counties possessing the greatest numbers of persons employed in manufacturing, and, a century later, had one of the highest per-capita values of manufactures of any region in the South. It should come as no surprise that a region that resembled Southeastern Pennsylvania in ethnicity likewise bore a resemblance to its economic landscape. It is the dearth of industry in much of the South that stymied the Confederacy's war effort, with railroad facilities not fully developed until after the Civil War. In contrast to the Deep South, a number of railroads—the Manassas Gap Railroad, Virginia Central Railroad, Baltimore and Ohio (B&O), and Winchester and Potomac—operated in the Valley during the antebellum period.[115]

Due, in part, to the location of the B&O Railroad in the Lower Valley, a number of woolen mills developed in Martinsburg and Winchester during the late nineteenth century. The diaspora of textile mills to the South from their epicenter in New England was precipitated by lower labor costs and lower energy rates. Whereas an abundance of waterfalls was a prerequisite for the early development of the textile industry in New England, the development of electric-powered factories leveled the playing field for the South, with the textile mills at Martinsburg attributed as being the first in the nation to utilize electric power.[116]

The Valley's woolen mills were profitable enterprises that produced cloth, blankets, and uniforms during the World Wars I and II, yet synthetic materials gradually led to the demise of the woolen industry. The first synthetic textile was viscose, subsequently renamed rayon, and purportedly the largest rayon plant in the world was at one time located in Front Royal. The plant was operated by the American Viscose Corporation (Avisco), whose parent company, Courtaulds Limited, was headquartered in England. That a neighborhood in Front Royal (Warren County) is named Viscose City is a testament to the plant's influence on the town. Completed in 1940, the Front Royal plant was one of at least eight American Viscose plants that manufactured rayon, used in making parachutes and jumpsuits during World War II. Later renamed Avtex Fibers, Inc., the Front Royal plant continued to operate until the late 1980s and was declared an U.S. Environmental Protection Fund Superfund site in 1986—one of the largest contaminated sites in the Commonwealth of Virginia. Estimated costs to remediate contaminated land and water in the aftermath of rayon production are at a staggering $150,000,000 and advisories regarding the consumption of fish in the South Fork of the Shenandoah River are still being issued due to the presence of PCBs (polychlorinated biphenyl). Farther to the south in the Upper Valley was another rayon plant, run by DuPont at Waynesboro (Augusta County). Many well-known synthetics were developed here at the Benger Laboratory, including Orlon, Lycra (Spandex), and Nomex. In 2004, the plant's name changed to Invista, and, today, only Lycra continues to be produced here. As with Avtex, there are known contaminants that were leached into the (South) River, specifically mercury, an ongoing concern today. Thus, the entire length of the South Fork of the Shenandoah River, including several of its tributaries, is under a fish-consumption advisory.[117]

Just as natural resources initially dictated the development of mills in certain locales, so, too, did the availability of limestone lead to the establishment of numerous quarries up and down the Valley. A specific type of limestone—dolomite—was quarried in the area between Harpers Ferry and Charles Town. While a number of quarries operated in this vicinity, the site operated by Standard Lime and Stone Company near Millville, West Virginia, employed more than 600 people, which constituted half the quarry work force in the area. The quarry operated by Standard Lime and Stone, a Baltimore-based business, was said to be one of the purest deposits of dolomite in the nation. Standard operated a quarry here from 1901 until 1958, and it shipped dolomite via the B & O Railroad to Pittsburgh for use in the steel-manufacturing process. Specifically, it was used to line furnaces in steel mills because of its heat-resistant properties.[118]

In addition to its quarrying and refractory operation, where stone was crushed and then burned in lime kilns, there was a mineral wool plant which opened around 1933. Mineral wool, also known as "rock wool," is a fire-resistant insulation used in building construction to prevent the spread of fire, and the rock wool plant in Millville was only one of a few dozen operating in the United States at that time. Finally, a "P32" magnesium oxide plant was built around 1938–1939, which entailed enriching the quarried dolomite with magnesium. Whereas the refractory, rock wool, and P32 plants were located on the east side of present-day WV 27, the majority of residences for workers were on the west side of the road on land now incorporated into Harpers Ferry National Historical Park.[119]

Approximately seventy-nine houses stood on the former Standard Lime and Stone Company property; and, along with a number of stores, a school, post office, and railroad depot located in the adjacent Town of Millville, the locale had all of the attributes of a company town—rare for the Shenandoah Valley. A number of Italian-American immigrants came to work and live in Millville, giving the town a degree of ethnic diversity that made it akin to company towns in the coal-producing regions of the Mid-Atlantic. The presence of a rural Italian-American community was equally rare in the Valley, which was populated primarily by Protestants of German, Scots-Irish, or English lineage. The company fielded a baseball team, complete with its own ball field, and could even boast of a Catholic chapel constructed near the workers' residences. Following the model of typical company towns, the residences for workers were constructed and owned by the company and located in close proximity to the work site. Although the motives of the Standard Lime and Stone Company cannot be deduced, many employers provided housing as means of attracting and retaining a reliable workforce. To maximize efficiency and minimize the amount of land needed for development, locating worker's housing close to the industrial site was desirable. In case an emergency arose, workers and, especially, management would be close at hand. Also, the grouping of worker's housing enabled employers to manage and control their work force and, if necessary, evict troublemakers.[120]

Millville was not typical for a company town, since it was not owned by a single business enterprise. Several other independently owned quarries also operated in the same vicinity, all with their own clusters of company housing. However, evaluated together with Millville proper, the area possessed all the characteristics of a company town, where the other institutions commonly associated with a settlement—houses, schools, churches, and stores—were subordinate to the business endeavor. A number of scholars have attempted to classify the spatial organization of company towns, and the Standard Lime and Stone Company operation might be classified according to the "Rhode Island System," which is characterized by a small-time operation, with its buildings lining the road rather than conforming to a grid plan or curvilinear plan produced by professionals in the design field. Moreover, a subtype of this plan is especially pertinent to Millville, which is distinguished by several clusters of houses that line a particular river and share a common power source. Finally, these types of company towns depended on individuals not associated with the company to operate the various civic institutions and commercial enterprises adjacent to the industrial site.[121]

A number of houses built by the Standard Lime and Stone Company to house their workers still stand, albeit in poor or ruinous condition, and include a number of associated outbuildings, including garages, workshops, smokehouses, chicken houses, hog houses, and outhouses, which are likewise in poor condition. Most of them were built around 1912 and may have been designed and built by the same people who constructed the company houses at nearby Bakerton, West Virginia, another quarry operated by the Standard Lime and Stone Company. While most of the company houses at Millville were three-bay, single-pile, two-story, gabled-roofed, vernacular frame structures covered with wooden siding (that were subsequently stuccoed during the 1940s) the circa 1920s foremen's houses were more substantial buildings, built of brick with hipped roofs and other architectural features that were characteristic of Foursquare-styled houses of that time period. More

Worker's House at the Standard Lime and Stone Quarry, near Millville, West Virginia
OIL ON PANEL, 8"X 12," FEBRUARY 7, 2012 (PAINTING #63).

importantly, the foremen's houses had indoor bathrooms whereas the workers' houses had outdoor privies. Eventually, some workers added indoor bathrooms, usually in the rear ell of the house, adjacent to the kitchen. The differentiation in both materials and amenities between workers and management was typical of the hierarchical organization of company towns.

Like the plantation economy that characterized Jefferson County's pre-Civil War landscape, the industrial landscape of the company left little doubt as to who was in control. Nevertheless, both workers and foremen lived and labored alongside one another in hazardous conditions. According to a local historian, company houses became obsolete here during the 1950s, partially due to modern transportation and communication devices that allowed employees to live farther from the work site. It is no surprise that they are in poor condition today, since company houses were generally built with economy in mind, because the lifespan of extractive industries was not easily predicted. Indeed, after World War II ended in 1945, production decreased at the Standard Lime and Stone Company's plant in Millville. The rock wool plant closed in 1949; the P32 operation ceased in 1957–1958, and nearly all if not all buildings have been removed from the property, which is still privately owned.[122]

The extant workers' houses are situated on property transferred to Harpers Ferry National Historical Park in 2004 and administered by the National Park Service, the nation's foremost federal conservation and preservation agency. National parks are beloved by the American people, but fiscal constraints ensure that proper resource management will continue to be a challenge. Time will tell if resources will be allocated to restore at least one of the workers' houses as a rare example of its type in the Shenandoah Valley.[123]

Currently, about fifteen percent of the Valley's workforce is engaged in manufacturing. With production jobs having largely migrated to Mexico, South America, and Asia, distribution centers and logistics services have been the backbone of the industrial sector not only in the Shenandoah Valley, but also the adjacent valleys of the Interstate 81 corridor in Maryland and Pennsylvania. About half of the nation's population lives within a day's drive of the Shenandoah, Hagerstown, and Cumberland Valleys, leading to an extensive warehousing complex in this corridor, and notable mega-distribution centers have recently popped up in Harrisonburg (Wal-Mart) and Staunton (Best Buy and FedEx), adding more eighteen-wheelers to Interstate 81's traffic flow.[124]

Corporations of all kinds may be more inclined to locate to Virginia, which, unlike West Virginia and states located north of the Potomac River, is a Right-to-Work state; that is, workers do not have to belong to a union. Additionally, Virginia imposes a lower corporate business tax than these other states. These two factors no doubt contributed to the location of MillerCoors Brewing and Merck Pharmaceutical Company in Elkton along U.S. 340 and the South Fork of the Shenandoah River. Yet another compelling reason for corporations to locate in the Shenandoah portion of the Great Valley is the Virginia Inland Port, located just north of Front Royal in Warren County, which is a U.S. Customs-designated port of entry that links the network of distribution centers via rail to marine terminals at Hampton Roads and the world beyond. As fate would have it, this very linkage facilitates the provision of cheaply produced overseas goods to the areas where manufacturing jobs once held sway, an unfortunate outcome of the global economy that we live in.[125]

The communications and biomedical industries have also imprinted the Valley's landscape, as evidenced by the sizable footprint of the towers and facilities owned by Edinburg-based Shenandoah Telecommunications Company (Shentel), Merck Pharmaceutical in Elkton, and growing regional hospitals and affiliated medical services in Winchester, Harrisonburg and Fishersville in Augusta County. Still, with its central location within the eastern United States and served by Interstates 81, 66, and 64, trucking and distribution centers seem to be the dominant economic enterprises in the years to come.

MillerCoors Brewery, Elkton
OIL ON PANEL, 6" X 8," APRIL 26, 2015 (PAINTING #229).

Brownsburg Academy, Brownsburg
OIL ON PANEL, 6" X 8," MARCH 14, 2011 (PAINTING #17).

Education

> I have often said that if there had been free schools in the South there would have been no war simply because an enlightened public opinion in that section would not have submitted to the rule of a slave holding oligarchy . . .
>
> —John S. Mosby, Assistant Attorney, United States Department of Justice and former Colonel, 43rd Battalion Virginia Cavalry, Confederate States of America (1909)[126]

Although most schoolhouses have been converted to dwellings or community buildings, many dot the Valley's landscape as a testament to the region's rural character and movement to establish free public education in the Commonwealth of Virginia. Creating a public school system in the Old Dominion was an arduous process, due not only to a dispersed population, but also to the reticence to levy taxes to support education. Virginia would have been credited with the first statewide public school system had the General Assembly acted on Thomas Jefferson's 1779 legislation, "A Bill for the More General Diffusion of Knowledge," but this would not be realized until ninety years later when the Underwood Constitution was ratified in 1869—Virginia's first constitutional convention after the end of the Civil War. Prior to this time, education was largely a private affair, accomplished through private tutoring, "Old Field" schools, and academies. An extant example, although no longer serving its original purpose, is Brownsburg Academy in Rockbridge County, which operated for just over a decade before the lean years of the Civil War and Reconstruction took its toll and forced its closure in 1877. Indeed, many academies had difficulty remaining financially solvent during this dark chapter in Virginia's history. The state senator who led the charge to secure state appropriations to build public high schools in the Commonwealth was actually a Brownsburg Academy product—William Hodges Mann. To accomplish this, Mann introduced legislation known as the Mann High School Bill, which provided $50,000 to match local funding to construct new schools.[127]

The first public schoolhouses established were modest one-room concerns, with their construction peaking at the turn of the twentieth century. As consolidation took root during the second quarter of the twentieth century, the number of schoolhouses decreased while their size increased. A rare surviving Reconstruction-era schoolhouse built to educate African-American schoolchildren is Josephine City School. Josephine City was a black community adjacent to Berryville, the county seat of Clarke County, which had the highest percentage of slaves per capita of any county in the Shenandoah Valley prior to the Civil War. While the U.S. Supreme Court, in its *Brown v. Board of Education* (1954) decision, declared that state laws mandating separate schools for blacks and whites were unconstitutional—overturning the decision in *Plessy v. Ferguson* (1896) that set forth the "separate but equal" doctrine—Virginia schools nonetheless remained segregated for a time. Rather than integrate, a number of Southern states, including Virginia, vowed to fight the federal government by penning a document called the "Southern Manifesto" and by organizing "massive resistance" to the edict. In fact, it was a Berryville resident, U.S. Senator Harry F. Byrd, Sr., who was kingpin for the movement and credited with devising the aforementioned slogans associated with it. Rather than comply with the Supreme Court's ruling, Virginia decided to close several high schools in 1958, the first being Warren County High School in Front Royal, south of Berryville. It opened five months later as an integrated school in response to a Virginia Supreme Court of Appeals ruling and U.S. Circuit Court order decrying the closures as unconstitutional.[128]

Although technically a public school, John Handley High School in the City of Winchester is the first and only privately endowed public high school in Virginia and one of only a handful in the nation. Completed in 1923, the commanding building, with its neoclassical design and grounds designed by the fabled Olmsted Brothers landscape architecture firm, owes its existence to the benevolence of Judge John Handley, from Scranton, Pennsylvania.[129]

Southerners were the progenitors of the movement to establish state-supported military schools, and the Shenandoah Valley became the epicenter of college preparatory military schools in the Commonwealth, Virginia currently having more private military academies in operation than another other state in the nation. Both Fishburne Military School in Waynesboro, which remains active, and Augusta Military Academy in Fort Defiance (Augusta County), which is no longer operating, were the first military academies established in Virginia when they were founded as all-male schools in 1879. Randolph-Macon Academy in Front Royal and Massanutten Military Academy in Woodstock opened in 1892 and 1899, respectively, and both are co-educational today.

Perhaps the strong military academy tradition in the Valley can be attributed primarily to the Scots-Irish, who not only valued military service, but likewise emphasized education. Virginia Military Institute (VMI), one of only six Senior Military Colleges currently operating in the U.S. and the oldest state-supported military college in the nation, is located in the Scots-Irish heartland of Lexington and is often referred to as the "West Point of the South." Distinguished attendees include General George S. Patton, Jr. and Nobel Prize-winner General George C. Marshall. General Thomas J. "Stonewall" Jackson, the Confederate military genius who distinguished himself by outmaneuvering numerically superior Union forces in the Shenandoah Valley, was Instructor of Artillery and Professor of Natural and Experimental Philosophy at VMI when the Civil War broke out. All three generals were of Scots-Irish lineage.[130]

Washington and Lee University, situated adjacent to VMI, was founded by the Scots-Irish as Augusta Academy. Renamed Liberty Academy and chartered as a college by the Virginia Legislature, the academy was one of a small number of institutions of higher learning established in the American colonies. Later named Washington College after its major benefactor, George Washington, the college came to be associated with another famous Virginia general, Robert E. Lee, when Lee was offered its presidency after the Civil War. Like Washington before him, Lee rescued the college from its financial difficulties and used his vast intellectual abilities to expand its educational offerings that supplemented the liberal arts with the mechanical arts.[131]

Another notable Virginian involved in higher education in the Commonwealth was Woodrow Wilson, one of eight U.S. Presidents from Virginia—the most of any state—and the only one

[top] *Clarke County African-American Cultural Center (Josephine City School), Berryville**
OIL ON PANEL, 8" X 12," OCTOBER 10, 2011 (PAINTING #12).

[bottom] *Administration Building, Mary Baldwin University, Staunton*
OIL ON PANEL, 9" X 12," AUGUST 2, 2015 (PAINTING #258).

born in the Shenandoah Valley (in Staunton, where there is now a Wilson presidential library). Of Scots-Irish ancestry and the son of a Presbyterian minister, Wilson was educated at Princeton, formerly the College of New Jersey, which was the first college established during the Colonial period by Presbyterians. Wilson was, first, a Princeton professor, and, subsequently the President of Princeton, but the distinction of being the first Virginia-born U.S. President to attend Princeton falls on James Madison. In fact, a number of famous Virginians have attended Princeton, including Robert E. Lee's father and Revolutionary War hero, Henry "Light Horse Harry" Lee, and Princeton has been characterized as being the most Southern-friendly of the Ivy League institutions.[132]

Yet another college in the Scots-Irish heartland associated with the Presbyterian Church is Mary Baldwin College, established in Staunton in 1842 as the Augusta Female Seminary and renamed Mary Baldwin University in 2016. The nation's oldest Presbyterian-affiliated women's college, Mary Baldwin is one of only three same-sex colleges remaining in Virginia, and its all-female Army ROTC program, established in 1996, is a partnership with VMI in Lexington. Historically, Mary Baldwin has had a strong affiliation with Stuart Hall School in Staunton. Affiliated with the Episcopal Church, Stuart Hall School was chartered in 1844 as the Virginia Female Institute, making it the Commonwealth's oldest all-girls school. It was renamed in honor of Flora Stuart, who directed the school from 1880–1899. She was the widow of renowned Confederate cavalry General J. E. B. Stuart, who died at the Battle of Yellow Tavern near Richmond in 1864. In 1992, Stuart Hall began the process of going co-ed. Today, it is the Valley's premiere independent school for college preparation, and it attracts students not only from the Valley and region, but also throughout the world.[133]

Although the Scots-Irish have firmly left their imprint on the educational landscape of the Valley, other ethnic and religious groups likewise left their mark. There is a strong higher education focus by the Germanic Anabaptist groups, with Eastern Mennonite University in Harrisonburg founded by the followers of Menno Simons and Bridgewater College in Bridgewater being founded by the Church of the Brethren. Although Shenandoah University is now affiliated with the United Methodist Church and is located in Winchester, it was likewise founded by the Brethren and was originally located some seventy-six miles to the south in Dayton. Another Methodist-affiliated school at one time was Southern Seminary, which was established in the City of Buena Vista (Rockbridge County) in 1901. Originally a junior college for women, it is now a four-year, coeducational institute operated since 1996 as Southern Virginia University by The Church of Jesus Christ of Latter-day Saints (Mormon Church). The most recent college to be founded in the Valley is Christendom College in Front Royal, which was established in 1977 and is associated with the Roman Catholic Church. [134]

A number of institutions of higher learning in the Valley have no religious affiliation. James Madison University (JMU), founded in 1908 as the State Normal and Industrial School for Women at Harrisonburg, is easily the largest university in the region, with an enrollment surpassing 22,000 in 2015. JMU has consistently ranked as one of the best universities not only in the Commonwealth, but within the South. Also part of the Virginia state educational system are Lord Fairfax Community College in Middletown (Frederick County) and Blue Ridge Community College in Weyers Cave (Augusta County)—not to be confused with Blue Ridge Technical and Community College in Martinsburg (Berkeley County), which is part of the West Virginia state educational system—and Dabney S. Lancaster Community College in the City of Buena Vista. Shepherd University in Shepherdstown (Jefferson County) was founded as Shepherd College in 1871 as one of six normal schools (teacher's colleges) in the fledgling state of West Virginia, but, unlike the institution that is now JMU, it was coeducational from its inception. It became a four-year college in 1930 and a university in 2004 and now serves more than 4,200 undergraduate students.[135]

Wayside Inn, Middletown
OIL ON PANEL, 6" X 12," OCTOBER 17, 2011 (PAINTING #170).

Foodways

> Well as I said we raised our corn, we fattened our hogs and when butchering time come . . . that was a great big excitement for us . . . because pop would get out a day or two before and split up a lot of dry wood and build a kiln then and we'd all go carry wood and carry it up . . . put down about four or five or six foot square of this dry wood and then laid these huge rocks all over it and put more wood and put more rock and more wood and keep building it up about . . . didn't have salting pans then . . . them days . . . get up every morning about 3 or 4 o'clock and they'd set the kiln a fire and well you could see the smoke and light from neighbors houses every morning and you knew who was going to butcher, and directly you could see the kiln was a burning. . . . Yea well some people I don't think butchered on Thanksgiving Day. . . . It was usually on the 20th or 15th . . . or 20th . . . some people would butcher early because they got to running out of feed. Mom never did like to butcher after the 20th of November . . . anywhere from there up to the 5th or 10th of December. Depends on the weather. If they would have a good cold time along there . . . then . . . cause you like to have three or four good cold nights . . . on it . . . then you had better luck with your meat . . .
>
> —Mrs. Mamie Jenkins Dearing, resident of Dark Hollow (1981)[136]

The Shenandoah Valley's cultural traditions were shaped by forces emanating from both Philadelphia southward and from Virginia's Tidewater and Piedmont regions westward, resulting in unique foodways that distinguish the Valley from other regions of Virginia. Using pork as a metaphor for exploring the Valley's diverse culinary heritage, one can find "Pork and Sauerkraut"—endemic to Pennsylvania German cuisine—alongside "Country Ham with Grits and Red Eye Gravy"—staples of Lowland South cuisine. Indeed, smokehouses built by Pennsylvania Germans and their descendants share the landscape with those built by Tuckahoes, the traditional term for eastern Virginians. Because the Valley was influenced by both the Mid-Atlantic and Lowland South culture hearths, it is often placed by geographers and folklorists within the Upland South culture region, although other scholars place the Valley in the Midland, also called the Pennsylvania Culture Region. Regardless of nomenclature, the Shenandoah Valley has historically been just as varied in its cuisine as in its other aspects of folklife.

The Valley is located within the great Ham Belt of the world, which includes the Upper and Middle South states of Virginia, West Virginia, North Carolina, Tennessee, Kentucky, and Missouri and extends to Central and Southern Europe and to Southern China. In essence, if the climate is too northerly, hams freeze and stymie the cure from permeating the meat, while if the climate is too southerly, hams will spoil in warmer temperatures. Accordingly, November is the traditional butchering hog butchering month in the Valley, although some Mennonite farmers prefer to butcher in March, in time for Easter. Aside from ham, another pork product that proliferates in the Valley is panhas, more commonly known as scrapple, which is attributable to the Pennsylvania Germans. Scrapple, a corruption of the German word meaning a "scrap" or "scraping," consists of scraps of meat mixed with flour and cornmeal made into a pudding that is particularly enjoyed for breakfast in the Mid-Atlantic.[137]

As the Valley's culinary landscape was heavily influenced by Pennsylvania Germans, other foods consumed in both the Southeastern Pennsylvania region and the Shenandoah Valley include fasnachts (fat cakes), shoo-fly pie, and apple butter. Fastnachts are essentially doughnuts that are traditionally served on Shrove Tuesday (the Tuesday before Ash Wednesday, which is the first day of Lent). Shoo-fly pie is commonly served as a Mennonite dessert in both locales, and apple butter is a condiment that is a staple on both Pennsylvania and Virginia Germans' tables. Grandma Moses rendered one of her better known Valley paintings, *Apple Butter Making* (1947), set at one of the Virginia farms that she and her husband lived on near Staunton.[138]

Tidewater and Piedmont contributions to Valley cuisine include fried chicken, spoonbread, and peanut soup. Spoonbread is essentially a cornmeal soufflé—so named because it is eaten with a spoon—that may have American Indian origins. Peanut soup is thought to be a contribution by slaves, as it closely resembles maafe, a soup eaten in West Africa.[139]

The dichotomous nature of the Valley's gastronomic landscape also manifests itself in the types of eating establishments that are found here. A number of Valley restaurants serve simple country fare that is not unlike that served at kitchen tables in the many farmhouses that dot the region; but more upscale establishments can be found in the region's cities and in smaller locales in the Hunt Country of the Lower Valley, where sophisticated palates have existed among the gentry class since the colonial period and continue to the present, as evidenced by the presence of L'Auberge Provençale, a luxurious inn with fine dining near the village of White Post. L'Auberge, along with other renowned restaurants such as Zynodoa and the Shack in downtown Staunton, have embraced the "farm-to-table" paradigm, sourcing ingredients from local producers that include Marker Miller Orchards and Polyface Farms. While currently all the rage, eating local and in-season fare is actually "old school" and was once commonplace in the Valley before produce was shipped from far-flung places. While the localvore movement is gaining traction in the Valley and Virginia as a whole, there is still much ground to be gained on New England, which leads all regions in per-capita consumption of locally grown food, even though the Valley has more farms than any New England state and more than Connecticut and Rhode Island combined.[140]

A region that staunchly clings to tradition, many of the Valley's eating establishments have been in continuous operation for more than fifty years. Established in 1797, the Wayside Inn in Middletown purportedly has been operating as an inn without interruption since that time and is known for serving Colonial Virginia fare. The Bavarian Inn in Shepherdstown, West Virginia, appeals to the region's Teutonic tastes, although the overwhelming majority of Valley Germans were not of Bavarian lineage but, instead, hailed from the Rhineland-Palatinate, known in Germany as Rheinland-Pfalz, adjacent Alsace, France, and the northwestern cantons of Switzerland.

L'Auberge Provençale, near White Post
OIL ON PANEL, 6" X 8," OCTOBER 16, 2011 (PAINTING #72).

Mrs. Rowe's Restaurant, Staunton
OIL ON PANEL, 5" X 8," JULY 11, 2011 (PAINTING #90).

The Snow White Grill in Winchester, Southern Kitchen in New Market, and Mrs. Rowe's near Staunton all serve hearty fare and have been operating continuously since the mid-twentieth century, gaining notoriety locally and afar through various means: the Snow White Grill was one of Patsy Cline's haunts and is the last of a group of Virginia/West Virginia/District of Columbia/Maryland hamburger chains by the same name still in use for its original purpose; Southern Kitchen was profiled in the popular book *Roadfood* (1977), and Mrs. Rowe's Restaurant published a number of popular cookbooks written by its late founder. None of the aforementioned establishments frequented by the Valley's overwhelmingly yeoman populace can be qualified as a diner per se, although the Valley, with U.S. 11 as its traditional artery and pockets of manufacturing, contains one of the highest concentrations of diners in Virginia, a state where diners are not nearly as prevalent as they are in the more industrialized states north of the Potomac River, where factory workers required quick and inexpensive sustenance. Winchester, with a variety of manufacturing concerns at one time, had a number of diners, and several are still extant, including the Triangle Diner and Amherst Diner.[141]

Whether highbrow or lowbrow, many of the Valley's restaurants still serve a number of specialties that have graced tables in the Valley for centuries. Social events such as the county fair, auctions, and church suppers also offer some of the Valley's authentic foods. Valley palates have expanded beyond traditional fare to encompass Asian, Indian, and Latino cuisine, as these and other immigrant groups have set down roots in the Valley and opened up eateries and food trucks featuring the foods of their homelands.

*Willow Shade, Childhood Home of Willa Cather, Gore**
OIL ON PANEL, 9" X 12," DECEMBER 26, 2011 (PAINTING #171).

The Arts

> Some call this [the Hoosick] a pretty valley, but give me the Shenandoah Valley, every time!
>
> —Grandma Moses (1949)[142]

Renowned for its association with the American Civil War more than any other facet of the region's history, it is not common knowledge that many notable artists of various mediums have made the Shenandoah Valley home, at one time or another, and that, today, the Valley boasts some of Virginia's best venues for art, dance, music, and theater. But that impression is changing, thanks, in part, to the growing reputation of the Valley's varied art scene.

Willa Cather, the Pulitzer Prize-winning novelist and one of the most important American literary figures of the early twentieth century, was born and raised in the Valley before her family migrated to Red Cloud, Nebraska, when she was nine. Although identified with the Cornhusker State, Cather's ancestors on both her mother's and father's sides of the family had deep roots in the Valley. The Cathers were in all likelihood Ulster-Welsh who immigrated to Pennsylvania from County Tyrone in Northern Ireland before migrating southward to Virginia, settling in the Back Creek Valley of Frederick County. Cather was born a few miles west of Winchester near Gore in a simple frame farmhouse owned by her mother's family. When she was one, the family moved just down the road to a house named Willow Shade, a substantial brick Greek Revival home that her paternal grandfather had built in 1851.[143]

Despite the Cather's relatively comfortable financial situation, the family sought out new opportunities on the frontier of Nebraska. Willa's grandfather, William Cather, and presumably her father and uncle had been Unionists during the Civil War, and these sympathies resulted in William being appointed Sheriff of Frederick County by Virginia's Reconstruction-era government. William, in turn, appointed his sons as deputy sheriffs, and there is conjecture by historians that hostilities towards the family by former Southern sympathizers compelled them to migrate to the Great Plains as evidenced by the mysterious burning of a barn on the farm that likely was attributable to arson.[144]

Although many of Cather's novels and short stories are set in Nebraska, memories of her youth spent in the Shenandoah Valley stayed with Willa throughout her life, as Willow Shade served as the setting for Cather's last novel, *Sapphira and the Slave Girl* (1940). A lesser-known short story, "A Night in Greenway Court," was published forty-four years earlier, with Lord Fairfax's country seat near White Post (Clarke County) serving as the setting.[145]

Just as Willa Cather's Valley roots are not widely known, neither is the Valley tenure of Anna Roberston Moses, better known as Grandma Moses. A housewife-turned artist—a transformation that did not occur until her mid-seventies—Grandma Moses is one of the most iconic American artists of the twentieth century. She was a self-taught painter of folk/primitive/outsider art that featured the landscapes and rural pastimes that she encountered during her lifetime. Her paintings were discovered hanging in a drug store located in the village of Hoosick Falls near her home in Eagle Bridge, New York, and she first exhibited at St. Etienne Gallery in New York City when she was eighty years of age. Moses became nationally and internationally known for her work and was even commissioned by President Eisenhower to paint his farm in Adams County, Pennsylvania, near Gettysburg.[146]

The vast majority of the landscapes Grandma Moses painted were in the Hoosic Valley of Upstate New York and adjacent Vermont and Massachusetts, but what is often overlooked is her eighteen-year stint living in the vicinity of Staunton. She lived in no fewer than five different houses, several of which she depicted with her brush. The first house she and her husband purchased as a married couple and the only house they owned in the Shenandoah Valley was Mount Airy, located in Verona. Currently owned by the County of Augusta, the house stands in deteriorated condition and was named by Preservation Virginia as one of the most threatened historic resources in the Commonwealth.[147]

Whereas bucolic river valleys in East Coast locales such as the Brandywine and Delaware valleys of Pennsylvania and Hudson Valley of New York had art colonies that captured the scenic beauty of these locales, this concept never took root in the Shenandoah Valley. Frederic Edwin Church, one of the heavyweights of the Hudson River School, was neither native to the Valley nor worked extensively there, and he only captured individual landscape features such as Natural Bridge in Rockbridge County. Conversely, George Caleb Bingham, another prominent nineteenth-century landscape painter, was an Augusta County native, yet he moved at a young age to Missouri and worked west of the Mississippi River. Grandma Moses actually resided in the Valley, although she did not paint while in residence. In fact, by the time she rendered her Valley paintings, she was more than forty years removed from her time in the Valley. She was fond of the region, and, when her husband desired to return to Upstate New York, Grandma Moses penned in her memoirs that she became homesick for the Shenandoah Valley.[148]

Several prominent photographers have also lived and worked in the Valley. During the depression, a number of established photographers were employed by the Farm Security Administration (FSA) to document conditions in rural locales like the Valley. FSA was one of President Franklin D. Roosevelt's New Deal programs, which was established, in part, to help address rural poverty. Russell Lee, Arthur Rothstein, Ben Shahn, John Vachon, and Marion Post Wolcott worked in the region, particularly in Shenandoah National Park and the various communities of the Shenandoah Homesteads project, where displaced residents of Shenandoah National Park were relocated. During the 1950s, O. Winston Link extensively photographed scenes along the Shenandoah Valley Railroad, which ran from Hagerstown, Maryland, to Roanoke, Virginia, where a museum pays tribute to his work. Born in New York City, Link is buried in Shepherdstown, West Virginia (Jefferson County), and his images of the last runs of steam engines are iconic. A contemporary photographer but one who works in the old method using the wet-plate process, Sally Mann is among only a handful of artists profiled in this essay who were born, raised, and worked in the Valley. Her

[top] *Grandma Moses's Home, Verona**
OIL ON LINEN, 9" X 12," OCTOBER 24, 2011 (PAINTING #51).

[bottom] *View to the East from Grandma Moses's Home, Verona*
OIL ON PANEL, 6" X 8," OCTOBER 24, 2011 (PAINTING #52).

[top] *Statler Brothers Monument, Wharf Area, Staunton**
OIL ON PANEL, 8" X 12," JULY 12, 2012 (PAINTING #156).

[bottom] *Patsy Cline's Home, Winchester**
OIL ON PANEL, 12" X 16," OCTOBER 17, 2011 (PAINTING #59).

photographs are displayed and collected in some of the nation's most prominent museums, and she was named America's Best Photographer by *Time* magazine in 2001. She still resides in the Valley near her birthplace of Lexington in Rockbridge County.[149]

Just as the Shenandoah Valley's contributions to literature, art, and photography are often overlooked, so, too, is its rich musical heritage. In fact, few regions outside of the Nashville Basin possess a country music legacy as rich as the Valley's. The Valley can claim two Country Music Hall of Fame inductees: Patsy Cline (née Virginia Patterson Hensley, from Winchester) and the Statler Brothers, none of whom were actually named Statler, only two of whom were brothers, but three of the members having been born in Staunton or Augusta County. In addition, two International Bluegrass Music Hall of Fame members have Valley roots: Mac Wiseman, born in Augusta County, and Bill Clifton, who was born in Maryland but later moved to Virginia and is credited with organizing the first-ever bluegrass festival at Oak Leaf Park near Luray in 1961. Although bluegrass has been super popular not only in the Valley, but also throughout the region, it quickly gained attention in the mainstream with the release of the Coen Brothers' unforgetable film, *O Brother Where Art Thou?* (2000), the soundtrack for which prominently featured Ralph Stanley, who was one of the acts (The Stanley Brothers) invited to Oak Leaf Park back in 1961.[150]

The simple house at 608 South Kent Street in Winchester, where Patsy Cline spent her early adulthood, is still extant. The Rainbow Road Club, a honkytonk located in Jefferson County, West Virginia, just over the Clarke County/Virginia state line, was featured in the popular film on Cline's life, *Sweet Dreams* (1985). Local legend persists that Cline actually performed there during her lifetime when it was called the Old Orchard Inn, while the Rainbow Inn was actually located near Winchester before it was torn down in the late 1950s. Cline was the first woman inducted into the Country Music Hall of Fame and is credited as the most popular female country singer in recording history. On the opposite end of the Valley, the Statler Brothers got their start singing gospel music in a church near Lyndhurst (which has since been replaced with a newer structure), while their office was located in Staunton, which honored its native sons with a statute in the Wharf Area Historic District. From 1970 to 1994, the Statler Brothers put on free concerts in nearby Gypsy Hill Park as part of a July 4 celebration known as "Happy Birthday USA" that attracted up to 100,000 spectators.[151]

The Statler Brothers continued the strong tradition of Southern Gospel in the Shenandoah Valley, which is attributed as the birthplace of both Southern Gospel and Shape-Note Singing. The Ruebush-Kieffer Company of Dayton in Rockingham County was the foremost publisher of seven-note scale of shape notes during the late nineteenth century. One of the proprietors of the company was Aldine Kieffer, who was the grandson of Joseph Funk, a Mennonite and noted publisher of music books and religious texts at his press in Singers Glen (also in Rockingham County), including the widely used hymnal, *Harmonia Sacra* (first published in 1832). Funk set up various singing schools, including one in the village he founded, which was aptly renamed, at a later date, to Singers Glen from its original name of Mountain Valley. Funk's house is still located in the middle of the village.[152]

The county fairs of the Valley regularly showcase country-western music, including various well-known acts. Likewise, the Shenandoah Valley Music Festival, which takes place at Orkney

Springs in Shenandoah County, has for half a century brought some of the nation's outstanding musical talent to the Valley. The Valley is also home to current acts of national reputation, including the Shenandoah Valley Bach Festival in Harrisonburg; Heifitz International Music Institute's events in Staunton, the brilliant American violinist Hilary Hahn (born and still residing in Lexington); and the bluegrass/folk/old-time/ acoustic country duo Robin and Linda Williams, of Lexington, who have been regulars on Garrison Keillor's acclaimed radio show, *A Prairie Home Companion*, since its inception in 1975. On several occasions, *Prairie Home Companion* has also hosted Old Crow Medicine Show (O.C.M.S.), which is another folk/old-time music outfit with roots in the Valley, founded in Harrisonburg in 1998. O.C.M.S. has two Grammy Awards under their belt and was inducted into the Grand Ole Opry in 2013. And the Waynesboro Symphony Orchestra has a well-deserved reputation for quality performances.[153]

Gypsy Hill Park is the scene of a summer concert series put on by the Stonewall Brigade Band. Established in 1855 as the Mountain Saxhorn Band and purportedly the oldest, continuous community band in existence in the nation, the band was mustered into Confederate General Thomas J. "Stonewall" Jackson's brigade at the outset of the Civil War and renamed after this famous Confederate until in 1875. It subsequently marched in six Presidential Inaugural Parades and continues to play at various civic occasions.[154]

For theater-goers, several long-standing venues exist(ed) in the Valley, including the Winchester Little Theatre (established 1929) and Wayside Theater in Middletown (which operated from 1961 to 2013), both in Frederick County, the Oak Grove Theater near Staunton (since 1954), and the Lime Kiln Theater in Lexington (Rockbridge County), which was established in 1967 and offers terrific musical events as well. The Staunton Performing Arts Center was established in 2012, utilizing a 100-year-old building originally built as a theater. Just down the street is the American Shakespeare Center, which opened its Blackfriars Playhouse in 2001 and is the only re-creation of the famous indoor playhouse in London where Shakespeare performed.[155]

Of course, the Valley's many colleges and universities offer countless venues for the fine arts and performing arts throughout the year. Of special note is the $92,000,000 world-class Forbes Performing Arts Center at James Madison University and its five theaters and acoustical perfection designed especially for dance, music, and theater that opened in 2010 as well as the grand Ohrstrom-Bryant Theatre (opened in 1998) at Shenandoah University.

[top] *Shenandoah Music Festival at Orkney Springs**
OIL ON PANEL, 8" X 12," SEPTEMBER 6, 2015 (PAINTING #263).

[bottom] *Lime Kiln Theater, Lexington*
OIL ON PANEL, 6" X 8," AUGUST 3, 2015 (PAINTING #257).

Shenandoah County Fair, Woodstock
OIL ON CANVAS, 12" X 24," SEPTEMBER 1, 2011 (PAINTING #120).

Recreation and Sports

Come to the mitt, shoot-gun, come to the mitt . . . knee-high and 90.

—David "Scratch" Clanagan, Rappahannock Monarchs, Rappahannock Monarchs-Woodstock Raiders Rivalry, Apple Valley Baseball League (1990s)[156]

A region blessed with an abundance of open space, sports and recreational activities are firmly rooted in the culture of the region. These activities take the form of rural pastimes, field sports, and athletic contests.

In an era of school violence, it may surprise some that, until the late 1980s and even later in some counties, Valley students routinely wore hunting knifes at school and kept their hunting rifles in their pickup trucks on school grounds. Many students to this day take off school the opening day of deer season, and Valley sportsmen, old and young, continue to supplement their diet with wild game just as their forebears did. Despite the availability of high-tech weaponry, some still stalk their prey with bow and arrow as well as modern-day versions of the Pennsylvania Long Rifle (more often called the Kentucky Rifle because of its use by Daniel Boone in the Bluegrass State), which originated with hunting rifles in Switzerland and the Palatinate of Germany, was carried to the Southeastern Pennsylvania region, and eventually made its way to the Southern backcountry.[157]

At the time of European contact, American Indians primarily used the Valley as a hunting ground, and, today, the region is still abundant in game. Some of the largest harvests of deer, bear, and wild turkey in Virginia occur in the Valley, and, though controversial in various quarters, some quarry, be they bears or foxes, are still hunted with hounds (hunting deer with dogs is prohibited in those Virginia counties west of the Blue Ridge Mountains). Indeed, foxhunting has been part of the Virginia landscape since the colonial era and has long been associated with the Valley's gentry class, centered on Clarke and Jefferson counties (Blue Ridge Hunt), although long-standing hunts and hunt clubs such as Glenmore and Rockbridge are located in Augusta and Rockbridge counties, respectively, to the south. Horse racing was likewise an important pastime of the gentry, which continues to the present in Jefferson County with the Charles Town Races, which opened for business in 1933.[158]

Fishing is an important pastime, with excellent bass and trout waters among other species. Two of the nation's preeminent fly-fishing experts, father and son duo Harry and Jeff Murray, operate a tackle shop in downtown Edinburg. Waynesboro continues to be active in creating events associated with fishing the South River of the Shenandoah, as is the South River Fly Shop downtown. One of the top 100 trout streams in the nation—Mossy Creek—is located in Augusta and Rockingham Counties, with the second being the Rapidan River, located within Shenandoah National Park on the eastern side of the Blue Ridge Mountains—technically the Blue Ridge Province rather than the Ridge and Valley. It is here that President and Mrs. Hoover established their aptly named Rapidan Camp in 1929 to escape the rigors of the Presidency and engage in fly-fishing and other outdoor activities.[159]-

Along with hunting and fishing, the county fair remains an important cultural institution in rural communities throughout the Shenandoah Valley. Here, a fair operates in every single county, making it the only region in the Commonwealth to have this distinction. The Shenandoah County Fair is one of the oldest fairs in Virginia, with roots as far back as 1886. Although the central tenet of county fairs was to showcase the agricultural industry that formed the backbone of the rural economy as well as put on a variety of homemaking exhibitions, there was limited entertainment such as horse racing. Entertainment was greatly expanded after the 1893 World's Fair in Chicago to include traveling carnivals. In essence, the focus shifted away from the exhibition sheds and to the midway, where the grittier side of fairs was on display. The heyday of freak and hoochie shows was in the decades immediately preceding World War II, yet this was part of the fair landscape in some Valley locales until recent years. Billed as a family affair, the Shenandoah County Fair featured the last traveling hoochie-coochie tent show in the nation, which came to a head in the mid-1990s, when nudity laws and moral values were put to the test. Given the conservative religious underpinnings in the region, the presence of these girlie shows was a cultural anomaly, and the phenomenon caught media attention beyond the region and state. The last show occurred in 1996 after more than seventy-five years in operation, after several years of legal issues and protests by a local anti-pornography group.[160]

County fairs in the Shenandoah Valley occur throughout the summer, with the Shenandoah County Fair occurring during the week leading up until Labor Day. The prominence of Shenandoah County's agricultural heritage was evident when future farmers were excused from the first week of school to attend to their livestock being exhibited at the fair, a situation that has since been remedied by school being started after Labor Day. Coinciding with the beginning of the high school football season, the Shenandoah County Fair was a fitting end to summer and the start of a new school year, and it remains one of the Valley's most enduring traditions.

Baseball has been a pastime in the Shenandoah Valley for more than a century. Nearly every town and village fielded a "town ball" team that competed against rivals from neighboring towns. Some of the Valley's larger cities such as Martinsburg, which competed in the Blue Ridge League, and Harrisonburg and Staunton, which competed in the Virginia League and Virginia Mountain League, fielded minor-league teams during the first half of the twentieth century; and while these leagues have since faded from the landscape, town ball remains. One of the oldest and most competitive of these leagues is the Rockingham County Baseball League (RCBL), founded in 1924, of which many minor and major leaguers can be counted among its alumni. The league has since expanded to adjacent Augusta and Shenandoah Counties, but its core group of teams is still located in Rockingham. Fan loyalty to the teams is fierce.[161]

The oldest ballpark still in use in the RCBL is Buck Bowman Park, home of the Clover Hill Bucks and named for the stadium's benefactor. The wooden grandstands, a rare survivor, were completed in 1954, and the park was the first in the league to make use of lights for night games. The tiny hamlet of Clover Hill bustles with activity on summer nights when there is a Bucks home game. Adding to the nostalgic scene is the use of wood bats, the league having banned aluminum in the late 1990s.[162]

Another town ball league that has been in existence for many years is the Apple Valley Baseball League, historically centered in the counties of Shenandoah, Frederick, Page, and Warren but at one time including teams from Rockingham County. The league also included teams from the Piedmont in Prince William, Culpeper, and Rappahannock counties, the Rappahannock Monarchs up until recent years being a predominantly African-American team, with roots going back to the days of segregated baseball. The Apple Valley Baseball League dates to 1969, but its predecessor league may be older than the Rockingham County League. The Valley Baseball League has also been in existence for many years, going back to 1923. It once filled out its rosters with both locals and highly touted college players, but is now strictly a collegiate summer league. It, too, has helped launch the careers of some major league players.[163]

Sports legends who have called the Valley home include Jack Ham, longtime Pittsburgh Steelers outside linebacker and NFL Hall of Fame inductee who attended Massanutten Military Academy in Woodstock; NFL Hall of Fame inductee Charles Haley, an outside linebacker and defensive end who played at James Madison University before starring for the San Francisco 49ers and Dallas Cowboys; Harrisonburg native Ralph Sampson, who starred at the University of Virginia and went on to a Hall of Fame basketball career with the Houston Rockets; and Dell Curry, also a Harrisonburg native, who starred at Virginia Tech and played in the N.B.A., holding numerous records for the Charlotte Hornets. While only a visitor, golfing legend Bobby Jones, one of the greatest golfers ever to play the game, opened the first nine holes in 1927 at Shenvalee Golf Resort in New Market. Other historic golf courses include Ingleside and Gypsy Hill Park in Staunton.[164]

Of course, elementary and secondary school athletics continue to dominate the Valley's sports scene, like everywhere else in the nation, but with so many colleges and universities in the Valley, residents also have ample opportunities to share in collegiate sports offerings. James Madison University, for example, won the 2004 national championship in Division 1-AA football and, in 2011, expanded Bridgeforth Stadium to a seating capacity of 25,000. Of note, ESPN's College GameDay visited JMU on October 24, 2015, resulting in one of the biggest and most festive crowds the acclaimed show has ever experienced, prompting hosts Reese Davis and Kirk Herbstreet to proclaim on air, respectively, "This is what college football is all about" and "This is the best GameDay we have ever had."

New Market Battlefield Military Museum
OIL ON PANEL, 6" X 10.5," MARCH 22, 2015 (PAINTING #215).

Hallowed Ground

> It would be impossible, of course, for the scholar to prove that the Southerner in battle has possessed more courage or displayed better fighting qualities than his compatriot from any other part of the country. However, from a statistical point of view, there is irrefutable evidence of the fact that, throughout American history, no other section of the country has sent its picked youth into battle so freely and so heedlessly as has the South. What is even more remarkable, throughout American history the section has furnished the outstanding generals. No state in the Union, for example, can rival Virginia's long list of illustrious military men, from George Washington to George Marshall. . . . It is not enough that the South should have the only state-supported military colleges in the nation. It is also studded from the Potomac to the Rio Grande with private military preparatory schools. A favorite location for such schools is the Valley of Virginia . . .
>
> —John C. Bonner, "The Historical Basis of Southern Military Tradition" (1951)[165]

The Shenandoah Valley is a name recognized around the world not only for its beauty but also for the role it played during the American Civil War. Yet the Valley's venerable military history is not isolated to this conflict from April 1861 to April 1865 but, instead, has many important chapters that both pre-date and post-date that war.

It starts with the Valley's strategic location. Because the Valley served, during the colonial era, as a buffer between English settlements east of the Blue Ridge and French possessions in the Ohio and Mississippi River Valleys west of the Alleghenies, a number of armed conflicts involving Euro-American settlers and American Indian war parties occurred in the French and Indian War, Cherokee War, and Pontiac's War. Architectural historians tend to refute the notion, but military historians contend that a series of stockade dwellings were utilized by settlers to take refuge during Indian incursions, some of which are still extant and referred to locally as "forts."

The largest and most significant of this defense network was Fort Loudoun, a fort proper in what is now the City of Winchester, not to be confused with the Fort Loudoun of similar age that is located in the Tennessee Valley. No longer extant, Fort Loudoun's construction was supervised by a young George Washington, who was put in command of the Virginia Regiment (militia) by Royal Governor Robert Dinwiddie and whose responsibilities included protecting the Virginia frontier. It is thought that the office that Washington used while supervising the construction of Fort Loudoun is the middle section of the building still standing at the intersection of Braddock and Cork streets in Winchester.[166]

Although there are no Revolutionary War battlefields located in the Valley, the region is well represented in terms of noteworthy commanders and regiments. George Washington, even before he lived in Winchester during his tenure as Commander of the Virginia Regiment and subsequent election as Commander-in-Chief of the Continental Army, was a teenage surveyor in the Valley for Lord Fairfax and speculated in a number of land holdings in the Upper Valley.

Another one-time Valley resident who became a general in the Continental Army was John Peter Gabriel Muhlenberg, the son of the Reverend Henry Melchior Muhlenberg, who was patriarch of the Lutheran Church in America. Born and raised in Philadelphia County (now Montgomery County), Pennsylvania, Peter Muhlenberg was an ordained minister who was called to the Shenandoah Valley after serving Lutheran congregations in the Raritan Valley of New Jersey. During his tenure in Virginia, he traveled to London, England, and was ordained an Anglican clergyman, serving both Emanuel Lutheran Church and Emmanuel Anglican (now Episcopal) Church in Woodstock. A true Renaissance man, Muhlenberg raised the Eighth Virginia Regiment (known as the German Regiment, for the large number of soldiers of Germanic ancestry) during the American Revolution, later commissioned a brigadier general in the Continental Army and brevetted a major general.[167]

One of the legends associated with Muhlenberg is the supposed stripping off of his clerical robe and the revealing of his officer's uniform underneath during a fiery sermon, declaring, "There is a time to pray and a time to fight, and that time has now come!" The veracity of this momentous occasion, however, has been analyzed for accuracy by historians, even being profiled on the "History Detectives" series on PBS (Public Broadcasting Service). There is doubt among several scholars that this event unfolded as legend holds it, which, instead, may have been an embellishment by family members and German-Americans seventy-five years after the fact. Regardless, Muhlenberg is venerated in the Valley, particularly in Woodstock, where not just one but two statutes are dedicated to him in front of the old Shenandoah County Courthouse and where the local elementary school is named after him.[168]

Yet another Shenandoah Valley resident who rose to prominence during the Revolution was Daniel Morgan. A resident of Frederick County (the portion of which is now Clarke County) at the outbreak of the war after having migrated southward from Hunterdon County, New Jersey, Morgan's heroics during that conflict earned him the Gold Medal from the Continental Congress. The Continental Congress had called for the formation of a number of rifle companies in Pennsylvania, Maryland, and Virginia, and Morgan was placed in charge of the Virginians. Some of the battle dress and tactics of Daniel Morgan's Riflemen were borrowed from American Indians, which fit well with waging a war on the American landscape, but their weapon of choice was a Swiss-German import—the Pennsylvania Long Rifle. With its rifled rather than smoothbore barrel, the Pennsylvania rifle was highly accurate and employed by the Continental Army to compete with some of Europe's finest soldiers, even though it was a hunting rather than a military firearm.[169]

Morgan owned a number of houses in what is now Clarke County, including Soldier's Rest and Saratoga, both of which are extant and listed in the Virginia Landmarks Register, as is the house named for him in the City of Winchester. Just down the street from his home in Winchester was his place of worship—the Old Stone (Presbyterian) Church, a late eighteenth-century edifice where his remains were interred before being reinterred in nearby Mount Hebron Cemetery.[170]

The war that had the greatest impact on the Shenandoah Valley was, of course, the Civil War, alternatively called, depending on one's allegiance, the War between the States, the War of Northern Aggression, and War of the Rebellion. The list of significant Civil War battles that occurred on Shenandoah Valley soil is lengthy—the 1st, 2nd, and 3rd Winchester; 1st and 2nd Kernstown; Cedar Creek; Fishers Hill; Toms Brook; Cool Spring; Front Royal; New Market; Port Republic; Cross Keys; and Piedmont. So, too, is the list of noteworthy commanders—Lee, Jackson, Ewell, Early, Grant, Sheridan, Custer, Crook, and more. Since tales of tactics, heroism, and atrocities are well-documented in the literature, their treatment is limited in this vignette.[171]

The famous exploits of Confederate General Thomas J. "Stonewall" Jackson in the Valley speak for themselves and are studied at military colleges around the world, but what is compelling about the engagements in the Valley is the tactical prowess showed by non-professional soldiers such as Turner Ashby, Elijah V. White, Harry Gilmor, John Hanson McNeill, and John Singleton Mosby—Confederate partisan commanders par excellence, even as both Mosby and McNeil were actually opposed to secession. Except for Mosby, who was an attorney, these men were all farmers, and these pre-war civilians turned out to be suited perfectly for unconventional warfare, which required a departure from conventional military maxims taught at the U.S. service academies. Their pursuit of the Union Army was relentless—Mosby and McNeill both making legendary nighttime raids that netted high-ranking officers in their beds.[172]

Operating primarily in Virginia's Piedmont region, Mosby's Rangers, perhaps the most proficient and feared of all Confederate Partisan Ranger units, carried out two of their most signature victories in the Shenandoah Valley. The "Berryville Wagon Train Raid" occurred in August 1864 near Berryville, the county seat of Clarke County, and resulted in Mosby's Rangers capturing 500 to 600 horses, 200 beef cattle, 200 prisoners, and 100 wagons that were serving as Union Army's General-in-Chief Philip Sheridan's supply train for his Valley Campaign. The "Greenback Raid" occurred in October 1864 near what is now Bardane, several miles east of Kearneysville (Jefferson County). The raid was so named, because the rangers attacked a federal paymaster and absconded with $173,000 and numerous federal prisoners after derailing and wrecking the train.[173]

Partisans depended on the help of the local populace who not only quartered and fed these men, but also kept them apprised of Union troop movements. Non-combatants paid dearly for their allegiance when the Union Army waged a legendary (and still-remembered) scorched-earth campaign against residents of the Loudoun and Shenandoah Valleys, burning houses, barns, mills, and crops.

The exemplary service of Valley citizen-soldiers continued beyond the Civil War. During World War I, three regiments of the Virginia National Guard were incorporated into the 116th Infantry Regiment, 29th Division, U.S. Army, and distinguished themselves in the Meuse-Argonne Offensive in France, which was the largest and costliest military engagement ever fought in by the U.S. military and resulted in Allied victory and the signing of the armistice that ended the war. Attached to the French 18th Division, the 116th regiment was awarded the French Croix de Guerre (Cross of War) for bravery, as did one is its members, Earle Gregory, who became the first Virginia Guardsman to earn the Congressional Medal of Honor, America's highest military honor.

Descended from Jackson's "Foot Cavalry" and with antecedents as early as the French and Indian War, the 116th was again called to service during World War II, where the unit will always be remembered for the valor displayed in assaulting Omaha Beach in Normandy, France, as part of the D-Day Invasion. Against formidable German defenses, 797 members of the 116th perished during the assault, but they lived up to their motto—"Ever Forward!"—and, eventually, the Americans were able to seize the stronghold, with the 116th being awarded the Distinguished Unit Citation for heroism and the 29th Division being awarded the French Croix de Guerre.[174]

No discussion of World War II would be complete with mentioning two VMI products—George C. Marshall and George S. Patton—who both had Virginia lineages. Marshall was instrumental in planning America's invasion of Europe and was later promoted a five-star general. He served as Army Chief of Staff, Secretary of Defense, and Secretary of State, in which capacity he helped design and implement the landmark European Recovery Program, dubbed the Marshall Plan after him. Patton, a combatant in both world wars and a progenitor of tank warfare, was one of the greatest generals in American history—even Hollywood made a movie, *Patton* (1970), about him.[175]

On the home front, the Valley's martial associations during World War I and World War II are manyfold. In addition to its equipment manufactories, a U.S. Army remount station was located just south of Front Royal on the current property of the Smithsonian Conservation Biology Institute (affiliated with the National Zoo in Washington, D.C.) that bred, trained, and supplied mules and dogs for the military. Located in an area of the nation renowned for quality breeding and the training of horses, the remount station operated from 1911 to 1948. German prisoners of war provided labor at the facility during World War II. In fact, this was one of four P.O.W. (Prisoner of War) camps located in the Shenandoah Valley, the others being in Winchester, Timberville, and Lyndhurst, with occasional work in Fishersville at the Woodrow Wilson General Hospital, now the Woodrow Wilson Rehabilitation Center. The Valley camps housed from 205 to 435 prisoners. The Valley's farm produce was critical to the war effort, yet enlistment in the armed forces by the region's farmers created labor shortages in the agricultural work force. Despite initial concern about the use of Nazi POWs on domestic soil, they successfully harvested crops on local farms without major incident and, where necessitated, engaged in forestry duties. Some remained in the Valley after the war.[176]

Additional wartime labor was provided by conscientious objectors, which included the Valley's Mennonites, Brethren, and Quakers. They were engaged in improvement projects on the Blue Ridge Parkway and in Shenandoah National Park, similar to the work of the Civilian Conservation Corps (CCC), and were quartered in former CCC camps. Another one of the four Civilian Public Service camps located in the Valley was under the direction of the Soil Conservation Service and operated by the Mennonite Central Committee. Here, conscientious objectors were engaged in soil-conservation work on agricultural land that had succumbed to erosion—work that undoubtedly resonated with the agrarian Anabaptists.[177]

Mennonites continue to serve peace-keeping missions during wartime. The Mennonite Central Committee, which established the well-known *Ten Thousand Villages* retail stores that is accredited with sparking the fair-trade movement, is currently helping citizens in Afghanistan,

Iraq, and Syria to establish market gardens, provide vocational training, and assisting with the relocation of displaced families who are fleeing famine and violence. With funds generated by the well-attended annual Virginia Mennonite Relief Sale, currently located at the Rockingham County Fairgrounds, financial assistance is provided around the world for families in need of food and shelter.[178]

Today, the pacifist presence is not insignificant in the Valley. Roughly 26,412 Valley residents belong to one of three peace churches—Church of the Brethren (16,848 members), Mennonite Church U.S.A. (5,275 members), and Seventh-Day Adventist Church (4,289 members). Of the nation's 3,144 counties (or county equivalents such as Virginia's independent cities), eight Valley localities are ranked in the top 100 for Church of the Brethren adherents, with West Virginia ranking first and Virginia second, respectively, among states and the District of Columbia; four Valley localities are ranked in the top 100 for percent of total population belonging to the Mennonite Church U.S.A., while Virginia is ranked seventh out of the fifty states and the District of Columbia; and five Valley localities are ranked in the top 100 for Seventh-Day Adventist Church adherents.[179]

Juxtaposed against the population statistics for pacifists are those for military personnel. Virginia is second only to California in the number of current active-duty members, and, as a percent of total population, Virginia ranks fourth out of the fifty states and the District of Columbia—no surprise given its adjacency to Washington, D.C., and twenty-seven military installations being located in the Commonwealth. With nearly half of all military recruits coming from military families, it is no surprise that Virginia is ranked among the top-ten states per capita for military enlistments. Continuing the historical trend of military service, the South as a region (including both Virginia and West Virginia, per the U.S. Department of Defense methodology) leads the nation in enlistments, having 1.5 times more enlistments than states north of the Potomac River, which have the lowest enlistment rate in the nation.[180]

The many monuments to the Valley's servicemen and servicewomen are a testament to the deep appreciation of sacrifices made in the name of freedom. The symbolic center of a community—the county courthouse—is a fitting location for placing these monuments, which include the conflicts in Korea and Vietnam in addition to the wars aforementioned. Denizens of the Valley continue to serve their nation in the conflicts in Iraq and Afghanistan. The 116th Regiment, reconstituted as the 116th Infantry Brigade Combat Team, continues as a Virginia National Guard unit and is headquartered in Staunton with an armory in Winchester. It has served in Operation Enduring Freedom (originally confined to Afghanistan and now part of the Global War on Terrorism), Operation Iraqi Freedom, and Operation New Dawn (Iraq).[181]

Whether fighting for the United States or Virginia and the Confederacy, on American or foreign soil, the Shenandoah Valley's residents have answered the call to serve for more than 250 years. Likewise, the Valley's sizable number of pacifists have contributed to national defense, albeit in civilian roles. Coupled with the Valley's plethora of military academies and as the setting for numerous engagements during the Civil War, the Valley's military legacy is rivaled by few regions in the nation.

Picnic at Watermelon Park, near Berryville
OIL ON CANVAS, 12" X 16," OCTOBER 11, 2010 (PAINTING #103).

Afterword

Edward L. Ayers

As someone who makes his living with words, I look at the paintings of Andrei Kushnir with a sense of mystery. How can anyone turn tubes of paint into luminous images? And how can anyone capture so powerfully the feeling of a place as expansive and, as Warren Hofstra reminds us in his eloquent essay, as layered as the Shenandoah Valley? It is beyond me, so all I can do is turn my impressions of the paintings and what they convey back into my own medium of words.

There is something about these images that evokes a sense of shared memory. While often focused on remnants of the past, they are not nostalgic. They represent time as a matter of fact, as a living presence on the landscape. The mountains and rivers speak of ancient time. The stone walls and barns speak of enduring time. The cars and trucks and stores and parking lots speak of time passing before our eyes. While beautiful, the paintings are neither glossy nor evasive.

There is also something about these images, framed in intimate perspective, that evokes personal memory. My relationship with the Valley is itself layered. I grew up in one of the other, lesser valleys of the Great Valley. We lived in the Holston Valley of East Tennessee, just south of the Virginia line. The valley there is narrower and more broken, with none of the vistas of the Shenandoah. The mountains did not hover and shimmer in the distance but stood nearby, making sure we did not look too far into the distance. The farms were small and the land hilly and rocky, with no sturdy walls or big houses or fine horses.

A few dozen miles makes a big difference. Passing north through the even narrower valleys of southwestern Virginia into the expanse of the Shenandoah on U.S. 11, even a child could feel the change. Suddenly, the sky opened, and farms stretched beyond sight. Although, by the 1950s and 1960s, the days of high farming had passed, an air of prosperity and quiet grandeur still hung over the Valley's landscape. The paintings of Andrei Kushnir capture that air with a sure touch.

The road through the Valley took on a new meaning for me during the 1970s, beginning my first trip out of the South when I followed it to work with a carnival then stopped in Wilmington, Delaware. My new wife and I followed it again as a route for our honeymoon journey to New York

City and Maine and then many times after as the way home during five years of graduate school at Yale in Connecticut. Those years were revelatory to both of us, revealing that we were unavoidably Southern and that we were fine with that.

Coming back to Tennessee every year at Christmas and then in the summer, we developed a routine: We drove the eight hours from New Haven to the Valley before we allowed ourselves to stop for the evening. Interstate 81 was new then, one piece after another having opened over the preceding three decades. Compared to the interstate highways of the Northeast, I-81 seemed almost bucolic then, relatively empty and with few trucks, a fitting complement to the relaxed landscape of the Valley itself. When we got out of the car to stay in Harrisonburg, we unexpectedly found ourselves in a landscape like the one where we had both grown up, a landscape of fast-food restaurants and strip malls scattered upon a rural landscape still visible next to the parking lots. We found ourselves among people whose manner of speaking and acting toward strangers was like our own. We knew we were home in the Valley. And we knew, as I could not help but say at some point on every trip, that "if there was a more beautiful place in America, I don't know where it is. I'd give anything to live here."

As luck would have it, we had the chance to live, if not in the Valley itself, just over the Blue Ridge Mountains in Charlottesville. For a quarter of a century, we crossed the always-exhilarating (if sometimes tricky) Afton Mountain at Rockfish Gap (1,903 feet elevation), struck by the same vistas that had greeted the Knights of the Golden Horseshoe, Thomas Jefferson, Stonewall Jackson, and countless pioneers. We bought bikes for our kids in Waynesboro and cheese from Mennonite stores in Dayton. We hiked in Shenandoah National Park and listened to music at Lime Kiln Theater. We found the best barbecue places and places to buy apples and daylilies.

And one day around 1990, driving on I-81, I was hit with a revelation that would shape my professional life: I saw a sign for the New Market battlefield, and a synapse jumped from my childhood years in Sunday School—the valley of the shadow of death. One of the most beautiful places in the United States had seen some of the most notorious destruction in American history. The Gulf War was then on everyone's mind, and another synapse fired: The people of the Valley, this Valley, had gone to war with one another in a matter of months. People living on the same soil, with the same climate and crops, sharing the same language, faith, and political ideals, had killed each other for four years. How could such people, on such a gentle and forgiving landscape, learn to hate so quickly? And what did that war and its aftermath mean for the people who lived here for the generations that followed?

I launched into what would become a twenty-five-year effort to understand those questions. Early in the history of the world-wide Web, my colleagues and I built a digital archive, *The Valley of the Shadow: Two Communities in the American Civil War*. That site—in retrospect, an entirely unreasonable undertaking—gathered every piece of written evidence we could find for Augusta County in Virginia and Franklin County in Pennsylvania, both in the Great Valley of which the Shenandoah is an integral part. Following that evidence, anyone in the world could, and still can, track the descent of the Valley, day-by-day, into the burning and killing of the Civil War and back out into the days of emancipation that followed. The letters, diaries, and newspapers are as remarkable as the landscape on which they were written.

Those documents reveal a history that time and memory have effaced. The Valley of Virginia had been cleared and cultivated not only by industrious Scots-Irish and German families, so fondly recalled, but also by enslaved African Americans. The stones in the walls and the foundations of the barns had often been laid by enslaved people. In fact, the more imposing the farm, the more likely it was to have demanded the labor of men, women, and children working for people other than themselves. After emancipation, those people, constituting as much as a quarter of the population in some counties, departed the Valley, finding more opportunity and more freedom beyond the Blue Ridge, beyond the Alleghenies.

That rich history is visible on the landscapes painted with such skill and passion by Andrei Kushnir. The slavery and the war are not the overt subject of his paintings, but their presence can be seen in the quiet farms and lonely roads, in the shadows. And with those shadows of history, the landscapes of the Valley become even more meaningful, more haunting. Whether it is a quiet river scene, a cemetery, a church, or an impressive house, the paintings here evoke places where enslaved people lived, where soldiers died, where mothers and fathers wept.

The days of high farming and big historic houses have passed in the Valley, replaced with industrial-sized poultry farms, with subdivisions and malls. It is hard for that not to feel like loss, for the new presences represent less regional character and more fleeting ambitions. The rich landscapes of Andrei Kushnir's paintings—unified in tone and spontaneity and yet varied in subject and perspective, unafraid of car dealers and empty streets—remind us that change has always been the lot of the Valley, that new things as well as old repay our close attention.

Evening on the Pond, Gypsy Hill Park, Staunton
OIL ON PANEL, 7" X 12," AUGUST 2, 2015 (PAINTING #253).

Notes

Epigraphs (page 5)

(Top) Washington Irving to Sarah Irving, June 22, 1853, in Ralph M. Aderman, Herbert L. Kleinfield, and Jenifer S. Banks, eds., *Washington Irving: Letters*, 5 vols. (Boston, MA: Twayne, 1973–1982), Vol. 4: 413–14; and (bottom) Charles James Faulkner, "The Speech of Charles Jas. Faulkner (of Berkeley [County]) in the House of Delegates of Virginia on the Policy of the State with Respect to Her Slave Population," January 20, 1832 (Richmond, VA: Thomas W. White, 1832), 9.

The Shenandoah Valley (Hofstra)

1. Washington Irving to Sarah Irving, June 22, 1853, in Ralph M. Aderman, Herbert L. Kleinfield, and Jenifer S. Banks, eds., *Washington Irving: Letters*, 5 vols. (Boston, MA: Twayne, 1973–1982), Vol. 4: 413–14.

2. See Andrei Kushnir, *Painted History: The Landscapes of Valley View Farm* (Richmond: Virginia Historical Society, 2004).

3. Indicative of the iconic status of the Shenandoah Valley might be its inclusion in *The Atlas of Legendary Places* as only one of three sites in the United States rising to this high status among thirty-seven "timeless landscapes" and other natural wonders of the world. See James Harpur and Jennifer Westwood, *The Atlas of Legendary Places* (New York: Konecky & Konecky, 1997).

4. William L. Alden, "Sailor Songs," *Harper's New Monthly Magazine*, Vol. 65, No. 386 (July 1882): 283.

5. David W. Bone, *Capstan Bars* (New York: Harcourt, Brace, 1932), 104–06; Norm Cohen, *Folk Music: A Regional Exploration* (Westport, CT: Greenwood Press, 2005), 100–01; and John A. Lomax, *American Ballads and Folk Songs* (New York: Macmillan, 1934), 543–46.

6. David Boaz, "Liberty at the Movies," *Cato Institute* (June 20, 2005); available at: http://www.cato.org/publications/commentary/liberty-movies. See, also, Mark Skousen, "Oscar Shrugged," *MSkousen.com* (September 5, 1999); available at: http://www.mskousen.com/1999/09/oscar-shrugged/.

7. Edward Porter Alexander, ed., *The Journal of John Fontaine: An Irish Huguenot Son in Spain and Virginia, 1710–1719* (Williamsburg, VA: Colonial Williamsburg, 1972), 106.

8. Ibid.

9. Ibid. See, also, William Alexander Caruthers, *The Knights of the Golden Horse-Shoe: A Traditionary Tale of the Cocked Hat Gentry in the Old Dominion* (Wetumpka, AL: Charles Yancey, 1845; New York: Harper & Brothers, 1882). Spotswood and his party were not the first Europeans to see the Shenandoah Valley. The Virginia explorer John Lederer visited the region in 1669 and 1670. On the exploration of Virginia, see Clarence Walworth Alvord and Lee Bidgood, *The First Explorations of the Trans-Allegheny Region by the Virginians, 1650–1674* (Cleveland, OH: Arthur H. Clarke, 1912); and Alan V. Briceland, *Westward from Virginia: The Exploration of the Virginia-Carolina Frontier, 1650–1710* (Charlottesville: University Press of Virginia, 1987).

10. Information about Brooke's appointment as a surveyor in the Shenandoah Valley can be found in William P. Palmer, Sherwin McRae, Raleigh Colston, and H. W. Flourney, eds., *Calendar of Virginia State Papers and Other Manuscripts, 1652–1781*, 12 vols. (Richmond, VA: 1875–1893; New York: Kraus Reprint, 1968), Vol. 1: 217–18; H. R. McIlwaine, Wilmer L. Hall, and Benjamin J. Hillman, eds., *Executive Journals of the Council of Colonial Virginia*, 6 vols. (Richmond: Virginia State

Library, 1925–1966), Vol. 4: 321; and Sarah S. Hughes, *Surveyors and Statesmen: Land Measuring in Colonial Virginia* (Richmond: Virginia Surveyors Foundation and Virginia Association of Surveyors, 1979), 98–99. Cognates of the name "Shenandoah" for the namesake valley and river can be found throughout the *Calendar of Virginia State Papers* and the *Executive Journals of the Council.*

11. John Lederer, *The Discoveries of John Lederer*, March of America Facsimile Series 25 (Ann Arbor, MI: University Microfilms, 1966), 24.

12. Michel's 1707 map of the Shenandoah Valley can be found in CO 5/1316, f. 79, Colonial Office Papers, Public Records Office, London, UK; and, for Michel's descriptive text, see Charles E. Kemper, "Documents Relating to Early Projected Swiss Colonies in the Valley of Virginia, 1706–1709," *Virginia Magazine of History and Biography*, Vol. 29, No. 1 (January 1921): 2–3.

13. George Washington to Robert Dinwiddie, April 27, 1756, in W. W. Abbot, et al., eds., *The Papers of George Washington*, 10 vols., Colonial Series (Charlottesville: University Press of Virginia, 1983–1995), Vol. 3: 59.

14. Fort Valley within the Massanutten Mountains centered in the lower Shenandoah Valley served as the particular site Washington had identified as a last resort for the Continental Army, according to a legend reported by a number of authors. See Julia Davis, *The Shenandoah* (New York: Farrar & Rinehart, 1945), 11 and 331; Samuel Kercheval, *A History of the Valley of Virginia*, 5th ed. (Strasburg, VA.: Shenandoah Publishing House, 1973), 364–65; and John Walter Wayland, *A History of Shenandoah County, Virginia* (Strasburg, VA: Shenandoah Publishing House, 1927), 174–75. For a more contemporary rendering of this story in the tourist literature, see Andrea Sutcliffe, *Touring the Shenandoah Valley Backroads* (Winston-Salem, NC: John F. Blair, 2010), 89. On the local history of Hessian mercenaries captured at the battle of Saratoga and later quartered in several Virginia towns, including Winchester, see Thomas K. Cartmell, *Shenandoah Valley Pioneers and Their Descendants: A History of Frederick County, Virginia, from Its Formation in 1738 to 1908* (Winchester, VA.: Eddy Press, 1909; Berryville, VA: Chesapeake Book Company, 1963), 518–19; and Freeman H. Hart, *The Valley of Virginia in the American Revolution, 1763–1789* (Chapel Hill: University of North Carolina Press, 1942), 28–29.

15. On the population of the Shenandoah Valley, see Robert D. Mitchell, *Commercialism and Frontier: Perspectives on the Early Shenandoah Valley* (Charlottesville: University Press of Virginia, 1977), 95–100 and Table 9.

16. *Virginia Centinel and Gazette; or, the Winchester Mercury* (October 21, 1789).

17. Kercheval, *History of the Valley of Virginia*, 305 and 52. For an indication that it may have been John Walter Wayland who helped perpetuate this myth into the twentieth century in his self-published book, *The German Element of the Shenandoah Valley of Virginia* (Charlottesville, VA: 1907), 17, see its contemporary iterations in Deane Winegar and Garvey Winegar, *Highroad Guide to the Virginia Mountains* (Atlanta, GA: Longstreet Press, 1998), 211. The eighteenth-century surveying and documentary evidence, however, does not substantiate this myth. See Robert D. Mitchell, Warren R. Hofstra, and Edward F. Connor, "Reconstructing the Colonial Environment of the Upper Chesapeake Watershed," in Philip D. Curtain, Grace S. Brush, and George W. Fisher, eds., *Discovering the Chesapeake: The History of an Ecosystem* (Baltimore, MD: The Johns Hopkins University Press, 2001), 167–90.

18. See Kercheval, *History of the Valley*, 35–48; Mitchell, et al., "Reconstructing the Colonial Environment." On the archaeology of the Indian peoples in the Shenandoah Valley, see William M. Gardner, *Lost Arrowheads & Broken Pottery: Traces of Indians in the Shenandoah Valley* (Front Royal, VA: Thunderbird Museum, 1986); Robert S. Grumet, *Historic Contact: Indian People and Colonists in Today's Northeastern United States in the Sixteenth through the Eighteenth Centuries* (Norman: University of Oklahoma Press, 1995): 283–87; Mary Ellen N. Hodges, "The Archaeology of Native American Life in Virginia in the Context of European Contact: Review of Past Research," in Theodore R. Reinhart and Dennis J. Pogue, eds., *The Archaeology of 17th-Century Virginia,* Special Publication No. 30 (Courtland, VA: Archeological Society of Virginia, 1993), 1–65; Warren R. Hofstra and Clarence R. Geier, "Native American Settlement within the Middle and Upper Drainage of Opequon Creek, Frederick County, Virginia," *Quarterly Bulletin of the Archeological Society of Virginia*, Vol. 54, No. 3 (September 1999): 154–65; Michael J. Klein and Thomas Klatka, "Late Archaic and Early Woodland Demography and Settlement Patterns," in Theodore R. Reinhart and Mary Ellen N. Hodges, eds., *Late Archaic and Early Woodland Research in Virginia: A Synthesis,* Special Publication No. 23 (Courtland, VA: Archeological Society of Virginia, 1991), 139–83; Douglas C. McLearen, "Virginia's Middle Woodland Period: A Regional Perspective," in Reinhart and Hodges, eds., *Middle and Late Woodland Research in Virginia: A Synthesis,* Special Publication No. 29 (Courtland, VA: Archeological Society of Virginia, 1992), 39–63; and E. Randolph Turner III, "Paleoindian Settlement Patterns and Population Distribution in Virginia," in J. Mark Wittkofski and Theodore R. Reinhart, eds., *Paleoindian Research in Virginia: A Synthesis*, Special

Publication No. 19 (Courtland, VA: Archeological Society of Virginia, 1989): 71–93.

19. Kercheval, *History of the Valley of Virginia*, 323 and 324.

20. Edward Beyer, *Album of Virginia; or Illustration of the Old Dominion* (Richmond, VA: self-published, 1858; Richmond: Virginia State Library, 1980). The term "New Virginia" was commonly employed throughout Virginia by 1800 to distinguish the dynamic, commercially oriented, and urbanizing economy of Virginia west of the Blue Ridge Mountains and particularly the Shenandoah Valley from the stagnant and conservative mentality dominating the economic outlook of eastern Virginia. See Warren R. Hofstra, *The Planting of New Virginia: Settlement and Landscape in the Shenandoah Valley* (Baltimore, MD: The Johns Hopkins University Press, in association with the Center for American Places, 2004), 5 and 326.

21. Harriet Martineau quoted Shakespeare ("Come on, sir; here's the place—Stand still. How fearful / And dizzy 'tis to cast one's eyes so low!" [*King Lear*, 4.6.15–16]) in her description of a visit to the Natural Bridge in the 1830s. With less "veneration" than the "very idea of Niagara inspires," this astute critic of American nature nonetheless found the site "most beautiful" and by any measure sublime: "The sunshine was slowly withdrawing from under the arch, and leaving us in the shadows of evening, while all was glowing like noon in the region to which we looked up from our lowly seats." See Martineau, *Retrospect of Western Travel*, 2 vols. (New York: Saunders and Otley, 1838), Vol. 2: 270–76. Thomas Jefferson described the Natural Bridge as the "most sublime of Nature's works," see Jefferson, *Notes on the State of Virginia* (London, UK: J. Stockdale, 1787), 35–36.

22. The publication of Thomas Buchanan Read's poem, "Sheridan's Ride," appeared on the front page of *The New York Tribune* on election day, November 8, 1864, less than three weeks after the battle of Cedar Creek. See Geraldine Wojno Kiefer and James K. Bryant II, "Strategy and Sublimity: A Gallery of Valley Pike Images during the Civil War," in Warren R. Hofstra and Karl Raitz, eds., *The Great Valley Road of Virginia: Shenandoah Landscapes from Prehistory to the Present* (Charlottesville: University of Virginia Press, in association with the Center for American Places, 2010), 135–52.

23. By order of Ulysses S. Grant, City Point, Virginia, July 14, 1864, *The War of the Rebellion: A Compilation of the Official Record of the Union and Confederate Armies*, 128 vols. (Washington, DC: Government Printing Office, 1880–1901), Ser. 1, Vol. 37, Pt. 2, 300–01; and John Heatwole, *The Burning: Sheridan in the Shenandoah Valley* (Charlottesville, VA: Rockbridge, 1998).

24. Carl N. Degler, "The American Civil War and the German Wars of Unification: The Problem of Comparison," in Stig Förster and Jörg Nagler, eds., *On the Road to Total War* (Cambridge, UK: Cambridge University Press, 1997), 68.

25. David Hunter Strother, "Personal Recollections of the War by a Virginian," *Harper's New Monthly Magazine*, Vol. 33, No. 193 (June 1866): 1.

26. George M. Neese, *Three Years in the Confederate Horse Artillery* (New York: Neale Publishing Company, 1911; Dayton, OH: Morningside Bookshop, 1983), 361.

27. Kenneth E. Koons, "'The Staple of Our Country': Wheat in the Regional Farm Economy of the Nineteenth-Century Valley of Virginia," in Koons and Warren R. Hofstra, eds., *After the Backcountry: Rural Life in the Great Valley of Virginia, 1800–1900* (Knoxville: University of Tennessee Press, 2000), 3–20, Table 1.1, and Table 1.2.

28. Kenneth W. Keller, "The Best Thoroughfare in the South," in Hofstra and Raitz, *The Great Valley Road of Virginia*, 181–82.

29. Harry F. Byrd Sr., as quoted in *The Staunton Daily News* (July 25, 1917). Harry F. Byrd Sr., a noted publisher, farmer, and politician from Berryville, was a descendent of one of Virginia's "first families."

30. Virginius Dabney, *Virginia: The New Dominion* (New York: Doubleday, 1971), 475; Keller, "Best Thoroughfare," 181–82; and Karl Raitz, "The Lay of the Land," in Hofstra and Raitz, *The Great Valley Road of Virginia*, 52.

31. George F. Thompson, the publisher of this book who has pioneered the study of *landscape* and of *place* since 1984, also speaks of discovering *landscape* as a boy when his family drove through the Shenandoah Valley. See his book, *Landscape in America* (Austin: University of Texas Press, 1995), 289.

32. See John Fraser Hart, "Reading the Landscape," in George F. Thompson, ed., *Landscape in America*, 23–42; and Janet Mendelsohn and Chris Wilson, eds., *Drawn to Landscape: The Pioneering Work of J. B. Jackson* (Staunton, VA: George F. Thompson Publishing, 2015).

33. The seminal book for understanding the bank barn is Robert F. Ensminger, *The Pennsylvania Barn: Its Origin, Evolution, and Distribution in North America* (Baltimore, MD: The Johns Hopkins University Press, in association with the Center for American Places, 1992; second edition, 2003).

34. "The Harvest," *Valley Farmer, and Gardeners' Monthly Chronicle*, Vol. 2 (August 1845): 10, as quoted in Kenneth E. Koons, "'The Staple of Our Country,'" 4.

35. Kenneth E. Koons, "'The Staple of Our Country'," especially Fig. 1.3 and note 99. Wheat production in the Valley peaked in 1920 at 3,836,504 bushels.

36. The seminal article for understanding the identification and development of the I-house is Fred Kniffen, "Folk Housing: Key to Diffusion," *Annals of the Association of American Geographers*, Vol. 55, No. 4 (December 1965): 549–77.

37. See Ensminger, *The Pennsylvania Barn.*

38. Washington Irving to Mary E. Kennedy, July 12, 1853, in Aderman, et al., *Irving: Letters*, Vol. 4: 419–20.

39. Jefferson, *Notes*, 278–79.

40. Ibid., 274.

41. Ibid., 274–75.

42. See, for instance, Washington's letter to John Posey, his debtor, in which he recommends that Posey invest in Shenandoah Valley lands where his money could increase fivefold in twenty years: "For proof of which only look to Frederick, & see what Fortunes were made by the Hite's & first takers up of those Lands: Nay how the greatest Estates we have in this Colony were made; Was it not by taking up & purchasing at very low rates the rich back Lands which were thought nothing of in those days, but are now the most valuable Lands we possess?" Washington to John Posey, June 24, 1767, in Abbot, et al., *The Papers of George Washington*, Vol. 8: 1–4.

43. François Jean de Beauvoir, Marquis de Chastellux, *Travels in North America in the Years 1780, 1781 and 1782*, 2 vols., translated by Howard C. Rice Jr. (Paris, France: Prault, 1786; Chapel Hill: University of North Carolina Press for the Institute of Early American History and Culture, 1963), Vol. 1: 359. Chastellux died in 1788 and did not play a role in the French Revolution.

44. François Alexandre Frédéric, duc de la Rochefoucauld-Liancourt, *Travels through the United States of North America . . . in the Years 1795, 1796, and 1797*, 4 vols., Second Edition, translated by H. Neuman (London, UK: R. Phillips, 1800), Vol. 3: 197, 213–14, and 216–18.

45. Andrew Burnaby, *Travels through the Middle Settlements in North America in the Years, 1759 and 1760*, Third Edition (London, UK: T. Payne, 1798; New York: Augustus M. Kelley, 1970), 73–74.

46. Isaac Weld, *Travels through the States of North America*, 2 vols. (London, UK: John Stockdale, 1807; New York: Johnson Reprint, 1968), Vol. 1: 232–33. Weld's great grandfather was a close friend of Sir Isaac Newton, and the name descended for three generations to the American traveler.

47. Board of Trade to King George I (September 8, 1721), CO 324/10, Public Records Office, London, UK. The fear that escaped Virginia slaves would live as maroons in the colony's western mountains and threaten the security of a slave society, as Jamaican maroons were already doing, is evident in the governor's correspondence with the Board of Trade. See William Gooch to the Board of Trade (June 29, 1729), CO 5 /1322, Colonial Office Papers, London, UK.

48. For these orders, see McIlwaine, et al., *Executive Journals of the Council of Colonial Virginia*, Vol. 4: 223–24, 229, 249–50, 253, 270, and 295.

49. Gooch to the Board of Trade (May 24, 1734), CO 5 /1323, Colonial Office Papers.

50. *John Hite et al. v. Lord Fairfax et al.*, transcript by Hunter Branson McKay, 1532 and 1547, Additional Manuscript 15317, The British Museum, London, UK.

51. Answer of William Rodgers, *Hite v. Fairfax*, transcript by McKay, 1575–76 and 1713.

52. Transcript of the Record, *Hite and McCoy v. Fairfax*, Folio 717, Folder 100, Clark-Hite Papers, Filson Historical Society, Louisville, KY; *Hite v. Fairfax*, transcript by McKay, 1547.

53. The names of the Shenandoah Valley's three regions—Lower, Middle, and Upper—reflect elevation. Thus, the Lower Valley is in the northernmost part, with Winchester as its center, and the Upper Valley is in the southernmost part, with Staunton as its center. See the *Map of the Shenandoah Valley* (page 245).

Andrei Kushnir's Vision of the Picturesque Virginia Landscape (Rasmussen)

1. Philip Fithian, *The Journal of Philip Vickers Fithian*, as quoted in Michael P. Branch and Daniel J. Philippon, eds., *The Height of Our Mountains: Nature Writing from Virginia's Blue Ridge Mountains and Shenandoah Valley* (Baltimore, MD: The Johns Hopkins University Press, in association with the Center for American Places, 1998), 101. The original spelling has been maintained.

2. Walt Whitman, as quoted in Branch and Philippon, *The Height of Our Mountains*, 189.

3. Thomas Jefferson, *Notes on the State of Virginia*, William Peden, ed. (Chapel Hill: University of North Carolina Press, 1955), 24–25 and 263–64, note 5.

4. Edmund Burke, *A Philosophical Inquiry into the Origin of Our Ideas of the Sublime and Beautiful* (London, UK: R. and J. Dodsley, 1757).

5. Ibid., 68–69, 131, and 137.

6. James Kirke Paulding, *Letters from the South Written during an Excursion in the Summer of 1816*, 2 vols. (New York: James Eastburn, 1817), Vol. 2: 65–66.

7. Archibald Alexander, as quoted in James W. Alexander, *The Life of Archibald Alexander, D.D., L.L.D., First Professor in the Theological Seminary at Princeton,*

New Jersey (New York: Charles Scribner, 1854); as cited in Branch and Phillippon, *The Height of Our Mountains*, 169.

8. Edward A. Pollard, *The Virginia Tourist: Sketches of the Springs and Mountains of Virginia* (Philadelphia, PA: J. B. Lippincott and Company, 1870), 55. Mary Allan-Olney, *The New Virginians*, 2 vols. (Edinburgh, Scotland, and London, UK: William Blackwood and Sons, 1880), Vol. 2: 201; and *A Description of the Natural Bridge of Virginia and Its History* (Philadelphia, PA: Billstein and Sons, 1887), 57.

9. Jefferson, *Notes on the State of Virginia*, 19–20.

10. Paulding, *Letters from the South*, Vol. 2: 251.

11. Isaac Weld, *Travels through the States of North America during the Years 1795, 1796, and 1797*, 2 vols., Third Edition (London, UK: J. Stockdale, 1800), Vol. 1: 239–41 and 244–45.

12. William Gilmore Simms, *Southward Ho! A Spell of Sunshine* (New York: Redfield, 1854); as cited in Branch and Philippon, *The Height of Our Mountains*, 174–75.

13. William Gilpin, *Essay on Prints* (1768), summarized in C. P. Barbier, *William Gilpin: His Drawings, Teaching, and Theory of the Picturesque* (Oxford, UK: Clarendon Press, 1963), 98–147; both as cited in George B. Tatum, "Nature's Gardener," in *Prophet with Honor, The Career of Andrew Jackson Downing, 1815–1852*, ed. by Tatum (Washington, DC: Dumbarton Oaks Research Library, 1987), 59–60.

14. Uvedale Price, *Essays on the Picturesque* (London, UK: J. Mawman, 1810), as cited in Tatum, "Nature's Gardener," 59–60.

15. Jefferson, *Notes on the State of Virginia*, 19.

16. Louis Philippe, *Diary of My Travels in America*, trans. by Stephen Becker (New York: Delacorte, 1977), as quoted in Branch and Philippon, *The Height of Our Mountains*, 132–33.

17. Simms, *Southward Ho!*, as quoted in Branch and Philippon, *The Height of Our Mountains*, 174; and Samuel Mordecai, *Description of the Album of Virginia: or The Old Dominion, Illustrated* (1857; reprinted Richmond, VA: Virginia State Library, 1980), 7.

18. Annie Dillard's *Pilgrim at Tinker Creek* (New York: Harper's Magazine Press, 1974) earned a Pulitzer Prize for General Non-fiction in 1975.

19. William Wordsworth, "The Tables Turned" (1798), as quoted in Kenneth Clark, *The Romantic Rebellion, Romantic versus Classic Art* (New York: Harper Collins, 1973), 282; and Kenneth Clark, *Landscape into Art* (New York: Harper & Row, 1976), 279.

20. Charles Joseph La Trobe, *The Rambler in North America*, 2 vols. (New York: Harper and Bros., 1835), Vol. 1: 61.

21. Andrew Burnaby, *Travels through the Middle Settlements in North America in the Years, 1759 and 1760*, Third Edition (London, UK: T. Payne, 1798; New York: Augustus M. Kelley, 1970).

22. Thomas Jefferson to Angelica Schuyler Church, February 17, 1788, Missouri History Museum, Columbia.

23. Simms, *Southward Ho!*, as quoted in Branch and Philippon, *The Height of Our Mountains*, 175.

24. George Bagby, in William Cullen Bryant, ed., *Picturesque America*, 2 vols. (New York: D. Appleton and Company, 1872; revised edition, 1874), Vol. 1: 337.

25. Russell Smith, notes written on his Virginia landscape drawings, Library of Virginia, Richmond.

26. Henry Ruffner, *Judith Bensaddi*, as quoted in Branch and Philippon, *The Height of Our Mountains*, 166–68.

27. Clark, *Landscape into Art*, 33 and 49.

28. Henry Ruffner, *Judith Bensaddi*, as quoted in Branch and Philippon, *The Height of Our Mountains*, 166–68.

29. Benjamin Henry Latrobe, *Essay on Landscape*, 2 vols. (Richmond, VA: self-published, 1798 and 1799), as cited in Edward C. Carter II, John C. Van Horne, and Charles E. Brownell, eds., *Latrobe's View of America, 1795–1820: Selections form the Watercolors and Sketches* (New Haven, CT: Yale University Press, 1985), 18, 20–21, and 64.

30. Dillard, *Pilgrim at Tinker Creek*, 5.

31. Clark, *Landscape into Art*, 109 and 53.

32. La Trobe, *The Rambler in North America*, Vol. 1: 40.

Land and Life in the Shenandoah Valley (Everett)

1. Frank Albert Waugh, *The Landscape Beautiful* (New York: Orange Judd Company, 1910), 105.

THE NATURAL LANDSCAPE

2. John Lee Coulter, "Industrial History of the Valley of the Red River of the North," in O. G. Libby, ed., *Collections of the State Historical Society of North Dakota,* Vol. 3 (Bismarck: State Historical Society of North Dakota, 1910), 530.

3. Nevin M. Fenneman, *Physiography of the Eastern United States* (New York and London, UK: McGraw-Hill Book Company, Inc., 1938), 38 and 121; William D. Thornbury, *Regional Geomorphology of the United States* (New York: John Wiley & Sons, Inc., 1965), 72; and William D. Thornbury, *Principles of Geomorphology*, Second Edition (New York: John Wiley & Sons, 1969), 228–29.

4. Thornbury, *Principles of Geomorphology*, 228–29; Thornbury, *Regional Geomorphology of the United States*, 109–10; Fenneman, 122 and 195–96; Lynn S. Fichter and Steve J. Baedke, "A Description of the Geology of Virginia," http://csmres.jmu.edu/geollab/ vageol/vahist/physprov.html#valleyandridge; and Henry Trapp, Jr. and Marilee A. Horn, "Ground Water Atlas of the United States: Valley and Ridge Aquifers," http://pubs.usgs.gov/ha/ha730/ch_l/.

5. John T. Hack and Robert S. Young, *Intrenched Meanders of the North Fork of the Shenandoah River, Virginia*, U.S. Geological Survey, Professional Paper 354-A (Washington, DC: Government Printing Office, 1959), 1–7; Rhesa M. Allen, Jr., *Geology and Mineral Resources of Page County Mineral Resources,* Bulletin 81 (Charlottesville: Virginia Division of Mineral Resources, 1967), Plate 1; E. K. Rader and T. M. Gathright, II, *Publication 159: Geologic Map of the Augusta, Page, and Rockingham Counties Portion of the Charlottesville 30 x 60-Minute Quadrangle* (Charlottesville: Commonwealth of Virginia Department of Mines, Minerals and Energy, Division of Mineral Resources, 2001); and John Gerrard, "Geology and Landforms," in T. P. Burt, R. J. Chorley, D. Brunsden, N. J. Cox, and A. S. Goudie, eds., *The History of the Study of Landforms or the Development of Geomorphology*, 4 vols. (Bath, UK: The Geological Society of London, 2008), Vol. 4: 40.

6. Fenneman, *Physiography of the Eastern United States*, 245–46; and G. W. Stose and H. D. Miser, *Manganese Deposits of Western Virginia*, Bulletin No. XXIII (Charlottesville: University of Virginia, 1922), 6–8.

7. The Aldine, "Scene on the Shenandoah," *The Aldine*, Vol. 7 (June 1874): 122.

8. U.S. Geological Survey, "The USGS Water Science School, Earth's Water: Rivers and Streams," http://ga.water.usgs.gov/edu/ earthrivers.html; and William H. Snowden, *The Story of the Expedition of the Young Surveyors* (Alexandria, VA: G. H. Ramey & Son, 1902), 13–14.

9. John Warner, "A Survey of the Northern Neck of Virginia, being the lands belonging to the Rt. Honourable Thomas Lord Fairfax Baron Cameron," http://www.loc.gov/item/99446122/; Carl Van Doren and Julian P. Boyd, *Indian Treaties Printed by Benjamin Franklin, 1736–1762* (Philadelphia: Historical Society of Pennsylvania, 1938); and Lewis H. Morgan, *League of the Ho-De'-No-Sau-Nee or Iroquois* (New York: Dodd, Mead and Company, 1922), 101.

10. U.S. Forest Service, "Appendix D—Wild and Scenic Rivers Eligibility Determination, Draft Environmental Impact Statement, George Washington National Forest, April 2011," http: //www.fs. usda.gov/ Internet/ FSE_DOCUMENTS/stelprdb5297843.pdf.

11. Robert Mitchell, "The Shenandoah Valley Frontier," *Annals of the Association of American Geographers*, Vol. 62, No. 3 (September 1972): 471–72; U.S. Census Bureau, "Ancestry: 2000, Census 2000 Brief," http://www.census.gov/prod/2004pubs/c2kbr-35.pdf; Tim Palmer, *The Wild and Scenic Rivers of America* (Washington, DC: Island Press, 1993), 24 and 69; Tim Palmer, *Endangered Rivers and the Conservation Movement*, Second Edition (Lanham, MD: Rowman & Littlefield, 2004), 165; Dyan Zaslowsky and T. H. Watkins, *These American Lands: Parks, Wilderness, and the Public Lands* (Washington, DC: Island Press, 1994), 246; Jimmy Carter, "Public Papers of the Presidents of the United States: Jimmy Carter, 1977 (Washington, DC: Government Printing Office, 1977), 980; and U.S. Forest Service, "Final Environmental Impact Statement for the Revised Land and Resource Management Plan, George Washington National Forest, January 1993, http://www.fs.usda.gov/Internet/ FSE_DOCUMENTS/stelprdb5176376.pdf; and U.S. Forest Service, "Draft EIS, April 2011."

12. Ernest Ingersoll, *Through the Shenandoah Valley: The Chronicle of a Leisurely Journey through the Uplands of Virginia* (Roanoke: VA: Passenger Department of the Shenandoah Valley Railroad Co., 1887), 14.

13. Virginia Department of Game and Inland Fisheries, "Virginia Rivers & Streams," http://www.dgif.virginia.gov/fishing/waterbodies/?type=2.

14. John Lewis Peyton, *History of Augusta County, Virginia* (Staunton, VA: Samul M. Yost & Son, 1882), 273–74.

15. Joshua Fry and Peter Jefferson, "A Map of the Most Inhabited Part of Virginia Containing the Whole Province of Maryland with Part of Pensilvania [sic], New Jersey and North Carolina"; Library of Virginia, "About the Virginia Land Office Patents and Grants/Northern Neck Grant and Surveys," http://www.lva.virginia.gov/ public/guides/opac/lonnabout.htm; and Katharine L. Brown and Kenneth W. Keller, "Searching for Status: Virginia's Irish Tract, 1770s–1790s," in Warren R. Hofstra, ed., *Ulster to America: The Scots-Irish Migration Experience, 1680–1830* (Knoxville: University of Tennessee Press, 2012), 123–24.

16. Anonymous, "Virginia Springs," *Southern Literary Messenger*, Vol. 3, No. 5 (May 1837): 281–84.

17. Thornbury, *Regional Geomorphology*, 120–24; W. Cullen Sherwood, "A Brief Geologic History of Rockingham County," http://csmres.jmu.edu/geollab/vageol/outreach/ fieldtrips/rockingham/whole.html; Sara E. Hyland, Lisa M. Kennedy, Tamim Younos, and Shane Parson, "Analysis of Sinkhole Susceptibility and Karst Distribution in the Northern Shenandoah Valley, Virginia: Implications for Low

Impact Development (LID) Site Suitability Models," Virginia Water Resources Research Center Special Report SR31-2006 (Blacksburg: Virginia Polytechnic Institute and State University, 2006), 9–11; Virginia Department of Mines, Minerals and Energy, Division of Geology and Mineral Resources, "Sinkholes and Karst Terrain," http://www.dmme.virginia.gov/DMR3/sinkholes.shtml; and Randall C. Orndorff and George E. Harlow, Jr., "Hydrogeologic Framework of the Northern Shenandoah Valley Carbonate Aquifer System," http://water.usgs.gov/ogw/karst/ kig2002/rco_field.html.

18. Thornbury, *Principles of Geomorphology*, 325; American Association for the Advancement of Science, *Science*, Vol. 56, No. 1444 (September 1922): 240–41; and Luray Caverns, "History: Today," http://luraycaverns.com/History/Today/tabid/532/Default.aspx.

19. Thornbury, *Principles of Geomorphology*, 303–27; and Holmes A. Semken, Jr., Russell W. Graham, and Thomas W. Stafford, Jr., "AMS ^{14}C analysis of Late Pleistocene Non-Analog Faunal Components from 21 Cave Deposits in Southeastern North America," *Quaternary International*, Vol. 217, Nos. 1–2 (April 2010): 240–55.

20. Jacques W. Delleur, *The Handbook of Groundwater Engineering*, 2d ed. (Boca Raton, FL: CRC Press, 2007), 2–38; Orndorff and Harlow, "Hydrogeologic Framework"; Stan Cohen, *Historic Springs of the Virginias: A Pictorial History* (Charleston, WV: Quarrier Press, 1981), vi–viii; Charlene M. Boyer Lewis, *Ladies and Gentlemen on Display: Planter Society at the Virginia Springs* (Charlottesville: University Press of Virginia, 2001); and Shrine Mont, "About Us," http://shrinemont. poweredbyindigo.com/v.php?pg=28.

21. Francis H. Chapelle, *Wellsprings: A Natural History of Bottled Water* (Piscataway, NJ: Rutgers University Press, 2005), 4; D. Q. Eggleston, *Annual Report of the Secretary of the Commonwealth to the Governor and General Assembly of Virginia for the Year Ending September 30, 1903* (Richmond, VA: J. H. O'Bannon, Superintendent of Public Printing, 1903), 109; *Poor's Railroad Manual Co., Poor's Manual of Industrials; Manufacturing, Mining and Miscellaneous Companies* (New York: Poor's Railroad Manual Co, 1913), 74; Jim Forte Postal History, http://www.postalhistory.com/photo.asp?url=scans_N%2FNY140428; National Reporter System—State Series, *The Atlantic Reporter*, Vol. 71 (St. Paul, MN: West Publishing Co., 1909), 386; and Berkeley Springs International Water Tasting, http://berkeleysprings.com/water/awards2012.htm.

22. Franklin B. Hough, "Report on Forestry Submitted to Congress by the Commissioner of Agriculture" (Washington, DC: Government Printing Office, 1882), 168.

23. Craig G. Lorimer, "Historical and Ecological Roles of Disturbance in Eastern North America Forests: 9,000 Years of Change," *Wildlife Society Bulletin*, Vol. 29, No. 2 (Summer 2001): 432; Robert D. Mitchell, Warren R. Hofstra, and Edward F. Connor, "Reconstructing the Colonial Environment of the Upper Chesapeake Watershed," in Philip D. Curtin, Grace S. Brush, and George W. Fisher, eds., *Discovering the Chesapeake: The History of an Ecosystem* (Baltimore, MD: The Johns Hopkins University Press, 2001), 171; Stephen H. Spurr, "George Washington, Surveyor and Ecological Observer," *Ecology*, Vol. 32, No. 3 (July 1951): 545; David Lee Ingram, Professional Land Surveyor, Ingram-Hagen & Co., conversation with the author (December 18, 2012); and Bryan A. Black and Marc D. Abrams, "Influences of Native Americans and Surveyor Biases on Metes and Bounds Witness-Tree Distribution," *Ecology*, Vol. 82, No. 9 (September 2001): 2574–81.

24. James M. Dyer, "Revisiting the Deciduous Forests of Eastern North America," *BioScience*, Vol. 56, No. 4 (April 2006): 341; James M. Dyer, "Land Use Legacies in a Central Appalachian Forest: Differential Response of Trees and Herbs to Historic Agricultural Practices," *Applied Vegetation Science*, Vol. 13, No. 2 (April 2010): 195; Lorimer, "Historical and Ecological Roles," 430–31; Cynthia Fowler and Evelyn Konopik, "The History of Fire in the Southern United States," *Human Ecology Review*, Vol. 14, No. 2 (Winter 2007): 169; and Hutch Brown, "Reports of American Indian Fire Use in the East," *Fire Management Today*, Vol. 64, No. 3 (Summer 2004): 17. For a convenient list of sources referencing Indian burning of the Shenandoah Valley, see Gerald W. Williams, "References on the American Indian Use of Fire in Ecosystems," found on the Website of the Virginia Department of Forestry, http://www.dof.virginia.gov/fire/prescribed-smoke-mgmt.htm; see, also, Thomas Meehan, "Notes on Treeless Prairies," *Proceedings of the Academy of Natural Sciences of Philadelphia*, Vol. 33 (1881): 11–14. For more contemporary research, see Hutch Brown, "Wildland Burning by American Indians in Virginia," *Fire Management Today*, Vol. 60, No. 3 (Summer 2000): 29–39; Cecil Frost and Steve Lindeman, "Eastern Prairie-Woodland Mosaic," U.S. Forest Service: Fire Regimes of the Conterminous United States, http://www.fs.fed.us/database/feis/fire_regime_table/fire_regime_table.html; Lorimer, 432; J. S. Clark and P. D. Royall, "Transformation of a Northern Hardwood Forest by Aboriginal (Iroquois) Fire: Charcoal Evidence from Crawford Lake, Ontario, Canada," *The Holocene*, Vol. 5, No. 1 (March 1995): 1–9; Marc D. Abrams, "Distribution, Historical Development and Ecophysiological Attributes of Oak Species in the Eastern United States," *Annales des Sciences Forestières*, Vol. 53, Nos. 2–3 (1996): 508; Durland L.

Shumway, Marc D. Abrams, and Charles M. Ruffner, "A 400-Year History of Fire and Oak Recruitment in an Old-Growth Oak Forest in Western Maryland, U.S.A.," *Canadian Journal of Forest Research*, Vol. 31, No. 8 (August 2001): 1437–43; and Mitchell, Hofstra, and Connor, "Reconstructing the Colonial Environment," 179 and 182.

25. Fowler and Konopik, "The History of Fire," 170–71; Thomas M. Schuler and W. Russ McClain, "Fire History of a Ridge and Valley Oak Forest," 5–6; Brown, "Reports," 20–21; Hough, "Report on Forestry," 168; Scott L. Stephens and Lawrence W. Ruth, "Federal Forest-Fire Policy in the United States," *Ecological Applications*, Vol. 15, No. 2 (April 2005): 532–33; Daniel Dey, "The Ecological Basis for Oak Silviculture in Eastern North America," in William J. McShea and William M. Healy, eds., *Oak Forest Ecosystems: Ecology and Management for Wildlife* (Baltimore, MD: The Johns Hopkins University Press, 2002), 60–79; Marc D. Abrams, "Native Americans, Smokey Bear and the Rise and Fall of Eastern Oak Forests," *Penn State Environmental Law Review*, Vol. 18, No. 2 (Winter 2010):142–43; Warren R. Hofstra, *The Planting of New Virginia: Settlement and Landscape in the Shenandoah Valley* (Baltimore, MD: The Johns Hopkins University Press, in association with the Center for American Places, 2004), 124–31; George Davis McJimsey, "Topographic Terms in Virginia (IV)," *American Speech*, Vol. 15, No. 4 (December 1940): 389; Chris Ludwig, Chief Biologist, Natural Heritage Program, Virginia Department of Conservation and Recreation, conversation with the author (November 8, 2012); Barry Lopez and Debra Gwartney, ed., *Home Ground: Language for an American Landscape* (San Antonio, TX: Trinity University Press, 2006); and Roger C. Anderson, James S. Fralish, and Jerry M. Baskin, eds., *Savannas, Barrens, and Rock Outcrop Plant Communities of North America* (Cambridge, UK: Cambridge University Press, 1999), 1–2.

26. Hofstra, *The Planting of New Virginia*, 124–31; George Davis McJimsey, "Topographic Terms in Virginia (II)," *American Speech*, Vol. 15, No. 2 (April 1940): 153; Thornbury, *Regional Geomorphosis*, 195 and 201; Jerry M. Baskin, Carol C. Baskin and Edward W. Chester, "The Big Barrens Region of Kentucky and Tennessee: Further Observations and Considerations," *Castanea*, Vol. 59, No. 3 (September 1994): 245; Reed F. Noss, *Forgotten Grasslands of the South* (Washington, DC: Island Press, 2013), 144; Jim Vanderhorst, "The Hot Zone: The Shale Barrens of Eastern West Virginia," *West Virginia Wildlife* (Fall 2005): 4–6; Carl S. Keener," Distribution and Biohistory of the Endemic Flora of the Mid-Atlantic Shale Barrens," *Botanical Review*, Vol. 49, No. 1 (January–March 1983): 65–66; H. A. Allard and E. C. Leonard, "Shale Barren Associations on Massanutten Mountain, Virginia," *Castanea*, Vol. 11, No. 3 (September 1946): 71–124; Gary P. Fleming and Karen D. Patterson, "The Natural Communities of Virginia; Ecological Groups and Community Types," http://www.dcr.virginia.gov/natural_heritage /documents/comlist02_12.pdf; Baskin, Baskin, and Chester, 248; Daniel C. Laughlin and Christopher F. Uhl, "The Xeric Limestone Prairies of Pennsylvania," *Castanea*, Vol. 68, No. 4 (December 2003): 300–01; J. Christopher Ludwig, "The Flora of Dolomite and Limestone Barrens in Southwestern Virginia," *Castanea*, Vol. 64, No. 3 (September 1999): 216–17; Fleming and Patterson; Rodney L. Bartgis, "The Limestone Glades and Barrens of West Virginia," *Castanea*, Vol. 58, No. 2 (June 1993): 69; and Peter Heus, "An Historical Prairie Remnant in Virginia," *Native Plants Journal*, Vol. 4, No. 2 (Fall 2003): 104–06.

27. Frost and Lindeman, "Eastern Prairie-Woodland Mosaic"; Lorimer, "Historical and Ecological Roles," 433–34; Erhard Rostlund, "The Myth of a Natural Prairie Belt in Alabama: An Interpretation of Historical Records," *Annals of the Association of American Geographers*, Vol. 47, No. 4 (December 1957): 407–09; Hofstra, Mitchell, and Connor, "Reconstructing the Colonial Environment," 170; Robert D. Mitchell, *Commercialism and Frontier: Perspectives on the Early Shenandoah Valley* (Charlottesville: University Press of Virginia, 1977), 24; Michael J. Leahy, "Prairies of the Old Dominion," *Missouri Prairie Journal*, Vol. 24, No. 3 (Summer 2003): 8–12; Daniel C. Laughlin, "Did Tallgrass Prairie Extend into Pennsylvania?," *The Prairie Naturalist*, Vol. 36, No. 1 (March 2004): 11–22; Stephens and Ruth, "Federal Forest-Fire Policy," 534; and Louise A. Pastro, Christopher R. Dickman, and Mike Letnic, "Burning for Biodiversity or Burning Biodiversity?: Prescribed Burn vs. Wildfire Impacts on Plants, Lizards, and Mammals," *Ecological Applications*, Vol. 21, No. 8 (December 2011): 3238–53.

28. Edward A. Pollard, *The Virginia Tourist: Sketches of the Springs and Mountains of Virginia* (Philadelphia, PA: J. B. Lippincott and Company, 1870), 40–41.

29. Fenneman, *Physiography*, 1938, 164–65; Thornbury, *Regional Geomorphology*, 100; Christine Mlot, "A Clearer View of Why Plants Make Haze," *Science*, Vol. 268, No. 5211 (May 1995): 641.

30. Fenneman, *Physiography*, 168–71; Thornbury, *Regional Geomorphology*, 102–03; Arthur M. Miller, "Wind Gaps," *Science*, Vol. 42, No. 1086 (October 1915): 571–73.

31. Dennis E. Simmons, "Conservation, Cooperation, and Controversy: The Establishment of Shenandoah National Park," *The Virginia Magazine of History and Biography*, Vol. 89, No. 4 (October 1981): 387–402; Gene Wilhelm, Jr., "Shenandoah Resettlements,"

Pioneer America, Vol. 14, No. 1 (March 1982): 15–38; Katrina M. Powell, ed., *"Answer at Once": Letters of Mountain Families in Shenandoah National Park, 1934–1938* (Charlottesville: University of Virginia Press, 2009), 70; Darwin Lambert, *The Undying Past of Shenandoah National Park* (Lanham, MD: Rowman & Littlefield, 1989), 217; and Ronald L. Heinemann, *Depression and New Deal in Virginia: The Enduring Dominion* (Charlottesville: University Press of Virginia, 1983), 123–24.

32. Audrey J. Horning, "In Search of a 'Hollow Ethnicity': Archaeological Exploration of Rural Mountain Settlement," in Maria Franklin and Garrett Fesler, eds., *Historical Archaeology, Identity Formation, and the Interpretation of Ethnicity* (Richmond, VA: Dietz Press, 1999): 121–37; Charles L. Perdue Jr., and Nancy J. Martin Perdue, "Appalachian Fables and Facts: A Case Study of the Shenandoah National Park Removals," *Appalachian Journal*, Vol. 7, Nos. 1–2 (Autumn–Winter 1979–80): 88–89 and 101; and Reed Engle, "Shenandoah: An Abused Landscape?," http://www.nps.gov/shen/historyculture/abused_landscape.htm.

33. Reed L. Engle, "Shenandoah: Not Without the CCC," *Cultural Resource Management*, Vol. 21, No. 1 (1998): 22–24; Perdue and Perdue, ibid., 89; and Timothy Davis, "'A Pleasant Illusion of Unspoiled Countryside': The American Parkway and the Problematics of an Institutionalized Vernacular," *Perspectives in Vernacular Architecture*, Vol. 9 (2003): 236–39.

34. National Park Service, "Visitor Spending Effects," (http://www.nature.nps.gov/socialscience/vse.cfm); National Park Service, "Visitor Use Statistics," (https://irma.nps.gov/Stats/).

35. Samuel K. Rosenman, ed., *The Public Papers and Addresses of Franklin D. Roosevelt*, Vol. 5 (New York: Random House, 1938), 170–73.

36. Christine Michaels, *Massanutten* (Charleston, SC: Arcadia Press, 2007), 7.

37. Chris Bolgiano, *The Appalachian Forest* (Mechanicsburg, PA: Stackpole Books, 1998), 97–98; William E. Shands, *The Lands Nobody Wanted: The Legacy of the Eastern National Forests* (Washington, DC: Pinchot Institute for Conservation, 1991), 31; Neil M. Maher, "A New Deal Body Politic: Landscape, Labor, and the Civilian Conservation Corps," *Environmental History*, Vol. 7, No.3 (July 2002): 435–37 and 452; and Dennis E. Simmons, "Conservation, Cooperation, and Controversy: The Establishment of Shenandoah National Park," *The Virginia Magazine of History and Biography*, Vol. 89, No. 4 (October 1981): 390–91.

38. Ray S. Bassler and Edwin C. Eckel, *Virginia Geological Survey Bulletin No. II-A: The Cement Resources of Virginia West of the Blue Ridge* (Charlottesville: University of Virginia, 1909), 41–42; U.S. Geological Survey, "Mineral Resources Online Spatial Data: Massanutten Sandstone," http://tin.er.usgs.gov/geology/state/sgmc-unit.php?unit=VASm%3B0; and Arthur Coe Spencer, *The Geology of Massanutten Mountain in Virginia* (Washington, DC: self-published, 1897), 24–25.

39. Thomas Jefferson, *Notes on the State of Virginia, Illustrated With A Map, including the States of Virginia, Maryland, Delaware and Pennsylvania* (London, UK: John Stockdale, 1787), 29.

40. Raymond S. Edmundson, "Origin of Little North Mountain in Northern Virginia," *The Journal of Geology*, Vol. 48, No. 5 (July–August 1940): 532. Grant and Mineral Counties in present-day West Virginia were both formed one year after the Civil War ended in 1865 from portions of Hardy and Hampshire Counties, respectively.

41. U.S. Department of Agriculture, Forest Service, "Land Areas of the National Forest System," http://www.fs.fed.us/land/staff/lar/LAR2011/LAR2011_Book_A5.pdf; The Forest History Society, "Chronology of National Forests Established Under the Weeks Act," http://www.foresthistory.org/ASPNET/Policy/WeeksAct/WeeksActForests.aspx; Ibid, "U.S. Forest Service: Eastern and Southern National Forests," http://www.foresthistory.org/ASPNET/Publications/eastern-southern/sec5.htm; U.S. Forest Service, "The George Washington and Jefferson National Forests," http://www.fs.usda.gov/detail/gwj/home?cid=stelprdb5313325; and William E. Shands, *The Lands Nobody Wanted: The Legacy of the Eastern National Forests* (Washington, DC: Pinchot Institute for Conservation, 1991), 34–35.

42. Janet Friedman, "The Iron Industry of Virginia, 1620 to 1920," National Register of Historic Places Multiple Property Documentation Form, 1999; Shands, *The Lands Nobody Wanted*, 23–24; and Chris Bolgiano, *The Appalachian Forest*, 68–70; and Chris Bolgiano, *Living in the Appalachian Forest: True Tales of Sustainable Forestry* (Mechanicsburg, PA: Stackpole Books, 2002), 62.

43. W. Henry McNab and Peter E. Avers, "Ecological Subregions of the United States," http://www.fs.fed.us/land/pubs/ecoregions/; Harold S. Adams and Steven L. Stephenson, "High Elevation Coniferous Forests in Virginia," *Virginia Journal of Science*, Vol. 42, No. 4 (Winter 1991): 391–94; William B. Leak, Dale S. Solomon, and Paul S. DeBald, *Silvicultural Guide for Northern Hardwood Types in the Northeast* (Broomall, PA: U.S. Forest Service Northeastern Forest Experiment Station, 1987), 1–2; Paul P. Kormanik, *Predicting Site Index for Virginia, Loblolly, and Shortleaf Pine in the Virginia Piedmont* (Asheville, NC: Southeastern

Forest Experiment Station, 1966), 1–3; and Virginia Department of Conservation and Recreation, "Virginia' Forest Resources," http://www.dcr.virginia.gov/virginia_naturally/education-resource-guide/virginias-forest-resources.shtml.

44. Virginia Department of Mines, Minerals and Energy, "Hydraulic Fracturing in Virginia and the Marcellus Shale Formation," http://www.dmme.virginia.gov/DGO/documents/ HydraulicFracturing.shtml; U.S. Environmental Protection Agency, "EPA Releases Draft Findings of Pavillion, Wyoming Ground Water Investigation for Public Comment and Independent Scientific Review," http://yosemite.epa.gov/opa/admpress. nsf/20ed1dfa1751192c8525735900400c30/ef35bd26a80d6ce3852579600065c94e!OpenDocument; and Shenandoah Valley Concerned Citizens, "Hydrofracking Virginia," http://hydrofracking.virginiajournal.org/.

THE CULTURAL LANDSCAPE

45. Illinois State Historical Society, "The Garden Spot of America," *Journal of the Illinois State Historical Society*, Vol. 37, No. 3 (September 1944): 273.

46. United Nations Educational Scientific and Cultural Organization, "Convention Concerning the Protection of the World Cultural and Natural Heritage," World Heritage Committee WHC-96/CONF.201/INF.21 Paris (October 22, 1996); and Hutch Brown, "Wildland Burning by American Indians in Virginia," *Fire Management Today*, Vol. 60 No. 3 (Summer 2000): 29–37.

47. National Park Service, "National Register Bulletin: How to Apply the National Register Criteria for Evaluation," National Park Service, National Register of Historic Places, http://www.nps.gov/nr/publications/bulletins/nrb15/; National Park Service, "National Heritage Areas," National Park Service National Heritage Areas Program Office, http://www.nps.gov/heritageareas/.

48. John William Wallace, ed., *Cases Argued and Adjudged in the Supreme Court of the United States, December Term, 1870*, Vol. XI (Washington, DC: W. H. & O. H. Morrison Publishers, 1870), 64.

49. Irvin D. Magin, *Shenandoah County Gazetteer & Historical Geography* (Stephens City, VA: Commercial Press, Inc., 1991), 102–03. The author has personally traveled to Alsace and researched its material culture and history. The Alsace metaphor was also presented by Tucker Brooke, Professor of English at Yale University, who hailed from West Virginia; rather than referring to the entire Valley, he made reference only to West Virginia's Eastern Panhandle counties of Morgan, Berkeley, and Jefferson, which, he believed, belonged to the Valley of Virginia "by natural as well as moral law." See Tucker Brooke, "Afoot in Alsace-Virginia," *The Sewanee Review*, Vol. 22, No. 3 (July 1914): 358–65, and, also, John Espy, Yale University Library Manuscripts and Archives, "Guide to the Charles Frederick Tucker Brooke Papers," http://drs.library.yale.edu:8083/ fedora/get/mssa:ms.1265/PDF.

50. Robert D. Mitchell, "The Shenandoah Valley Frontier," *Annals of the Association of American Geographers*, Vol. 62, No. 3 (September 1972): 466; Stephen R. Potter, *Commoners, Tribute, and Chiefs: The Development of Algonquian Culture in the Potomac Valley* (Charlottesville: University Press of Virginia, 1993), 126 and 174–76; Keith Egloff and Deborah Woodward, *First People: The Early Indians of Virginia* (Charlottesville: University Press of Virginia, 1992), 50; and Francis Jennings, *The Ambiguous Iroquois Empire: The Covenant Chain Confederation of Indian Tribes with English Colonies from its beginnings to the Lancaster Treaty of 1744* (New York: W. W. Norton, 1984), 278 and 354.

51. Warren R. Hofstra, *A Separate Place: The Formation of Clarke County, Virginia* (White Post, VA: Clarke County Sesquicentennial Committee, 1986), 34–35; Warren R. Hofstra, "These Fine Prospects: Frederick County, Virginia, 1738–1740." Ph.D. diss. (Charlottesville: University of Virginia, 1985), 42–43; Dieter Cunz, *The Maryland Germans: A History* (Princeton, NJ: Princeton University Press, 1948), 48–59; and Edwin Danson, *Drawing the Line: How Mason and Dixon Surveyed the Most Famous Border in America* (New York: John Wiley & Sons, 2001), 1.

52. Parke Rouse, *The Great Wagon Road: From Philadelphia to the South* (New York: McGraw-Hill, 1973), ix; James G. Leyburn, *The Scotch-Irish: A Social History* (Chapel Hill: University of North Carolina Press, 1962), 195–220; and Paul A. W. Wallace, *Indian Paths of Pennsylvania* (Harrisburg: Pennsylvania Historical and Museum Commission, 1965), 105 and 177.

53. Jennings, *The Ambiguous Iroquois Empire*, 294–96 and 354–62; and Wallace, *Cases Argued and Adjudged*, 180.

54. Mitchell, *The Shenandoah Valley Frontier*, 465–66; Stuart E. Brown, Jr., *Virginia Baron: The Story of Thomas 6th Lord Fairfax* (Berryville, VA: Chesapeake Book Company, 1965), 26–48 and 80–100.

55. Warren R. Hofstra, "Private Dwellings, Public Ways and the Landscape of Early Rural Capitalism in Virginia's Shenandoah Valley," in Elizabeth Collins Cromley and Carter L. Hudgins, eds., *Gender, Class, and Shelter: Perspectives in Vernacular Architecture, Vol. 5* (Knoxville: University of Tennessee Press, 1995), 213; C. Richard Beam, *Pennsylvania German Dictionary:*

English to Pennsylvania Dutch (Lancaster, PA: Brookshire Publications, Inc., 1991), 109; Denman Waldo Ross, *The Early History of Land-Holding Among the Germans* (Boston, MA: Soule and Bugbee, 1883), 175; Robert E. Dickinson, "Rural Settlements in the German Lands," *Annals of the Association of American Geographers*, Vol. 39, No. 4 (December 1949), 260–62; Glenn T. Trewartha, "Types of Settlement in Colonial America," *Geographical Review*, Vol. 36, No. 4 (October 1946): 584–85; Donald W. Linebaugh, "Folk Art, Architecture, and Artifact: Toward a Material Understanding of the German Culture in the Upper Valley of Virginia," in David Colin Crass, Steven D. Smith, Martha A. Zierden, and Richard D. Brooks, eds., *The Southern Colonial Backcountry: Interdisciplinary Perspective on Frontier Communities* (Knoxville: University of Tennessee Press, 1998), 205; Richard Pillsbury, "The Urban Street Pattern as Culture Indicator: Pennsylvania, 1682–1815," *Annals of the Association of American Geographers*, Vol. 60, No. 3 (September 1970): 432; and James A. Henretta, "Families and Farms: Mentalité in Pre-Industrial America," *William and Mary Quarterly*, Vol. 35, No. 1 (January 1978): 4 and 19.

56. Hofstra, "Private Dwellings, Public Ways," 211–24; Warren R. Hofstra and Robert D. Mitchell, "Town and Country in Backcountry Virginia: Winchester and the Shenandoah Valley, 1730–1800," *The Journal of Southern History*, Vol. 59, No. 4 (November 1993), 619–46; Robert D. Mitchell, "The Settlement Fabric of the Shenandoah Valley, 1790–1860: Pattern, Process, and Structure," in Kenneth E. Koons and Warren R. Hofstra, eds., *After the Backcountry: Rural Life in the Great Valley of Virginia, 1800–1900*, (Knoxville: University of Tennessee Press, 2000), 34–47; Warren R. Hofstra, *The Planting of New Virginia: Settlement and Landscape in the Shenandoah Valley* (Baltimore, MD: The Johns Hopkins University Press, in association with the Center for American Places, 2004), 1–16; and Pillsbury, "The Urban Street Pattern," 429–36.

57. Wilbur Zelinksy, "The Pennsylvania Town: An Overdue Geographical Account," *Geographical Review*, Vol. 67, No. 2 (April 1977), 130–45; and Coree Reuter, "Spitler Chest Sells for $150,000 at Auction," *Northern Virginia Daily* (2 February 2012).

58. Wilbur Zelinksy, "Where The South Begins: The Northern Limit of the Cis-Appalachian South in Terms of Settlement Landscape," *Social Forces*, Vol. 30, No. 2 (December 1951), 173–74.

59. Virginius Dabney, *Virginia: The New Dominion* (Charlottesville: University Press of Virginia, 1971), 290–94.

60. West Virginia Division of Culture and History, "West Virginia Statehood," http://www.wvculture.org/history/statehoo.html.

61. West Virginia Division of Culture and History, "Constitution of West Virginia," http://www.wvculture.org/history/ statehood/constitution.html; Millard K. Bushong, *A History of Jefferson County, West Virginia* (Charles Town, WV: Jefferson Publishing Company, 1941), 190–200; and West Virginia Division of Culture and History, "Controversy Over the Inclusion of Jefferson and Berkeley Counties in the State of West Virginia," http://www.wvculture.org/history/government/ berkjeff03.html.

62. Bushong, ibid., 190–200; and Jenni Vincent, "Secession Bill Planned to 'Stir Pot'," *The Martinsburg Journal* (January 25, 2011).

63. Jerra Jenrette, "Labor-Management Conflict in the Eastern Panhandle: Perfection Garment Company Battles the ILGWU," *West Virginia History*, Vol. 52 (1993): 109–26.

64. U.S. Census Bureau, "State & County Quick Facts," http://quickfacts.census.gov/qfd/index.html; U.S. Census Bureau, "State-based Metropolitan and Micropolitan Statistical Areas Maps," http://www2.census.gov/ geo/maps/metroarea/stcbsa_pg/Feb2013/cbsa2013_VA.pdf; Regional Plan Association, "America 2050: Megaregions," http://www.america2050.org/content/megaregions.html; Sara S. Hollberg, *The State of the Valley Report* (Staunton, VA: Valley Conservation Council), 72-73; American Farmland Trust, "Farming on the Edge," https://www.farmland.org/farming-on-the-edge; and Virginia Department of Conservation and Recreation, "Virginia Conservation Land Needs Assessment: Virginia Forest Economics Model," http://www.dcr.virginia.gov/natural-heritage/vaconvisforest.

65. The City of Staunton, Virginia, "The Origin of the City Manager Plan in Staunton, Virginia," http://www.icmaml.org/wp-content/uploads/2014/07/Origin-City-Manager-Plan-in-Staunton-VA.pdf; *The New York Times*, "Election Results 2008," http://elections.nytimes.com/2008/results/president/map.html#; *The New York Times*, "Election Results 2012" http://elections.nytimes.com/2012/results/president#.

66. Barton W. Currie, "Along the Shenandoah Valley Pike," *The Country Gentleman*, Vol. 78, No. 51 (December 20, 1913): 3.

67. Joshua Fry and Peter Jefferson, "A Map of the Most Inhabited Part of Virginia Containing the Whole Province of Maryland with Part of Pennsylvania, New Jersey and North Carolina," http://memory.loc.gov/cgi-bin/query/h?ammem/gmd:@field(NUMBER+@band (g3880+ct000370)); West Virginia Division of History and Culture, "West Virginia Highway Markers Database: Pack Horse Ford," http://www.wvculture.org/history/wvmemory/ hmresults.aspx?County=&Title=pack%20horse&Words=&Op=AND; Paul

A. W. Wallace, *Indian Paths of* Pennsylvania (Harrisburg, PA: Pennsylvania Historical and Museum Commission, 1965), 105, 177, and 180; and Nathaniel Mason Pawlett and Howard H. Newlon, Jr., "The Route of the Three Notch'd Road: A Preliminary Report, http://www.virginiadot.org/VTRC/ main/ online_reports/pdf/76-r32.pdf.

68. Harpers Ferry Planning Commission. Harpers Ferry Historic District National Register Nomination. Washington: National Park Service, National Register of Historic Places, 1978; Map Collections from the University of Texas at Arlington, "United States System of Highways: Adopted for Uniform Marking by the American Association of State Highway Officials, November 11, 1926," http://texashistory.unt.edu/ ark:/67531/metapth298433/m1/1/zoom/; U.S. National Archives and Records Administration, "Records of the Bureau of Public Roads," http://www.archives.gov/research/guide-fed-records/groups/030.html; and Dave Strong, "The Virginia Highways Project," http:// www.vahighways.com/route-log/va321-340.htm.

69. Lt. Gen. Jubal A. Early, *A Memoir of the Last Year of the War for Independence in the Confederate States of America* (New Orleans, LA: Blelock & Co., 1867), 33; John W. Wayland, *History of Shenandoah County, Virginia* (Strasburg, VA: Shenandoah Publishing House, Inc., 1927), 272–73; and Valley Conservation Council, *The Middlebrook-Brownsburg Corridor: A Survey of Cultural and Natural Resources* (Staunton, VA: Valley Conservation Council, 1997), 35 and 40.

70. Kenneth W. Keller, "The Best Thoroughfare in the South," in Warren R. Hofstra and Karl Raitz, eds., *The Great Valley Road: Shenandoah Landscapes from Prehistory to the Present* (Charlottesville: University Press of Virginia, in association with the Center for American Places, 2010), 177–79; and Ronald L. Heinemann, *Harry Byrd of Virginia* (Charlottesville: University Press of Virginia, 1996), 104 and 176; U.S. Department of Transportation, Federal Highway Administration, "Senator Harry Flood Byrd of Virginia—The Pay-As-You-Go Man," http://www.fhwa.dot.gov/infrastructure/byrd.cfm.

71. John W. Wayland, *Twenty-Five Chapters on the Shenandoah Valley* (Strasburg, VA: Shenandoah Publishing House, Inc., 1957), 187–89; Seth C. Bruggeman, "The Shenandoah River Gundalow: Reusable Boats in Virginia's Nineteenth-Century River Trade," *The Virginia Magazine of History and Biography*, Vol. 118, No. 4 (2010): 314–49; and Ronald E. Shaw, *Canals for a Nation: The Canal Era in the United States, 1790-1860* (Lexington: University Press of Kentucky, 1990), 104-116; 232.

72. Library of Virginia, "Out of the Box: Notes from the Archives," http://www.virginiamemory.com/blogs/ out_of_the_box/tag/ludwig-von-buchholtz/.

73. Michael Caplinger and John Bond, "The Baltimore and Ohio Railroad Martinsburg Shops," National Historic Landmark Nomination, 2003; W. F. Allen, ed., *The Official Railway Guide for the United States and Canada* (New York: The National Railway Publication Co., 1891), 27-28; Shenandoah Valley Railroad, LLC, "Shenandoah Valley Railroad, LLC History," http://www.svrr-llc.com/history.html; and AMTRAK, "Northeast Train Route," http:// www.amtrak.com/northeast-train-routes; AMTRAK, "Midwest Train Routes," http://www.amtrak.com/ midwest-train-routes.

74. U.S. Department of Transportation, Federal Highway Administration, "FHWA By Day: A Look at the History of the Federal Highway Administration," http://www.fhwa.dot.gov/ byday/fhbd0802.htm; Virginia Department of Transportation, "Interstate 81 History," http://www.virginiadot.org/projects/ const-STAN-I81-history.asp; Virginia Department of Transportation, "Interstate 81 Corridor Study," http://www.virginiainterstates.org/i81_corridor_study.asp; Federal Highway Administration, "Economic Development History of Interstate 81 in Virginia," http://www.fhwa.dot.gov/planning/ economic_development/studies/i81va.cfm; Thomas Hylton, Save Our Land, Save Our Towns (Harrisburg: PA: Seitz and Seitz, Inc., 1995), 30; and Alpine Initiative, "Article on the Protection of the Alps," http://www.alpeninitiative.ch/ alpine-initiative/topics/ article_on_the_protection_of_the_alps.html.

75. James Kirke Paulding, *Letters from the South By a Northern Man,* Vol. 1 (New York: Harper and Brothers, 1835), 105–06.

76. John Singleton Mosby, *The Memoirs of Colonel John S. Mosby*, Charles Wells Russell, ed. (Boston, MA: Little, Brown, 1917), 366; John Heckewelder, "Names which the Lenni Lenape or Delaware Indians Gave to Rivers, Streams and Localities within the States of Pennsylvania, New Jersey, Maryland and Virginia, with their Significations," in William C. Reichel, ed., *The Transactions of the Moravian Historical Society*, Vol. 1 (Nazareth, PA: 1872): 277; Stephen A. Runkle, *Native American Waterbody and Place Names within the Susquehanna River Basin and Surrounding Subbasins* (Harrisburg, PA: Susquehanna River Basin Commission, 2003), 28; Robert D. Mitchell, Warren R. Hofstra, and Edward F. Connor, "Reconstructing the Colonial Environment of the Upper Chesapeake Watershed," in Curtin, Brush, and Fisher, *Discovering the Chesapeake*, 181–82.

77. Wayland, *Twenty-Five Chapters on the Shenandoah Valley*, 15 and 285–86; New York State Historical Association, *Proceedings of New York State Historical Association* (Newburgh, NY: Newburgh Journal

Print, 1906), 203–05; and William R. Gerard, "Some Virginia Indian Words," *American Anthropologist,* New Series, Vol. 7, No. 2 (April–June 1905): 244.

78. Bruce Elliot Johansen and Barbara Alice Mann, *Encyclopedia of the Haudenosaunee* (Iroquois Confederacy) (Westport, CT: Greenwood Press, 2000), 296; and Nicolas A. Reynolds, Historical Researcher, Oneida History Program, who stated, in an email to the author (January 4, 2011): "In reference to Skenandoah, that name has a long history with the Oneida. Today, Skenadore, Skenandore, Skenandoah, Shenandoah, Skenado, etc, etc, etc. . . . are all last names that have been derived from that one name. Chief Shenandoah (in English) was a derivative of the Oneida equivalent: Skanu·tó (sp?), which is pronounced "skah-noon-DOH," with the emphasis, or accent on the last syllable. That word is directly taken from the Oneida word for a deer, which is Osk/\ nu·tú (o-skah-noon-DOO). The root of that word is Osk/\·ná (o-skah-NAH), and means 'peace.' The deer is considered a peaceful animal."

79. Craig Alexander Kopris, *All Wandat Word List* (Wyandotte, OK: Wyandotte Nation, 2012), 472; Charles Garrad and Conrad E. Heidenreich, "Khionontateronon (Petun)," in William C. Sturtevant, ed., *Handbook of North American Indians* (Washington, DC: Government Printing Office, 1978), 395; and John L. Steckley, *Words of the Huron* (Waterloo, ON: Wilfrid Laurier University Press, 2007), 54–55.

80. Marvin T. Smith, "Aboriginal Population Movements in the Postcontact Southeast," in Charles M. Hudson, ed., *The Transformation of the Southeastern Indians, 1540–1760* (Oxford: University Press of Mississippi, 2002), 6; and James F. Pendergast, "The Massawomeck: Raiders and Traders into the Chesapeake Bay in the Seventeeth Century," *Transactions of the American Philosophical Society, Vol. 81, Part 2* (Philadelphia: American Philosophical Society, 1991), 1–73.

81. Sara S. Hollberg, "Natural Bridge," National Register of Historic Places Registration Form, 1997.

82. Samuel R. Cook, "The Monacan Indian Nation: Asserting Tribal Sovereignty in the Absence of Federal Recognition," *Wicazo Sa Review*, Vol. 17, No 2 (Autumn 2002): 94; J. Douglas Smith, "The Campaign for Racial Purity and the Erosion of Paternalism in Virginia, 1922–1930: Nominally White, Biologically Mixed, and Legally Negro," *The Journal of Southern History*, Vol. 68, No. 1 (February 2002): 105; Richard B. Sherman, "The Last Stand": The Fight for Racial Integrity in Virginia in the 1920s," *The Journal of Southern History*, Vol. 54, No. 1 (February 1988): 72; Angela Gonzales, Judy Kertész and Gabrielle Tayac, "Eugenics as Indian Removal: Sociohistorical Processes and the De(con)struction of American Indians in the Southeast," *The Public Historian*, Vol. 29, No. 3 (Summer 2007): 63; Cook, ibid., 99; Vincent Shilling, "DOI Issues Determination: Pamunkey becomes No. 567; First Federally Recognized Tribe in Va." *Indian Country Today* (July 2, 2015): http://indiancountrytodaymedianetwork.com/ 2015/07/02/doi-issues-determination-pamunkey-becomes-no-567-first-federally-recognized-tribe-va; and Angela A. Gonzales and Timothy Q. Evans, "The Imposition of Law: The Federal Acknowledgment Process and the Legal De/Construction of Tribal Identity," in Amy E. Den Ouden and Jean M. O'Brien, eds., *Recognition, Sovereignty Struggles, & Indigenous Rights in the United States: A Sourcebook* (Chapel Hill: University of North Carolina Press, 2013), 37-64.

83. Hofstra, *The Planting of New Virginia*, 122; and J. William Frost, *A Perfect Freedom: Religious Liberty in Pennsylvania* (University Park: The Penn State University Press, 1993), 1.

84. In this book, the more recent term "Scots-Irish" is used rather than the historic American term "Scotch-Irish." In Northern Ireland, the term "Ulster-Scots" is preferred. For more discussion, see Michael Montgomery, "Scotch-Irish or Scots-Irish: What's in a Name?," *Tennessee Ancestors*, Vol. 20 (2004): 143–50; Calder Loth, ed., *The Virginia Landmarks Register*, Fourth Edition (Charlottesville: University Press of Virginia, 1999), 46; James G. Leyburn, *The Scotch-Irish: A Social History* (Chapel Hill: University of North Carolina Press, 1962), xiv–xvi, 85–87, and 158–66; and Katharine L. Brown and Kenneth W. Keller, "Searching for Status: Virginia's Irish Tract, 1770s–1790s," in Warren R. Hofstra, ed., *Ulster to America: The Scots-Irish Migration Experience, 1680–1830* (Knoxville: University of Tennessee Press, 2012), 123–24.

85. Donald B. Kraybill, *The Riddle of Amish Culture* (Baltimore, MD: The Johns Hopkins University Press, in association with the Center for American Places, 1989), 47; Klaus Wust, *The Virginia Germans* (Charlottesville: University of Virginia Press, 1969), 187-88); Richard K. MacMaster, *Land, Piety, Peoplehood: The Establishment of Mennonite Communities in America, 1683–1790* (Scottdale, PA: Herald Press, 1985), 20; and Wayland, *Twenty-Five Chapters on the Shenandoah Valley*, 84.

86. Wust, ibid., 29; Edward A. Chappell, "Acculturation in the Shenandoah Valley: Rhenish Houses of the Massanutten Settlement," *Proceedings of the American Philosophical Society*, Vol. 124, No. 1 (February 1980): 72–74; William Woys Weaver, "The Pennsylvania German House: European Antecedents and New World Forms," *Winterthur Portfolio*, Vol. 21, No. 4 (Winter, 1986): 243–64; and Virginia Historic Landmarks

Commission, "Mill Creek Church/Mauck's Meeting House," National Register of Historic Places Inventory-Nomination Form, 1975. When Mr. Weaver was queried for this book, he stated, in an email to the author (October 3, 2012), that the term *Flurkuchenhaus*, frequently used among scholars to describe this floor plan, should be avoided, due to its Nazi associations.

87. Robert D. Mitchell, "The Shenandoah Valley Frontier," 471; Loth, *The Virginia Landmarks Register*, 178; and Albert Cook Myers, *Immigration of the Irish Quakers into Pennsylvania, 1682–1750* (Swarthmore, PA: self-published, 1902), 178.

88. Loth, ibid., 121; Warren R. Hofstra, *A Separate Place: The Formation of Clarke County, Virginia*, 2–14; and Loth, ibid., 117–23.

89. Celeste Ray, ed., *The New Encyclopedia of Southern Culture*, Vol. 6: *Ethnicity* (Chapel Hill: University of North Carolina Press, 2007), 164–65; Stephen L. Longenecker, *Shenandoah Religion: Outsiders and the Mainstream, 1716–1865* (Waco, TX: Baylor University Press, 2002), 67–69; and U.S. Census Bureau, "State & County Quick Facts."

90. J. Randolph Kean, "The Development of the 'Valley Line' of the Baltimore and Ohio Railroad," *The Virginia Magazine of History and Biography*, Vol. 60, No. 4 (October 1952): 539; Ted McGee, "St. Peter's Roman Catholic Church," National Register of Historic Places Inventory-Nomination Form, 1972; John W. Wayland, *A History of Rockingham County* (Dayton, VA: Ruebush-Elkins Company, 1912), 238 and 256; Jacob Rader Marcus, *United States Jewry, 1776–1985*, Vol. 1 (Detroit, MI: Wayne State University Press, 1993), 29; Robert N. Rosen, *The Jewish Confederates* (Columbia: University of South Carolina Press, 2000), 120–21; Elizabeth B. McCue, "Gospel Hill Historic District," National Register of Historic Places Inventory-Nomination Form, 1983; and Josh Howard on Behalf of the Virginia Department of Historic Resources, "Selected Modernist Architects in Virginia: Biographical Sketches," http://www.dhr.virginia.gov/NewDominion/ArchitectBios_Howard_Final.pdf.

91. Monica Heppel, Joanne Spano, and Luis Torres, eds., "Changes in the Apple Harvest Work Force in West Virginia: Implications for the Community," *Changing Face*, Vol. 3, No. 4 (September 1997); and Eric Arnesan, ed., *Encyclopedia of U. S. Labor and Working-Class History*, Vol. 1 (New York: Routledge, 2007), 564;

92. Library of Virginia, "Union or Secession: Virginians Decide," http://www.virginiamemory.com/online_classroom/ union_or_secession/.

93. Rupert B. Vance, *Human Geography of the South: A Study in Regional Resources and Human Adequacy* (Chapel Hill: University of North Carolina Press, 1932), 89.

94. The Shenandoah Valley was referred to as the "Granary of the Confederacy" as early as 1866—only one year removed from the Civil War—although it is possible it earned this nickname during the war. See J. T. Trowbridge, *The South: A Tour of Its Battle-fields and Ruined Cities* (Hartford, CT: L. Stebbins, 1866), 35. Alternatively, the Valley has been called the "Breadbasket of the Confederacy." See Alva Agee, *Right Use of Lime in Soil Improvement* (New York: Orange Judd Company, 1919), 1; Lex Renda, "The Advent of Agricultural Progressivism in Virginia," *The Virginia Magazine of History and Biography*, Vol. 96, No. 1 (January 1998): 61 and 81; Douglas Helms, "Soil and Southern History," *Agricultural History*, Vol. 74, No. 4 (Autumn 2000): 731–35 and 755–56; and Franklin Knight, ed., *Letters on Agriculture from His Excellency George Washington, President of the United States, to Arthur Young, Esq. F.R.S. and Sir John Sinclair, Bart., M.aP., with Statistical Tables and Remarks, By Thomas Jefferson, Richard Peters, and Other Gentlemen, On the Economy and Management of Farms in the United States* (Washington, DC: self-published, 1847), 54.

95. R. Douglas Hurt, *American Agriculture: A Brief History* (Ames: Iowa State University Press, 1994), 43; and Avery O. Craven, *Soil Exhaustion as a Factor in the Agricultural History of Virginia and Maryland, 1606–1860* (Urbana: University of Illinois, 1926), 11.

96. James T. Lemon, *The Best Poor Man's Country: A Geographical Study of Early Southeastern Pennsylvania* (Baltimore, MD: The Johns Hopkins University Press, 1972), 19–22; James T. Lemon, "The Agricultural Practices of National Groups in Eighteenth-Century Southeastern Pennsylvania," *The Geographical Review*, Vol. 56, No. 4 (October 1966): 485–86; Lewis C. Gray, *History of Agriculture in the Southern United States to 1860: Volume II* (Washington, DC: The Carnegie Institution of Washington, 1933), 908 and 919; and Craven, *Soil Exhaustion*, 85–90.

97. John Lee Coulter, "Industrial History of the Valley of the Red River of the North," in O. G. Libby, ed., *Collections of the State Historical Society of North Dakota*, Vol. 3 (Bismarck: State Historical Society of North Dakota, 1910), 567; Oliver E. Baker, "Agricultural Regions of North America. Part I—The Basis of Classification," *Economic Geography*, Vol. 2, No. 4 (October 1926): frontispiece; Oliver E. Baker, "The Potential Supply of Wheat," *Economic Geography*, Vol. 1, No. 1 (March 1925): 32 and 37–38; Oliver E. Baker, "Agricultural Regions of North America. Part III—The Middle Country, Where South and North Meet," *Economic Geography*, Vol. 3, No. 3 (July 1927): 309; E. G. Nourse, "Our Wheat Surplus," *Foreign Affairs*, Vol. 11, No. 3 (April 1933): 451; Kenneth W.

Keller, "The Wheat Trade on the Upper Potomac, 1800–1860," in Koons and Hofstra, *After the Backcountry*, 29; G. Terry Sharrer, *A Kind of Fate: Agricultural Change in Virginia, 1861–1920* (Ames: Iowa State University Press, 2000), 71–72; and Kenneth E. Koons, "'The Staple of Our Country': Wheat in the Regional Farm Economy of the Nineteenth-Century Valley of Virginia," in Koons and Hofstra, *After the Backcountry*, 14–15.

98. Frank S. Melvin, "McCormick (Cyrus) Farm and Workshop," National Register of Historic Places Registration Form, 1972; and Virginia Polytechnic Institute and State University, "Shenandoah Valley Agricultural Research and Extension Center," http://www.arec.vaes.vt.edu/shenandoah-valley/about/index.html.

99. Sharrer, *A Kind of Fate*, 71–72 and 161; M. R. Cooper, "Outlook for the Apple Industry," *Journal of Farm Economics*, Vol. 11, No. 1 (January 1929): 144–45; Baker, "Agricultural Regions of North America. Part III," 315; Ronald L. Heinemann, *Harry Byrd of Virginia* (Charlottesville: University Press of Virginia, 1996), 125–40; William R. Henry, "Broiler Production Regions of the Future," *Journal of Farm Economics*, Vol. 39, No. 5 (December 1957): 1194; Richard Hartshorne, "A New Map of the Dairy Areas of the United States," *Economic Geography*, Vol. 11, No. 4 (October 1935): 349–51; and Loyal Durand Jr., "The Major Milksheds of the Northeastern Quarter of the United States," *Economic Geography*, Vol. 40, No. 1 (January 1964): 23–24.

100. Grady McWhiney and Forrest McDonald, "Celtic Origins of Southern Herding Practices," *The Journal of Southern History*, Vol. 51, No. 2 (May 1985): 165–66; Grady McWhiney and Forrest McDonald, "The Antebellum Southern Herdsman: A Reinterpretation," *The Journal of Southern History* Vol. 41, No. 2 (May, 1975): 156; Eugene J. Wilhelm, "Animal Drives: A Case Study in Historical Geography," *Journal of Geography*, Vol. 66, No. 6 (September 1967): 329–33; and Donald Cook, conversation with the author (ca. 1999).

101. Judy Egerton, *British Sporting Paintings: The Paul Mellon Collection in the Virginia Museum of Fine Arts British Sporting Paintings* (Richmond: Virginia Museum of Fine Arts, 1985), ix; Philip Smith, "New Squire in Virginia," *The Washington Post* (October 6, 1985); and Virginia Horse Center Foundation, "The Foundation," http://www.horsecenter.org/About/The-Foundation.aspx.

102. U.S. Department of Agriculture (USDA) Economic Research Service, "Virginia State Fact Sheet: Population, Income, Education, Employment, and Federal Funds," http://www.ers.usda.gov/StateFacts/.

103. Wines & Vines, "U.S. Winery Database," http://www.winesandvines.com/template.cfm?section=widc&widcDomain=wineries; U.S. Department of Agriculture, National Agricultural Statistics Service, Virginia Field Office, "Annual Statistical Bulletin: Grape Acres and Production by County and Variety," http://www.nass.usda.gov/Statistics_by_State/Virginia/Publications/Annual_Statistical_Bulletin/page5110.pdf; Virginia Wine Marketing Office, "2015 Governor's Cup Awards," https://www.virginiawine.org/governors-cup/awards#Gold; Virginia Department of Agriculture and Consumer Services, "Virginia Vineyards Association Names Jeff White Grower of the Year," http://www.vdacs.virginia.gov/ news/releases-a/013114wineaward.shtml; Dana Milbank," Vineyards that are putting Virginia on the fine-wine map," *The Washington Post Magazine*, (November 21, 2013); and Katie Kelly Bell, "Is Virginia Wine Country Poised to be the East Coast Napa?," *Forbes Travel* (August 15, 2013).

104. Michael A. Tomlan, Tinged with Gold: Hop Culture in the United States (Athens: University of Georgia Press, 1992), 9–42; U.S. Department of Agriculture, National Agricultural Statistics Service, Northwest Regional Field Office, "Hops," http://www.nass.usda.gov/Statistics_by_State/Washington/Publications/Hops/; Virginia Cooperative Extension, "2014 Virginia Hops Grower Survey—Scope of the Industry," http://www.agriculture.vsu.edu/files/docs/2014-virginia-hops-grower-survey-summary-final.pdf; and Michael Felberbaum, "Virginia Turning to Hops as Potential Cash Crop," *USA Today* (October 5, 2014).

105. Joseph W. Glass, *The Pennsylvania Culture Region: A View from the Barn* (Ann Arbor, MI: UMI Research Press, 1986), 9–15; and Robert F. Ensminger, *The Pennsylvania Barn: Its Origin, Evolution, and Distribution in North America* (Baltimore, MD: The Johns Hopkins University Press, in association with the Center for American Places, 1992; second edition, 2003), xvi, 10–17, 51–55, and 147–48.

106. Family Central, "Jacobus Lichte," http://www.familycentral.net/index/family.cfm?ref1=8097:287&ref2=8097:288; and Ensminger, ibid., 89 and 108–109.

107. Joseph G. Dawson, III, "The First of the Modern Wars?," in Susan-Mary Grant and Brian Holden Reid, eds., *Themes of the American Civil War: The War between the States,* Second Edition (New York: Routledge, 2010), 68–80; James M. McPherson, "From Limited War to Total War in America," in Grant and Reid, 307–09; Stephen B. Oates, *Abraham Lincoln: The Man Behind the Myths* (New York: HarperCollins, 1984), 136; Virginia Historic Landmarks Commission, "Lincoln Homestead and Cemetery," National Register of Historic Places Inventory-Nomination Form, 1972; John L. Heatwole, *The Burning: Sheridan's Devastation of the Shenandoah Valley* (Charlottesville,

VA: Howell Press, 1998), 114; Richard Martin, "Rife's Mill," National Register of Historic Places Registration Form, 1999; LDA Creations, Inc., "History at Silver Lake Mill," http://www.silverlakemill.com/history.php; Virginia Historic Landmarks Commission, "Edinburg Mill," National Register of Historic Places Inventory-Nomination Form, 1979; Clayton Chun, *U.S. Army in the Plains Indian Wars*, 1865–1891 (Oxford, UK: Osprey Publishing, 2004), 16; and Thom Hatch, *The Custer Companion: A Comprehensive Guide to the Life of George Armstrong Custer and the Plains Indian Wars* (Mechanicsburg, PA: Stackpole Books, 2002), 83–84.

108. Sally McMurry, *Transforming Rural Life: Dairying Families and Agricultural Change, 1820–1885* (Baltimore, MD: The Johns Hopkins University Press, 1995), 33–37; H. J. Barre and L. L. Sammet, *Farm Structures* (New York: John Wiley & Sons, 1950), 213; and N. S. Fish, *Building the Dairy Barn*, Bulletin 369 (Madison: University of Wisconsin Agricultural Experiment Station, 1924), 31.

109. Allen G. Noble, *Wood, Brick, and Stone: The North American Settlement Landscape, Volume 2: Barns and Farm Structures* (Amherst: The University of Massachusetts Press, 1984), 43–46.

110. U.S. Department of Agriculture, *Dairy Barn Construction*, Farmers' Bulletin No. 1342 (Washington, DC: Government Printing Office, 1923), 12; and R. E. Hundertmark and A. B. Nystrom, *The Dairy Barn and Milk House, How to Construct Them*, Popular Bulletin No. 95 (Pullman, WA: State Agricultural Experiment Station, 1915), 11.

111. Ernest Kelly and Clarence Clement, *Market Milk* (New York: John Wiley & Sons, 1923), 107; Hundertmark and Nystrom, ibid., 14; and USDA, *Dairy Barn Construction*, 4.

112. Fish, *Building the Dairy Farm*, 5; USDA, *Dairy Barn Construction*, 18–20; and Hundertmark and Nystrom, ibid., 34–35.

113. Michael Pollan, "No Bar Code," *Mother Jones* (May/June 2006), http://www.motherjones.com/ environment/2006/05/no-bar-code; *Food, Inc.*, directed by Robert Kenner (New York: Magnolia Pictures, 2008); *Polyfaces: The Film,* directed by Isaebella Doherty and Lisa Heenan (Eppalock, Australia: Regrarians Media, 2015); and Michael Pollan, *The Omnivore's Dilemma* (New York: Penguin Press, 2006). See, also, Monique Calello, "Healing the Land and Ourselves 1 Meal at a Time: A Swope Farm Charts the Way," *The News Leader* (November 6, 2015): 1A and 2A.

114. Forrest G. Hoffmaster and James L. "Dixie" Wiltshire, *The Town of Millville (Jefferson County) West Virginia and the People* (Charles Town, WV: self-published, 2004).

115. University of Virginia Library, "Historical Census Browser," http://mapserver.lib.virginia.edu/; T. J. Woofter, Jr., "The Tennessee Valley Regional Plan," *Social Forces*, Vol. 12, No. 3 (March 1934): 332; and Stephen J. Goldfarb, "A Note on Limits to the Growth of the Cotton-Textile Industry in the Old South," *The Journal of Southern History*, Vol. 48, No. 4 (November 1982): 549.

116. Knit Goods Industry, 370–80; Paul E. Rivard, *A New Order of Things: How the Textile Industry Transformed New England* (Hanover, NH: University Press of New England, 2002), 9; Goldfarb, ibid., 550–58; and West Virginia Humanities Council, "Textile Industry," http://www.wvencyclopedia.org/articles/706.

117. Wilbur S. Johnston, *Weaving a Common Thread: A History of the Woolen Industry in the Top of the Shenandoah Valley* (Winchester, VA: Winchester-Frederick County Historical Society, 1990), 54–63 and 133–35; Mira Wilkins, *The History of Foreign Investment in the United States, 1914–1945* (Cambridge, MA: Harvard University Press, 2004), 22; Amy T. Peterson and Ann T. Kellogg, ed., *The Greenwood Encyclopedia of Clothing through American History, 1900 to the Present* (Westport, CT: Greenwood Press, 2008), 166; "Front Royal Rayon Plant Will Be Largest in World," *The Free Lance-Star* (March 3, 1937): 1; U.S. Environmental Protection Agency, "Avtex Fibers," http://www.epa.gov/superfund/accomp/success/avtex.htm; Edna Johnston and Kathryn Gettings Smith, "Front Royal Historic District," National Register of Historic Places Registration Form, 2002; "The Story of American Viscose Corporation," *The Free Lance-Star* (June 12, 1956): 14; Virginia Department of Health, "Fish Consumption Advisories—Shenandoah River," http://www.vdh.virginia.gov/Epidemiology/ dee/ PublicHealthToxicology/ Advisories/ShenandoahRiver.htm; Ashley E. Stanley, "A Short History of the Waynesboro DuPont Plant: Its Impact on Waynesboro, 1997," http://static.mgnetwork.com/wnv/core/media_path/multimedia/pdf/DuPontpaper.pdf; and Elizabeth Spilman Massie and Cortney Skinner, *Images of America: Waynesboro* (Charleston, SC: Arcadia Publishing, 2009), 89.

118. G. P Grimsley and I. C. White, *West Virginia Geological Survey: Jefferson, Berkeley, and Morgan Counties* (Wheeling, WV: Wheeling News Litho. Co., 1916), 396 and 401–02; Jill A. Chappel, "Standard Lime & Stone Quarry (Millville Quarry): Photographs and Written Historical and Descriptive Data" (Philadelphia, PA: Historic American Engineering Record, Mid-Atlantic Region, National Park Service, 1991); and James L. "Dixie" Wiltshire, *Millville: Boom Town Big "M" Country* (Charles Town, WV: self-published, 1998), 2–8.

119. James L. "Dixie" Wiltshire, "Millville—Boom Town," (Unpublished manuscript, n.d.); and Chappel, ibid., 1991.

120. Wiltshire, *Millville*, 2–3; Wiltshire, "Millville—Boom Town"; Marcia J. Drucker, ed., *A Bicentennial History of Jefferson County* (Martinsburg, WV: Quebecor Printing, 2001), 61; and Margaret M. Mulrooney, *A Legacy of Coal: The Coal Company Towns of Southwestern Pennsylvania*, in Thomas Carter and Bernard L. Herman, eds., *Perspectives in Vernacular Architecture, IV* (Columbia: University of Missouri Press, 1991), 130–36.

121. John S. Garner, *The Company Town: Architecture and Society in the Early Industrial Age* (Oxford:, UK Oxford University Press, 1992) 3–4; and L. Martin Perry, *Coal Company Towns in Eastern Kentucky, 1854–1941: A Historic Context* (Frankfort: Kentucky Heritage Council, 1991).

122. Drucker, *A Bicentennial History*, 62–63; Wiltshire, "Millville—Boom Town," 5; and Chappel, "Standard Lime & Stone Quarry," 5.

123. Jeffrey C. Everett, "Allstadt Farm Cultural Landscape Inventory, Harpers Ferry National Historical Park" (Washington, DC: National Park Service, National Capital Region, Cultural Landscapes Program, 2005).

124. Virginia Economic Development Partnership, "Community Profiles: Northern Shenandoah Valley and Shenandoah Valley," http://virginiascan.yesvirginia.org/communityprofiles/MapSearch.aspx?type=VIRTUALVIRGINIAREGION.

125. The Center for Rural Pennsylvania, "Economic and Transportation Impact of Warehousing on Rural Pennsylvania," http://www.rural.palegislature.us/documents/reports/ Warehousing_Report08.pdf; National Conference of State Legislatures, "Right-to-Work Resources," http://www.ncsl.org/research/labor-and-employment/right-to-work-laws-and-bills.aspx; Federation of Tax Administrators, "Range of State Corporate Income Tax Rates," http://www.taxadmin.org/fta/rate/corp_inc.pdf; and Port of Virginia, "Virginia Inland Port," http://www.portofvirginia.com/facilities/virginia-inland-port-vip/.

126. John S. Mosby Letter to Alexander Spottswood Campbell, (February 25, 1909), http://www.gilderlehrman.org/collections/83baf3b2-aeeb-4c21-90eb-942828989229.

127. Virginius Dabney, *Virginia: The New Dominion* (Charlottesville: University Press of Virginia, 1971), 165, 245–250, 367–373, and 381–382; Foney G. Mullins, "A History of the Literary Fund as a Funding Source for Free Public Education in the Commonwealth of Virginia." Ph.D. diss. (Blacksburg: Virginia Polytechnic Institute and State University, 2001), 8–16; Margaret B. Gunter, ed., "A History of Public Education in Virginia," http://*www.cteresource.org/TFTfinalWebFiles/.../ history_public_ed.pdf*; Virginia Department of Historic Resources, "Brownsburg Historical Marker," 2001; and Library of Virginia, "A Guide to the Papers of William Hodges Mann, 1910–1914," http://ead.lib.virginia.edu/vivaxtf/view?docId= lva/vi03142.xml.

128. Virginia Historic Landmarks Commission, "Public Schools in Augusta County, Virginia 1870–1940," National Register of Historic Places Inventory-Nomination Form, 1984; Maral S. Kalbian, "Josephine City School," National Register of Historic Places Registration Form, 1995; U.S. Census Office, "Map Showing the Distribution of the Slave Population of the Southern States of the United States," (Washington, DC: U.S. Census Office, 1861); Mary Gray Farland and Beverley Bigelow Byrd, *In the Shadow of the Blue Ridge, Clarke County, Virginia, 1732–1952* (Richmond, VA: William Byrd Press, 1978), 112–13; Ronald L. Heinemann, *Harry Byrd of Virginia* (Charlottesville: University Press of Virginia, 1996), 325–344; and Virginia Department of Historic Resources, "DHR Approves 12 New Historical Highway Markers," http://www.dhr.virginia.gov/pdf_files/Dec2010markers.FINAL.pdf.

129. David Edwards, Joanie Evans, et al., "John Handley High School," National Register of Historic Places Registration Form, 1998.

130. Clarence L. Mohr, ed., *The New Encyclopedia of Southern Culture*, Vol. 17: *Education* (Chapel Hill: University of North Carolina Press, 2011), 82; Virginia Historic Landmarks Commission, "Augusta Military Academy," National Register of Historic Places Inventory-Nomination Form, 1982; Virginia Historic Landmarks Commission, "Augusta Stone Church," National Register of Historic Places Inventory-Nomination Form, 1973; Virginia Military Institute, "VMI Archives," http://www.vmi.edu/archives/home; Historic Rural Hill Cultural Center, "History of the Scots and Scots-Irish," http://www.ruralhill.net/ Heritage.asp#scots; and James Webb, *Born Fighting: How the Scots-Irish Shaped America* (New York: Broadway Books, 2004), 10–11.

131. Joshua Owens, "A Case Study of the Founding Years of Liberty Hall Academy: The Struggle Between Enlightenment and Protestant Values on the Virginia Frontier," *Journal of the Backcountry Studies*, Vol. 4, No. 2 (Fall 2009): 1–8; Virginia Historical Society, "Robert E. Lee After the War," http://www.vahistorical.org/ collections-and-resources/virginia-history-explorer/robert-e-lee-after-war; and Dabney, *Virginia*, 359.

132. James G. Leyburn, The Scotch-Irish: A Social History (Chapel Hill: University of North Carolina Press, 1962), 245; James Axtell, *The Making of Princeton University: From Woodrow Wilson to the Present* (Princeton, NJ: Princeton University Press, 2006), 1; Willard Thorp, ed., *The Lives of Eighteen from Princeton* (Princeton, NJ: Princeton University Press, 1946), 137, 112, and 84; Jerome Karabel, *The Chosen: The Hidden History of Admission and Exclusion at Harvard, Yale, and Princeton* (New York: Houghton Mifflin, 2005), 315; and William Gillette, *Jersey Blue: Civil War Politics in New Jersey, 1854–1865* (New Brunswick, NJ: Rutgers University Press, 2005), 3.

133. Loth, *The Virginia Landmarks Register*, 506; and Laura Peters, "Once Plenty, Now Single-sex Colleges in Va. Down to 3," *The News Leader* (March 15, 2015).

134. Shenandoah University, "History," http://www.su.edu/ 0D09904F2D694BFD862F895CC7DB02AA.asp; Virginia Landmarks Commission, "Southern Seminary Main Building," National Register of Historic Places Inventory-Nomination Form, 1971; Methodist Episcopal Church, South, *Minutes of the Annual Conferences of the Methodist Episcopal Church, South* (Nashville, TN: Publishing House of the Methodist Episcopal Church, South, 1902), 12 and 274; Southern Virginia University, "Mission and History," http://svu.edu/about/history/; and Christendom College, "A History of Christendom College: The First 35 Years (1977–2012)," http://www.christendom.edu/about/history.php; Loth, 510.

135. James Madison University, "JMU Historical Timeline," http://www.jmu.edu/centennialcelebration /timeline.shtml; Jerry Bruce Thomas, "Shepherd University." e-WV: The West Virginia Encyclopedia (September 9, 2015), http://www.wvencyclopedia.org/articles/393.

136. Mamie Jenkins Dearing, interview by Dorothy Noble Smith, transcribed by Sharon G. Marston, *Shenandoah National Park Oral History Collection*, James Madison University (November 5, 1980), http://mdid.cit.jmu.edu/snp/interview/SNP041/.

137. David Arnold and Candace Cansler, "Raw Talent: America's Ham Artisans Take on Europe's Masters," American Museum of Food, http://www.aamp.com/news/hamart.asp; Elmer Smith, *Shenandoah Valley Cooking: Recipes and Kitchen Lore*, Second Edition (Lebanon, PA: Applied Arts Publishers, 1971), 16; William Woys Weaver, *Sauerkraut Yankees: Pennsylvania-German Foods & Foodways* (Philadelphia: University of Pennsylvania Press, 1983), 42–43; William Woys Weaver, *A Quaker Woman's Cookbook: The Domestic Cookery of Elizabeth Ellicott Lea*, Second Edition (Mechanicsburg, PA: Stackpole Books, 2004), 342; and William Woys Weaver, *Country Scrapple: An American Tradition* (Mechanicsburg, PA: Stackpole Books, 2003), 1–3.

138. Smith, ibid., 17; Weaver, *A Quaker Woman's Cookbook*, 311–12; Jane Kallir, *Grandma Moses in the 21st Century* (Alexandria, VA: Art Services International, 2001), 91 and 160-61.

139. John T. Edge, ed., *The New Encyclopedia of Southern Culture, Vol. 7: Foodways* (Chapel Hill: University of North Carolina Press, 2007), 264–65; and Geneva Collins, "Where Settlers, Slaves and Natives Converged, a Way of Eating Was Born," *The Washington Post* (May 9, 2007).

140. L'Auberge Provençale, "Farm to Table," http://www.latableprovencale.com/farm-to-table-restaurant.html; Zynodoa Restaurant, "Producers," http://www.latableprovencale.com/farm-to-table-restaurant.html; Strolling of the Heifers, "2015 Locavore Index," http://www.strollingoftheheifers.com/locavoreindex/; and U.S. Department of Agriculture, "Census of Agriculture: 2012 Census Publications," http://www.agcensus.usda.gov/ Publications/2012/.

141. Diner Hunter, "Snow White Grill—Winchester Virginia," http://dinerhunter.com/2008/09/29/snow-white-grill-winchester-virginia/; Jane Stern and Michael Stern, *Roadfood: The Coast-to-Coast Guide to 800 of the Best Barbecue Joints, Lobster Shacks, Ice Cream Parlors, Highway Diners, and Much, Much More* (New York: Clarkson Potter Publishers, 2011), 200; and Marc C. Wagner, "Diners of Virginia," National Register of Historic Places Multiple Property Documentation Form, 1995.

142. Grandma Moses, *My Life's History* (New York: Harper & Brothers, 1952), 104.

143. James Woodress, *Willa Cather: A Literary Life* (Lincoln: University of Nebraska Press, 1987), 12–31; and Loth, *The Virginia Landmarks Register*, 177 and 180.

144. Ann Romines, *Willa Cather's Civil War: A Very Long Engagement,* in Steven Trout, ed., *Cather Studies, Vol. 6: History, Memory, and War* (Lincoln: University of Nebraska Press, 2006), 10–11.

145. Ann Romines, *Admiring and Remembering: The Problem of Virginia,* in Susan J. Rosowski, ed., *Cather Studies, Vol. 5: Willa Cather's Ecological Imagination* (Lincoln: University of Nebraska Press, 2003), 274 and 280–82.

146. Jane Kallir, "Grandma Moses," in Elsa Longhauser, Harald Szeeman, and Lee Kogan, eds., *Self-Taught Artists of the 20th Century: An American Anthology* (New York: Museum of American Folk Art, 1998), 78–79; Kallir, *Grandma Moses in the 21st Century*, 255; and Otto Kallir, *Grandma Moses* (New York: Harry N. Abrams, 1973), 315.

147. Franklin Johnston, "Grandma Moses in the Shenandoah Valley: November 1887–December 1905," *Augusta County Historical Bulletin,* No. 41 (2005); Franklin Johnston, "Grandma Moses in West Virginia," *West Virginia Historical Society Quarterly*, Vol. XX (July 2006): 2–3; and Preservation Virginia, "Virginia's Most Endangered Historic Sites 2007," http://www.apva.org/pressroom/pdf/ endangered_sites_07.pdf.

148. James C. Kelly and William M. S. Rasmussen, *The Virginia Landscape: A Cultural History* (Charlottesville, VA: Howell Press, 2000), 74; Paul C. Nagel, *George Caleb Bingham: Missouri's Famed Painter and Forgotten Politician* (Columbia: University of Missouri Press, 2005), 1-8; The Metropolitan Museum of Art, "Navigating the West: George Caleb Bingham and the River," http://www.metmuseum.org/about-the-museum/press-room/exhibitions /2015/navigating-the-west; and Moses, *My Life's History*, 104.

149. Lynne Warren, ed., *Encyclopedia of Twentieth-Century Photography,* 3 vols. (New York: Routledge, 2006), Vol. 1: 481–84; Library of Congress, "Farm Security Administration/Office of War Information Black-and-White Negatives," http://www.loc.gov/pictures/search/?q=shenandoah&co=fsa; Rebecca J. Rosen, "A Gorgeous Photographic Elegy to the Last Steam Train," *The Atlantic* (October 4, 2012); Margarett Loke, "O. Winston Link, Photographer, Dies at 86," *The New York Times* (February 2, 2001); David G. Helmer, "Memories of O. Winston Link," *Turntable Times: The Official Newsletter of the Roanoke Chapter, National Railway Historical Society, Inc.*, Vol. 33, No. 2 (February 2001): 8-9; Richard B. Woodward, "The Disturbing Photography of Sally Mann," *The New York Times Magazine* (April 16, 2015); and Blake Morrison, "Sally Mann: The Naked and the Dead," *The Guardian* (May 28, 2010).

150. Paul Kingsbury, Michael McCall, and John W. Rumble, eds., *The Encyclopedia of Country Music,* Second Edition (New York: Oxford University Press, 2012). It should be noted that Watermelon Park along the Shenandoah River in Clarke County makes the same claim of hosting the first-ever bluegrass festival.

151. Terri Higgins, "A Picture from the Past: The Frye Brothers, Patsy, and the Rainbow Inn," *The Winchester Star* (April 21, 1992); Ellis Nassour, *Honky Tonk Angel: The Intimate Story of Patsy Cline* (New York: St. Martin's Press, 1993), 27; Country Music Hall of Fame, "Patsy Cline," http://www.countrymusichalloffame.org/full-list-of-inductees/view/patsy-cline; and Brad Zinn, "Statler Brothers 50 Years Later," *The News Leader* (February 21, 2015).

152. W. K. McNeil, ed., *Encyclopedia of American Gospel Music* (New York: Routledge, 2005), 134–35, 336, and 341; and Loth, *The Virginia Landmark Register*, 472 and 474.

153. Robin & Linda Williams, "Bio," http://www.robinandlinda.com/bio.html; *Billboard*, "Artists: Old Crow Medicine Show," http://www.billboard.com/artist/277107/old-crow-medicine-show/biography; Prairie Home Companion, "Guests: Old Crow Medicine Show," http://prairiehome.org/guests/old-crow-medicine-show/; and Grand Ole Opry, "Artist Bio: Old Crow Medicine Show," http://www.opry.com/artist/old-crow-medicine-show.

154. Stonewall Brigade Band, "Stonewall Brigade Band," http://www.stonewallbrigadeband.com/.

155. Winchester Little Theatre, "History of the Theatre," http://www.wltonline.org/; F. C. Lowe, "Final Curtain Call Falls on Wayside Theatre; Ending 52-Year Run," *The Winchester Star* (August 8, 2013); Lime Kiln Theater, "History," http://www.limekilntheater.org/; Staunton Performing Arts Center, "Our History," http://www.stauntonperformingarts.org/our-history; and American Shakespeare Center, "Blackfriars Playhouse," http://www.americanshakespearecenter.com/v.php?pg=124.

156. David "Scratch" Clanagan, overheard by the author (ca. 1990).

157. Felix Reichmann, "The Pennsylvania Rifle: A Social Interpretation of Changing Military Techniques," *The Pennsylvania Magazine of History and Biography*, Vol. 69, No. 1 (January 1945): 9; and Carlton O. Wittlinger, "The Small Arms Industry of Lancaster County, 1710–1840," *Pennsylvania History*, Vol. 24, No. 2 (April 1957): 1–2.

158. Virginia Department of Game and Inland Fisheries, "Virginia's Game Wildlife," http://www.dgif.virginia.gov/wildlife/game/; Virginia Department of Game and Inland Fisheries, "Regulations-Bear," http://www.dgif.virginia.gov/hunting/regulations/bear.asp; Virginia Department of Game and Inland Fisheries, "Regulations-Deer," http://www.dgif.virginia.gov/hunting/ regulations/deer.asp; The Blue Ridge Hunt, "History of the Blue Ridge Hunt," http://www.blueridgehunt.org/history.html; Glenmore Hunt Club, "Glenmore Hunt Club: A Brief History," http://www.glenmorehunt.org; The Rockbridge Hunt, "The Rockbridge Hunt: A History of its First Sixty Years," http://home.wlu.edu/~mortonc /archive/education/History.html; and West Virginia Archives and History, "Opening of the Charles Town Racetrack," http://www.wvculture.org/history/sports/charlestownracetrack01.html.

159. Trout Unlimited, *Trout Unlimited's Guide to America's 100 Best Trout Streams* (Guilford, CT: Lyons Press, 2005), 131–38; and National Park Service, "President Herbert and Lou Henry Hoover's Rapidan Camp," http://www.nps.gov/nr/travel/presidents/hoover_camp_rapidan.html.

160. John W. Wayland, *A History of the Shenandoah County, Virginia* (Strasburg, VA: Shenandoah Publishing House, Inc., 1927), 27; Harvey H. Jackson, III, ed., *The New Encyclopedia of Southern Culture, Vol. 2: Sports and Recreation* (Chapel Hill: University of North Carolina Press, 2011), 74–77; A. W. Stencell, *Girl Show: Into the Canvas World of Bump and Grind* (Toronto, ON: ECW Press, 1999), 225; and Dan McCauley, "Fairs Drops Strip Show," *The Daily News-Record* (April 22, 1996).

161. Robert P. Savitt, *Images of America: The Blue Ridge League* (Charleston, SC: Arcadia Publishing, 2011), 7; Sports Reference LLC, "Baseball-Reference.com" http://www.baseball-reference.com/; and Harrisonburg-Rockingham Historical Society, "The Legend of Lineweaver: Rockingham County Baseball League," http://www.heritagecenter.com/Web_Pages/Museum/Collection/ Baseball/Baseball.html.

162. Harrisonburg-Rockingham Historical Society, "Rockingham County Baseball Collection," www.heritagecenter.com/Web_Pages/ Archives/.../ HRHS-14.pdf.

163. Darrell J. Howard, *"Sunday Coming": Black Baseball in Virginia* (Jefferson, NC: McFarland & Company, 2002), 188–89; Craig Orndorff, conversation with the author, (July 5, 2015); and Valley Baseball League, "About the VBL," http://www.valleyleaguebaseball.com/information/about_vbl.

164. The Pennsylvania Center for the Book, "Bios: Jack Ham," http://pabook.libraries.psu.edu/ palitmap/bios/Ham__Jack.html; Pro Football Hall of Fame, "Jack Ham," http://www.profootballhof.com/players/ jack-ham/; Pro Football Hall of Fame, "Charles Haley," http://www.profootballhof.com/players/charles-haley/; Naismith Memorial Basketball Hall of Fame, "Ralph Sampson," http://www.hoophall.com/hall-of-famers/tag/ralph-sampson; National Basketball Association, "Former Hornets Star Dell Curry Expands Role with Organization," http://www.nba.com/hornets/former-hornets-star-dell-curry-expands-role-organization#; and Shenvalee Golf Club, "Opened to the Public, July 7, 1927," *The Shenvaleader*, Vol. 26 (Winter 2011): 2.

165. James C. Bonner, "The Historical Basis of Southern Military Tradition," *The Georgia Review*, Vol. 9, No. 1 (Spring 1951), 74–78.

166. Virginia Department of Historic Resources, Historical Highway Markers, http://dhr.virginia.gov/HistoricMarkers/; Norman L. Baker, "Fort Loudoun as Virginia's French & Indian War Command Center," http://frenchandindianwar foundation.org/history/fort-loudoun/; and W. W. Abbot, et al., eds., *The Papers of George Washington, November 1756–October 1757* (Charlottesville: University Press of Virginia, 1984), 50–54.

167. Philip Columbus Croll, Henry Addison Schuler, and Howard Wiegner Kriebel, "Famous Pennsylvania Germans," *The Pennsylvania-German*, Vol. 1 (July 1900): 3–5; Donald S. Armentrout and Robert Boak Slocum, eds., *An Episcopal Dictionary of the Church: A User-Friendly Reference for Episcopalians* (New York: Church Publishing, 2000), 345; and Thomas Adam, ed., *Germany and the Americas: Culture, Politics, and History* (Santa Barbara, CA: ABC-CLIO, 2005), 792–93.

168. Public Broadcasting System, "History Detectives Episode 5: Muhlenberg Robe," http://www-tc.pbs.org/opb/historydetectives_old/pdf/505_muhlenbergrobe.pdf.

169. Neil L. York, "Pennsylvania Rifle: Revolutionary Weapon in a Conventional War?," *The Pennsylvania Magazine of History and Biography*, Vol. 103, No. 3 (July 1979): 302–08; and David Meschutt, "Portraits of Daniel Morgan, Revolutionary War General," *American Art Journal*, Vol. 17, No. 3 (Summer 1985): 35.

170. Maral S. Kalbian and J. Daniel Pezzoni, "Soldier's Rest," National Register of Historic Places Registration Form, 1996; Charles W. Snell, "General Daniel Morgan House, Saratoga," National Register of Historic Places Inventory-Nomination Form, 1973; George R. Schember and Jeanne S. Schember, "Daniel Morgan House," National Register of Historic Places Registration Form, 2012; and Virginia Historic Landmarks Commission Staff, "Presbyterian Meeting House (Old Stone Church)," National Register of Historic Places Inventory-Nomination Form, 1976.

171. National Park Service, *Study of Civil War Sites in the Shenandoah Valley of Virginia* (Washington, DC: National Park Service, 1992).

172. Stanley L. Sandler, ed., *Ground Warfare: An International Encyclopedia, Vol. I* (Santa Barbara, CA: ABC-CLIO, 2002), 428; Millard K. Bushong, *General Turner Ashby and Stonewall's Valley Campaign* (Waynesboro, VA: The McClung Companies, 1992), 12.

173. Virgil Carrington Jones, *Gray Ghosts and Rebel Raiders: The Daring Exploits of the Confederate Guerillas* (New York: Henry Holt, 1956), 46–48 and 74; Jeffry D. Wert, *Mosby's Rangers* (New York: Simon & Schuster, 1990), 190–92; John Singleton Mosby, *The Memoirs of Colonel John S. Mosby*, Charles Wells Russell, ed. (Boston, MA: Little, Brown, 1917), 314–25; and Thomas J. Evans and James M. Moyer, *Mosby's Confederacy: A Guide to the Roads and Sites of Colonel John Singleton Mosby* (Shippensburg, PA: White Mane, 1991), 77.

174. John W. Listman, Jr., "Serving Commonwealth and Country," http://vko.va.ngb. army.mil/virginiaguard/history/overview.html; Brian F. Neumann, "Preparations," in Edward G. Lengel, ed., *A Companion to the Meuse-Argonne Campaign* (Chichester,

UK: John Wiley & Sons, 2004), 33; Steven Trout, "The Greatest Battle Ever Forgotten: The Meuse-Argonne Offensive and American Memory," in Lengel, 496-514; Edward G. Lengel, *To Conquer Hell: The Meuse-Argonne, 1918* (New York: Henry Holt, 2008), 298; John Abram Cutchins and George Scott Stewart, Jr., *History of the Twenty-ninth Division, "Blue and Gray," 1917–1919* (Philadelphia, PA: self-published, 1921), 316–20; 29th Division Association, "116th Infantry," http://www.29thdivisionassociation.com/116th%20Infantry%20history.html; Alex Kershaw, *The Bedford Boys: One American Town's Ultimate D-Day Sacrifice* (Cambridge, MA: Da Capo Press, 2003), 240; and Joseph Balkoski, *The Last Roll Call: The 29th Infantry Division Victorious, 1945* (Mechanicsburg, PA: Stackpole Books, 2015), 305.

175. Ronald L. Heinemann, "George C. Marshall (1880–1959)," *Encyclopedia Virginia* http://encyclopediavirginia.org/Marshall_George_C_1880-1959#start_entry; and Robert Harvey, *Maverick Military Leaders: The Extraordinary Battles of Washington, Nelson, Patton, Rommel and Others* (New York: Skyhorse Publishing, 2008), 343–62.

176. Lt. Colonel S. C. Reynolds, Q.M.C., "The Front Royal Remount Depot," *Quartermaster Review* (September–October 1930), reprinted at U.S. Army Quartermaster Foundation, http://www.qmfound.com/front_royal.htm; George M. Rommel, *The Army Remount Problem* (Washington, DC: U.S. Department of Agriculture, 1911); 122–24; Smithsonian Institution, "Smithsonian Conservation Biology Institute (SCBI)," http://siarchives.si.edu/history/smithsonian-conservation-biology-institute-scbi; John Hammond Moore, "Hitler's Wehrmacht in Virginia, 1943–1946," *The Virginia Magazine of History and Biography*, Vol. 85, No. 3 (July 1977): 263–64; Woodrow Wilson Rehabilitation Center, "The History of Woodrow Wilson Rehabilitation Center (WWRC), http://www.wwrc.net/WWRCHistory.htm; Gregory L. Owen, "Prisoners of War in Rockingham County During World War II," *The Harrisonburg-Rockingham Historical Society Newsletter*, Vol. 29, No. 2 (Spring 2007): 1–5; and Gregory L. Owen, "Axis Prisoners of War Confined in the Shenandoah Valley of Virginia during World War II," http://www.thelongestpatrol.com/pwoverview.html.

177. John C. Paige, *The Civilian Conservation Corps and the National Park Service, 1933–1942: An Administrative History* (Washington, DC: National Park Service, 1985), 36; and Mennonite Central Committee, "The Civilian Public Service Story," http://civilianpublicservice.org/camps.

178. Jennifer A. Keahey, Mary A. Littrell, and Douglas Murray, "Business with a Mission: The Ongoing Role of Ten Thousand Villages within the Fair Trade Movement," in A. E. Weaver, ed., *A Table of Sharing: Mennonite Central Committee and the Expanding Networks of Mennonite Identity* (Telford, PA: Cascadia Publishing House, 2011), 265-83.; Ten Thousand Villages, "Our History," http://www.tenthousandvillages.com/about-history/; Ashlea Ebeling, "Ten Thousand Villages Grows with Fair Trade," *Forbes* (August 20, 2009); Mennonite Central Committee, "Middle East," http://mcc.org/learn/where/middle-east; and Mennonite Central Committee, "Relief Sales," https://mcc.org/get-involved/events/relief-sales.

179. The Association of Religion Data Archives, "QuickLists: U.S. Religious Groups," http://www.thearda.com/ QL2010/.

180. Governing, "Military Active-Duty Personnel, Civilians by State," http://www.governing.com/gov-data/military-civilian-active-duty-employee-workforce-numbers-by-state.html; U.S. Census Bureau, "Population Estimates: State Totals: Vintage 2013," http://www.census.gov/popest/data/state/totals/2013/index.html; Military Bases.com, "Virginia Military Bases," http://militarybases.com/virginia/; James Joyner, "Geography and the American Military," *Outside the Beltway*, (August 26, 2010); and Mike Miller, "Military Pride: These States Boast the Highest Enlistment Rates in America," *Independent Journal* (November 21, 2014).

181. Virginia National Guard, "116th Infantry Brigade Combat Team to conduct change of command ceremony at Fort A. P. Hill," http://vaguard.dodlive.mil/2014/07/31/5809/; and Virginia National Guard, "Winchester infantry battalion shows off new armory," http://vko.va.ngb.army.mil/virginiaguard/newsletter/CGnewsletter2009/ VaGuard2009Newsletter_14.pdf.

Museum of the Shenandoah Valley, Winchester
OIL ON PANEL, 9" X 12," MARCH 24, 2015 (PAINTING #214).

Notes on the Paintings with Selected Commentaries by the Artist

Each caption in the book includes the title and location of the painting (in *italics*) and the medium, dimensions, date, and chronological number of each painting in the Andrei Kushnir archive for this collection of his work. An asterisk (*) indicates that this painting appeared in the "Painting the Valley: Works by Andrei Kushnir" exhibition curated by Corwyn Garman for the Museum of the Shenandoah Valley. The list below includes the page number on which the painting appears in the book, geographical and historical information about the place, and selected commentaries (in *italics*) by Andrei Kushnir.

Front Matter

2. The North Fork of the Shenandoah River at its confluence with Tumbling Run, a tributary near Fishers Hill.

4. The Shenandoah Valley and South Fork of the Shenandoah River from the Skyline Drive near Front Royal.

This painting captures the themes running through all the paintings that follow. Foremost, I was attracted to the beautiful oak tree that framed the valley below on a partly cloudy day. I also liked what seemed, through the haze, to be an industrial works in the middle-right distance. Roads led to and past that subject, and, just to the left, was a bend in the river. Fields and forests filled out the middle third of the painting, and a curtain of trees rose between them and the overlook where I stood. Everything came together—the composition and subject.

6. Oak Leaf Park, near Luray, claims to be the site of the first-known bluegrass festival in the world. Bill Clifton, a noted bluegrass musician and singer who formed the Dixie Mountain Boys in 1952, organized the festival for July 4, 1961. Performers included Mac Wiseman, a Shenandoah Valley native, the Stanley Brothers, and Bill Monroe and the Bluegrass Boys. Watermelon Park (pages 76–78), near Berryville, makes the same claim.

What drew me to this scene was that, purportedly, this was the site of the first-ever bluegrass festival in the world. I received permission from the owner of the place to paint it, as it was no longer Oak Leaf Park but a cow pasture. He told me the structure in the middle was the festival stage, where the performers played. The owner said that cows now use the structure as shade, though there were no cows on the field that day—they were behind a wooden fence at my back. The field was very deeply furrowed—some mounds of earth rising two feet up and ruts running unevenly through the entire pasture. I found a nice spot facing the stage-structure, in the mid-distance, framed by two wind-blown trees, with Massanutten Mountain as the backdrop. The site seemed to be going back to its natural, wild state as I painted, the cows mooing behind me.

10. An exhibit of Andrei Kushnir's paintings at his gallery, *American Painting*, in Washington, D.C.

13. The North Fork of the Shenandoah River, looking south-southwest from an overlook at the New Market Battlefield.

14. The South Fork of the Shenandoah River near the canoe launch at Shenandoah River/Raymond R. "Andy" Guest Jr. State Park, known locally as Andy Guest State Park. The 1,604-acre park has more than five miles of river frontage along the South Fork of the Shenandoah River as well as twenty-four-plus miles of trails for hiking, biking, and horseback riding.

16. Buchanan (pronounced "Buck-CAN-un"), located 11.5 miles south of Natural Bridge on U.S. 11 (the old Valley Turnpike or Valley Road), is the self-proclaimed southern "Gateway to the Shenandoah Valley," even as the town is located within the James River watershed rather than the Shenandoah River watershed. The town, incorporated in 1832, was the western terminus of the James River and Kanawha Canal when construction of the canal ended.

I wanted to do a painting of Buchanan, since the town calls itself the "Southern Gateway to the Shenandoah Valley." Following Jeff Everett's comment that the Wilson Warehouse is an important historic structure, I decided to get it into the painting. I kept walking toward the James River, until I found a good view of the background mountain that also included the warehouse. The backyards of the town depicted a nice image of village life on a quiet afternoon in September.

21. Rockbridge Vineyard, near Raphine, is part of the growing viticulture in the Shenandoah Valley and adjacent Piedmont region on the eastern side of the Blue Ridge Mountains. Vineyards are rapidly replacing historic apple orchards throughout the Valley, and some of the Valley's wines are now prized worldwide.

22. Opequon (pronounced "Oh-PECK-un") is the site of one of the earliest eighteenth-century settlements in the Lower (northernmost region of the) Valley.

27. View of Meems Bottom, looking toward Smith Creek from Mt. Airy, an historic property (ca. 1795) in Shenandoah County. The property was once owned as a part-time residence by the Vanderbilts, known for their extraordinary wealth during the Gilded Age, which they used to acquire some of America's grandest estates that include the Biltmore in Asheville, North Carolina, Shelburne Farms in Burlington, Vermont, and the Breakers in Newport, Rhode Island. On "Dunmore Mr. Airy" (named after Shenandoah County's original name to distinguish it from the other Mt. Airy estates in Virginia), Harold S. Vanderbilt designed and constructed many of its then-innovative agricultural buildings and became an accomplished agriculturalist. Despite having no experience prior to his tenure at Mt. Airy, Vanderbilt became the first famer outside of the Corn Belt to win the DeKalb corn-raising championship.

After obtaining permission from the owners of this property, I set up at its northern edge in such a way that the bare trees would nicely frame the scene, and I could capture the distant topography, tree-lined Mt. Airy Lane, Smith Creek, and the stone wall that surrounds this historic private property. I was amazed at the vivid-green grass, compared with the other vegetation, in late March.

28. The ubiquitous "I-house" was once so popular that the one-bay-deep and two-story-high form was added to the front of an older residence on this property, which subsequently became the rear "ell." This house is located near Hamburg, a rural hamlet in Shenandoah County, not to be confused with Hamburg in Page County, where Mauck's Meeting House (page 300) is located.

31. Living remnants of nineteenth-century "high farming" are still in evidence throughout the Valley, as seen here on Headquarters Road in Shenandoah County.

35. The blacksmith shop (left) and grist mill (right) at the historic Robert McCormick Farm, founded in the late-eighteenth century as Walnut Grove in Steeles Tavern, near Raphine. This is where son Cyrus McCormick reportedly invented the mechanical reaper in 1831, forever changing North American agriculture.

Sometimes, one view will trump all others. Here, large trees embraced both structures, complete with water wheel and creek in the foreground. Just as important, my painting spot was in the shade the entire afternoon.

36. Mennonite farms dominate much of western Rockingham County, where horse-drawn buggies are part of the rural scene.

The owners of the property facing this scene were most accommodating, allowing me to set up in their front yard and offering me a cold beer when I finished. I had one more scene to capture before darkness fell.

39. View of Page Valley and the South Fork of the Shenandoah River from the Jewel Hollow Overlook on the Skyline Drive near Luray.

40. Thanks, in part, to the efforts of Thomas Jefferson, who proclaimed its beauty to the European world of his time, Natural Bridge was designated on some lists as one of the seven natural wonders of the New World.

43. The Potomac River, looking west (upriver) from Harpers Ferry, remains one of the East Coast's most sublime views.

I was shocked to learn that Byrne Island, on the right in this painting of the Potomac River at Harpers Ferry, was once the site of an amusement park, built by the B & O Railroad for its employees. The pedestrian bridge is long gone, and the island is uninhabited. This view, from the grounds of Hilltop House, a defunct resort hotel, is especially gorgeous in the springtime.

44. The famous view of three states and the Potomac River looking east (downriver) at the railroad crossing and tunnel at Harpers Ferry, as seen from Hilltop House, an historic hotel.

47. Reflections off the South Fork of the Shenandoah River at Shenandoah River/Andy Guest State Park, near Bentonville, an unincorporated community about nine miles south of Front Royal.

49. Summertime view from the top of Shenandoah Mountain, a seventy-three-mile-long mountain ridge (4,390 feet highest elevation) in the Allegheny Mountains, which defines the westernmost border of the Shenandoah Valley.

50. Shenandoah sycamore at evensong along the South Fork of the Shenandoah River near the historic White House in Page County near Luray. Massanutten Mountain is in the background.

This is a study for a slightly larger painting, "Shenandoah Sycamore, near the White House" (see page 109, bottom). I just wanted to enjoy the scene of the sycamore hanging over the Shenandoah River, on a late-autumn afternoon, as long as I could!

53. A boat landing near Shenandoah River/Andy Guest State Park near Bentonville in Warren County.

55. The well-known overlook from Afton Mountain and Rockfish Gap (1,903 feet elevation), where the Skyline Drive and Blue Ridge Parkway intersect at U.S. 250 and Interstate 64 east of Waynesboro.

The temperature was reported to reach 100 degrees Fahrenheit the day I created this small painting. Enough said.

56. The North Fork of the Shenandoah River at Red Banks between Edinburg and Mount Jackson.

This location was pointed out to me by Jeff Everett, who at one time lived nearby. The North Fork of the Shenandoah is crossed by a low, concrete bridge at this site on VA 698. Because of the wonderful view (looking to the north and east), with very little crossing traffic, it made an ideal place to create a larger scale painting. I made several small studies on the first day, as is my usual practice before beginning a large work. This allows me to "learn" the landscape, and it also helps in planning the larger painting's design.

I attached a bar to the back of the large canvas for ease of transporting it to and from the car and used a heavier, aluminum tripod to hold the canvas during painting. On the first day, while I was "laying in" the sky, a kind lady from the farmhouse just on the other side of the bridge came by and made a most-generous offer: Handing me her cell phone, she promised to spell me and stand by the painting whenever I needed a break.

This wonderful woman, an artist herself, and her husband were longtime residents of the area and, without hesitation, accepted me working in her "neck of the woods." She even took several photographs as I painted. During the days that I worked on the painting, she and various neighbors occasionally checked on me, brought refreshments, and offered encouragement and friendship. I felt most welcome.

62. Unforgettable views of the Shenandoah Valley and South Fork of the Shenandoah River from the Skyline Drive during peak autumn foliage, as seen from Gooney Run Overlook (top) and the Visitor's Center at Dickey Ridge (bottom) near Front Royal.

69. Looking downriver on the Potomac towards Harpers Ferry, from Sandy Hook, Maryland.

This is not a traditional view of Harpers Ferry, but it has spectacular scenic and historic elements. I loved the fact that one can still make out the spire of St. Peter's Catholic Church, up on the hill across the river, and the ruins of the former railroad trestle pilings, crossing the Shenandoah side where the Shenandoah meets the Potomac. Standing alongside the C&O Canal in Maryland from across the river and observing the scene on a luminous spring day, it was easy to be inspired.

70. Looking downriver on the Shenandoah towards Harpers Ferry and St. Peter's Catholic Church, from Jefferson Rock. Construction of this Gothic Revival church in Lower Town began in 1830 and was consecrated three years later on May 3, 1833.

71. Looking downriver at the Shenandoah River from beneath the U.S. 340 bridge at Harpers Ferry.

72. Thoroughbred horse racing is a year-round event at Charles Town Race Track, which opened on December 2, 1933, and became the Hollywood Casino at Charles Town Races in 1997.

73. The original deed for Edge Hill Cemetery in Charles Town was recorded on August 9, 1858. During the Civil War, 184 Confederate soldiers were buried in the military section pictured here, many of them killed at nearby battles at Antietam (1862) and Cameron's Depot, also known as Summit Point (1864).

74. The Rainbow Road Club in Rippon, West Virginia, on the Virginia state line, has long been popular with locals. It is also the site of a few unforgettable scenes from the movie *Sweet Dreams* (1985), about Country Music Hall of Fame singer Patsy Cline, from nearby Winchester, who fell in love here on the dance floor and parking lot with future husband Charlie. Originally called the Old Orchard Inn, local legend persists that Cline performed here during her lifetime, while the original Rainbow Inn—a documented haunt of Patsy's—was located near Winchester before it was torn down during the late 1950s.

75. The historic post office in the unincorporated town of Gaylord, just south of the Virginia/West Virginia line in Clarke County, operated from 1880–1956. The post office was originally located along the tracks of the Shenandoah Valley Railroad until it was moved to its current location during the 1940s.

On U.S. 340 in Clarke County, Virginia, just south of the Rainbow Road Club in Rippon, West Virginia, is this little historic post office building. You would miss it if you blinked. I felt touched by this tiny building, and could not resist painting it. At least this painting might survive, if the building should fall apart!

76–77. Watermelon Park and Campground, along VA 621 near Berryville in Clarke County, claims to be the site of the first Bluegrass Festival in the world, held here on August 10, 1960. Ever since, some of the greatest country and bluegrass musicians have played here, including Johnny Cash, Merle Haggard, Del McCowry, Bill Monroe, Ray Price, Earl Scruggs and Lester Flatt, and the Statler Brothers. Interestingly, Oak Leaf Park (page 6) near Luray makes the same claim.

78. Private property along the Shenandoah River just north of Watermelon Park near Berryville.

The "Private Property" sign in the lower-left corner almost begged me to paint this view, which can be enjoyed by everyone who looks at it.

79. The view of Clarke County from Bears Den along the Appalachian Trail (AT) in the Blue Ridge Mountains. Bears Den was first built in 1933 as a private summer retreat. In 1984, the property was purchased by the Potomac Appalachian Trail Club and sold soon thereafter to the Appalachian Trail Club for use as a hostel for hikers. This particular section of the AT is known for its "roller coaster" (up and down) character.

I arrived at this little park just as the sun was about to set and rushed to the outcropping of rocks from which this view is painted. The tourists surrounding me, most with cameras, seemed surprised to find someone capturing the view the old-fashioned way!

80. Winter evening along the Shenandoah River in Clarke County, looking upriver.

81. The Shenandoah River, looking upriver at Hardin Island, situated between Treasure Island and Bethel in Warren and Clarke Counties, respectively.

82. Wintertime view of Clarke County and the Shenandoah River from the top of Blue Ball, a mountain (1,070 feet elevation) near Ashby Gap between Poplartree Hollow and Hardin Island.

This view from the top of a mountain named "The Blue Ball" was painted on a very cold (temperature in the 20s Fahrenheit) and very windy January day. The wind was so extreme that the kind owner of the property lent me a balaclava to cover my face. Windy conditions are the most stressful to paint under, as one has to hold tightly to the brushes and weight down the palette, so it isn't blown away. The owner of the site also told me that this was the best time to paint from this spot, as a family of rattlesnakes, in hibernation at the time, has lived for generations under the rocks upon which I stood.

83. Some of the Lower Valley's most historic sites are located in or near the small village of Millwood: the Burwell-Morgan Mill (1785), Old Chapel (1793), Carter Hall (1792) of Project HOPE fame, Long Branch (1811), and River House or Ferry Farm (ca. 1820), all of them listed on the Virginia Landmarks Register and National Register of Historic Places.

84. Two riders enjoy an outing at the Blandy Experimental Farm, a property listed on the Virginia Landmarks Register and National Register of Historic Places near White Post that was once part of, but is now adjacent to, The Tuleyries, a private antebellum estate (1833) that was listed on the Virginia Landmarks Register in 1971 and the National Register of Historic Places in 1972.

85. Three non-native weeping willows adorn Blandy Experimental Farm, where exotic vegetation intermingles with native species on this bucolic landscape. In 1986, the 172-acre Orland E. White Arboretum here was designated the State Arboretum of Virginia.

86. Side entrance to the brick slave quarters aptly known as the Quarters Building at Blandy Experimental Farm. In 1926, Graham F. Blandy bequeathed a 712-acre portion of his estate, The Tuleyries (ca. 1833), to the University of Virginia to educate "boys farming in the various branches."

87. Once a slave quarters, the Quarters Building was enlarged and converted into laboratories and housing for Blandy Experimental Farm.

88. White Post is a deeply historic, unincorporated town named after the "White Post" at the intersection of White Post Road and Berrys Ferry Road in Clarke County, which originally pointed settlers to Greenway Court (1748), Lord Proprietor Thomas Fairfax's estate and hunting lodge (page 286). According to locals, the original signpost was destroyed numerous times by drunken drivers. The White Post Historic District (1983) now encompasses twenty-three contributing buildings. One of the most famous businesses in White Post is White Post Restorations, founded in 1940 and still managed by the same family. It is known worldwide as a leading restorer of antique classic cars.

89. For more than fifty years, Dinosaur Land has been a popular roadside attraction at Double Toll Gate, south of White Post. Joseph Geraci, the founder, reportedly was inspired by fiberglass dinosaurs at a putt-putt golf course in Florida. The enterprise today features more than sixty prehistoric creatures form the Mesozoic era.

I had great fun painting the fighting dinosaurs and the little one next to the green sign on one spring evening, as cars whizzed past the parking lot of this ol' time tourist attraction at Double Toll Gate, at the intersection of U.S. 340 and U.S. 522. A few weeks later, my wife and I took our three little granddaughters there, and they LOVED it! Many more dinosaurs lurked inside the park, as well as a giant gorilla and shark. If you take your kids to this retro park, they will surely remember it for the rest of their lives.

90–91. Evening landscapes of Front Royal.

I had gotten in touch with the owner of this property before coming here, as it had a great view of the bridge that leads into Front Royal with the interesting topography of the low fields next to the Shenandoah River. The best view was from the upstairs balcony of the house. When I arrived, the owner wasn't home. When I called, he said he was delayed and gave me permission to crawl into an upstairs window to get to the balcony! This is the resulting painting, as well as the two pastoral scenes on the preceding page. He arrived as I was finishing up, and I included his truck in this painting of the bridge.

92. Campground along the North Fork of the Shenandoah River in Front Royal.

93. Riverton in Front Royal is where the North and South Forks of the Shenandoah River merge into the Main Stem, which finds its confluence with the Potomac River at Harpers Ferry.

I wanted to paint the exact spot where the North and South Forks of the Shenandoah River joined. A neighborhood dog barked ferociously the entire time I worked on this painting, which was very unnerving and caused me to look continually over my shoulder.

94–95. Looking upriver (left) and downriver (right) from a boat landing in Front Royal.

As evening fell anglers began to appear. By the time it was dark, the shores and pier were crowded! I was the only person not holding a fishing pole.

96. Spelunker's Restaurant is known for its famous frozen custard and cavern burgers, the latter a reference to Skyline Caverns on the south side of town.

Spelunker's is my favorite burger joint in the Valley.

97. Front Royal, founded in 1788, is the county seat of Warren County and a northern gateway town to Shenandoah National Park and the Skyline Drive. More than 400 buildings contribute to the Front Royal Historic District, listed on the Virginia Landmarks Register and the National Register of Historic Places. The Warren County Courthouse, built in 1935–1936 to replace the original courthouse built in 1836, is part of the Front Royal Historic District and is individually listed in the aforementioned historic registers. In front are a Confederate Monument, dedicated in 1911, and an obelisk honoring veterans from World Wars I and II. Front Royal was called "Helltown" during the colonial period and still maintains a frontier mentalité, despite increasing gentrification of the northern Shenandoah Valley as a result of its proximity to the ever-spreading Washington, D.C., metropolitan area.

98. The Pioneer Motel in Front Royal, now called the Parkside Inn, evokes a sense of the past and present in its appeal to the automobile tourist.

99. Detrick is an unincorporated community on VA 678 in Shenandoah County's Fort Valley. Fort Valley lies between the North and South Forks of the Shenandoah River, bounded on each side by parallel ridges of the Blue Ridge and Massanutten Mountains.

100. A prototypical small-scale beef cattle operation in Fort Valley, near Dilbeck (794 feet elevation).

101. Dry Run Christian Church (ca. 1921) is located north of Detrick on VA 678 in Fort Valley.

I just had to paint this little church—a classic Valley scene. Its unadulterated form, bucolic setting, and non-denominational structure brings to mind the gospel classic, "Give Me That Old-Time Religion" (1873).

102–103. The sinuous character of the South Fork of the Shenandoah River is on display near Shenandoah River/Andy Guest State Park near Bentonville. Locally, these "oxbows" or entrenched stream meanders are called "bends."

The top painting on page 102 is the study for the larger painting "South Fork of the Shenandoah River" (page 104), which is a twilight view of the same location but made several years later. After completing the large painting "The Shenandoah River," I thought I might paint a wide, horizontal view of the entire oxbow. Thus, I first made a small plein-air study (page 103, bottom) and then worked up the larger study (top). After finding a very nice view on the shore on the right side of the river, as depicted in the oxbow paintings, and after making several studies of that view, I ultimately decided I would make a large painting from the shore, "Shenandoah River Skies" (page 106, top). So many choices, so little time!

104. The South Fork of the Shenandoah River from the overlook at Shenandoah River/Andy Guest State Park.

This is one of the earliest works in the collection, painted in 2002. I am a longtime artist member of the Blue Ridge Arts Council in Front Royal, and in 2002, when picking up paintings from an exhibit there, Ms. Kym Crump, the president, told me about a new state park that had opened up about eight miles away. Upon investigating the location, I found that it included the best landscape overlook that I had ever seen. I made a small oil sketch right then and there and decided to do a series of paintings at the location. This work, painted in the autumn of 2002, was the major painting resulting from that group. I painted several oil sketches, including this painting's study (page 102, top), done on the morning prior to beginning work on the larger painting, on July 16, 2002. I would drive down to the Andy Guest State Park, eat lunch, and then work on the large painting all afternoon. I did this during the latter half of July 2002 and through August, standing on a concrete platform overlooking the scene. Once it was evening but still light, I would usually make a small evening painting. "Canoe Launch" (page 53) and "Shenandoah Shore (Breezy Day)" (page 14) were two such paintings. I would then return to Front Royal, where I took a room at a small motel near the town's edge. Usually, I could work on the large painting for only two days in a row, because it was so hot and the only protection I had on the concrete platform was my hat and sunscreen. (I do not like painting with an umbrella.) It was fun to see the painting develop, but I was glad to finish the trees on the bottom of the painting, because working on site had taken me about a month and a half of on-and-off effort. While painting, I would hear the sounds of the people drifting down the river, past me, on rubber rafts, and fishing from canoes and boats. I included a canoe with paddler before signing the painting and considering it finished.

105. This spectacular view of the South Fork of the Shenandoah River is possible only from Wildcat Ledge Trail, a difficult .2-mile trek at Shenandoah River/Andy Guest State Park.

I returned to the Andy Guest State Park in 2007 and asked the ranger at the gate whether there were some good views from higher elevations other than the overlook I had previously painted. She told me the best view was from a place called "Wildcat Ledge." I immediately knew I had to paint from a place called Wildcat Ledge! As I hauled the painting gear and canvas up the mountain on a very hot and sweaty day, the trail got smaller and denser, and I got to a place where I could see both the mountain and river in front of it. Since there were trees and vines blocking much of the view, I decided to trudge on, and no more than fifty feet later was rewarded with the spectacular view in this painting. Thomas Cole never found a finer scene, I'm sure. I worked like the devil until almost sunset to capture it all, but the reward was a most difficult trip back down the mountain, tripping on roots and rocks in the darkness, getting numerous scratches and abrasions, taking care not to get my new painting smudged.

106–107. The various views of the South Fork of the Shenandoah River at Shenandoah River/Andy Guest State Park.

As noted before, in 2004, two years after painting the large "The Shenandoah River" (page 102, bottom), I decided to paint another large piece but from the shore. I had previously found a good site and made the painting "Shenandoah River, Guest Park" (page 106, top) at the spot on September 21, 2004. A day later, I came back and made a proportionally smaller oil sketch "On the Shenandoah River" and then an evening scene, "Twilight, Shenandoah River"—both depicted on page 107—at the location on September 22. I really liked the spot and was very pumped up. I came back with the larger canvas on September 30 and worked on the large painting that afternoon and late into the afternoon of October 1. However, as can be seen from the finished painting, clouds were moving in, with rain. It rained for the next few weeks, per my recollection, and, by then, the hues in the foliage had changed, and many of the leaves had dropped. I did not return to working on the large painting until 2011, at which time, in the studio, I repainted the sky. I revamped the right foreground on the large painting in late 2012, making it more like the foreground in the studies, previously mentioned, completed on site.

108–109. Autumn views of the South Fork of the Shenandoah River and the historic White House near VA 684 in Page County near Luray.

110. The White House is a historic landmark along the South Fork of the Shenandoah River near Luray, with Massanutten Mountain in the background. This was the home of Martin Kauffman, a minister who served a Mennonite congregation in the area—reputedly using the White House as a place of worship—and sometimes preaching at nearby Mauck's Meeting House. The adjacent bridge over the South Fork served as a critical crossing for Confederate troops during the 1862 Valley Campaign.

111. The view west from Kauffmans Mill Road near the White House in Page Valley.

After driving to the bend of Kauffmans Mill Road past the historic White House, I found a beautiful scene right by the Shenandoah River. But some very large, angry dogs would not let me get out of my car, so I had to drive on. Lucky for me, just a little further, after another bend and before the road rejoined U.S. 340, I came upon this gorgeous view. So, do not lament if angry, barking dogs confront you, because you can never tell what is around the next bend.

112–113. Since its modern-day discovery on August 13, 1878, by three locals, Luray Caverns has attracted visitors from all over the world—today, around 500,000 annually—who come to see such natural underground wonders as Saracen's Tent (page 112, top), Washington Column (page 112, bottom), and Dream Lake (page 113). The caverns were designated a National Natural Landmark in 1973.

I received permission from the owners of Luray Caverns to paint in the actual cavers. This produced some challenges, as could be expected. First, the lighting was very uncertain, as the lights would normally come on when a tour group approached and go off when the group left. Second, it was difficult to depict space inside the caverns, and the stalagmites and stalactites often added to this difficulty. My recollection is that the lights stayed on continuously while I painted "Dream Lake," the work on this page, but the scene was so confusing, that I left in the handrail, which appears on the left side of the painting, to create some sense of what one might be looking at. I decided to employ the figures in the two paintings on page 102 to solve the problem of depicting space.

114–115. Morning (page 114, top), afternoon (page 114, bottom), evening (page 115, bottom), and moonrise (page 115, top) views of the South Fork of the Shenandoah River at the boat ramp in Luray.

I took full advantage of the wonderful views of the fall scenery along the Shenandoah River at this boat ramp, painting from morning til night in every direction.

116. Jewell Hollow Overlook (3,333 feet elevation) along the Skyline Drive offers spectacular views of Page County.

117. Stevens Cottage in the Town of Shenandoah (Page County), completed on May 6, 1891, served as the original office of the Shenandoah Land and Improvement Company during the Valley's railroad boom. It is listed on the Virginia Landmarks Register and National Register of Historic Places.

118. Winter twilight at a town park along the South Fork in Shenandoah. The Town of Shenandoah, one of the few Valley towns actually located along the various forks of the Shenandoah River, has historically been subject to flooding.

It was snowing as I set up and made this tiny painting in the park in the town of Shenandoah. By the time I finished, my palette was totally covered with snow. When I got to the motel room and opened the paint box where I had slid the panel upon which the painting was done, the painting looked ruined, with water drops from melting snow crystals running down all over the painting. I call this my "miracle painting," because, to my surprise, with a few strokes of the brush, the painting was perfectly reconstituted!

119. What is now known as the Town of Shenandoah in Page County was not incorporated until 1884, but the community was settled fifty years earlier, having grown up around three iron furnaces that smelted raw iron into pig iron. Known at the time as the "Pittsburgh of the Valley," the town was a locally important industrial center for the Valley until 1957, when the railroad downgraded it facilities and automobile traffic become more commonplace. The Shenandoah Valley Railroad, which later became the Norfolk & Western, traversed Page Valley and was the last major railroad to convert to diesel engines from steam. This phenomenon attracted noted railroad photographer O. Winston Link, whose powerful black-and-white night photographs of the N&W include a number of Shenandoah Valley scenes.

A dreary, snowy, sleety day—perfect conditions for the die-hard plein-air painter!

120. (Top) Looking west at ballfields in Elkton, with Massanutten Mountain in the distance. This complex includes the home field of the Elkton Blue Sox, part of the Rockingham County Baseball League. (Bottom) Although permanent settlement in the area began around 1741 near a large lithia spring north of town, Elkton, formerly known as Conrad's Store, was officially incorporated on March 14, 1908. As elsewhere in the Valley, efforts are ongoing to revitalize the town's downtown Main Street.

Elkton might seem like a hardscrabble town, but I wanted to show its authentically charming side by making a painting of its sports fields in the sunny springtime (top) and a sense of what its Main Street might become.

121. Looking east toward the Blue Ridge Mountains from the Port Republic Cemetery, where the earliest gravestones are for Stephen Harnsbeerger (1787–1870), Matilda G. Kemper (1794–1881), and George W. Kemper, Jr. (1789–1872).

I worried about the red barn appearing in the exact center of this painting, but I could not be true to the place without using this composition, by far the best view of this memorable cemetery, high on a hill near Port Republic. It was a late afternoon I will never forget.

122. Port Republic was founded in 1802 at the confluence of the South and North Rivers, which form the South Fork of the Shenandoah River. Many mills were built in the area, the earliest in 1745. The village's location at the head of navigation influenced its development as a commercial enterprise. The Battle of Port Republic (June 9, 1862), was centered here. Today, Port Republic is a historic district on the National Register of Historic Places.

Only one word comes to mind about how I felt while making this painting—COLD!

123. Waynesboro, along the South River, one of two main tributaries of the South Fork of the Shenandoah River, was named for General Anthony Wayne of Revolutionary War and Northwest Indian War fame. It, along with Front Royal, long served as major sites for the textile industry, the environmental effects of which remain today.

After the guards at the industrial plant in Waynesboro refused to let me in, I found this better view just down the road. To get this view, I had to stand right in front of an overpass, with the wind howling through the tunnel from behind me on a twenty-degree Fahrenheit day. What do you do in such a situation? Paint fast!

124. Waynesboro (originally Waynesborough) was plotted as early as 1797, and a few buildings from this period remain, including the Plumb House and Coiner-Quesenbery House. Now centrally located between the cities of Staunton and Charlottesville along Interstate 64, Waynesboro is undergoing two kinds of development: large-scale commercial development outside corporate limits with its homogenized architecture and chain stores and preservation of its historic downtown, including the rehabilitation of the Wayne Theatre (1926), which reopened its doors in 2016 as the Wayne Theatre and Ross Performing Arts Center ("The Wayne").

125. Cowbane Prairie Natural Area Preserve, near Stuarts Draft, is an important conservation area managed jointly by the Virginia Department of Conservation and Recreation and The Nature Conservancy. Few reserves of wet and mesic prairie remain in the Valley, which makes this preserve all the more important.

After getting caught and entangled (and thus scratched up) in the brambles in the Nature Conservancy's sister site of this state-owned tract, I spent a very pleasant sunny afternoon here.

126. Sam Houston (1793–1863), who is known for his military heroics securing Texan independence from Mexico in 1836, was born nearby in a cabin on the Timber Ridge Plantation in Rockbridge County. A wayside north of Lexington, featuring a 38,000-pound monument of Texas pink granite, commemorates his birthplace.

127. Maple Hall, a Greek Revival mansion built in 1855 north of Lexington, is today a popular inn. The building is listed on the Virginia Historic Landmarks Register and National Register of Historic Places.

Portfolio II

133. Historic Williamsport, Maryland, from Riverview Cemetery. The town is located on the Potomac River at the southern terminus of Hagerstown Valley, the Maryland portion of the Ridge and Valley Physiographic Province, of which the Shenandoah Valley is also a part.

134. This is one of a number of former woolen mills in Martinsburg attributed as being the first in the nation to utilize electric power, ending New England's dominance of the textile industry.

Although there seemed to be many art spaces and thus, presumably, many local artists in Martinsburg, a reporter for the town newspaper interviewed me, emphasizing the novelty of an out-of-town artist painting Martinsburg's historic structures.

135. The former Baltimore and Ohio Railroad roundhouse and shops at Martinsburg, which replaced similar structures burned during the Civil War by legendary Confederate General Thomas J. "Stonewall" Jackson and which was the scene of the first protests by railroad workers during the Great Railroad Strike of 1877—recognized not only as the first railroad strike, but the first strike of any kind in the nation.

The subject of this painting is the railroad roundhouse on the right side of the scene, so I set up in such a way to capture the railroad setting. The left and center of the painting show the accommodations of the site to modern life: the parking lot on the left and the pedestrian walkway to the historic roundhouse structure. I could not believe how LOUD the trains were as they passed by, while I worked all afternoon on this painting.

136–137. Marker-Miller Orchards near Winchester has been in continuous operation by the same family for more than 100 consecutive years and is honored as a Century Farm by the Virginia Department of Agriculture and Consumer Services. The Lower Valley's counties of Frederick and Berkeley lead all Virginia and West Virginia counties, respectively, in apple production, and they have, historically, been one of the most prominent apple-producing districts in the nation.

138. Hopewell Friends Meeting House in Clear Brook is one of two extant historic Quaker meeting houses in Frederick County and the second-oldest Quaker house of worship in the Commonwealth.

139. The Daniel Morgan Statue adjacent to the Old Stone Presbyterian Church (1788) in Winchester. The esteemed Revolutionary War general was a congregant of the church, which is one of several extant eighteenth-century Presbyterian churches in the Valley.

You might think it is easy painting a statue, but the shadows that define its form are constantly changing. I chose to include the street in the scene, to give the image some contemporary context.

140. Gaunt's Drug Store in Winchester was an old haunt of country music singer Patsy Cline, who used to work at the soda fountain.

This painting was painted from the inside of my van during a rainy morning in Winchester. I made sure to include the cardboard cut-out of Patsy Cline (the blobs of red) standing in the front windows of Gaunt's Drug Store, where she had worked I have since learned the store has closed but hope it will be preserved, as it was full of Patsy Cline memorabilia.

141. Another one of Patsy Cline's purported haunts in downtown Winchester, the Snow White Grill was part of a group of mid-twentieth century hamburger chains located in the larger cities of the Potomac River's watershed.

142. Sarah's Glen, a garden on the Shenandoah University campus in Winchester.

Some day, I want to make a very large painting of this gorgeous garden on the grounds of Shenandoah University. It contains many interesting forms, perspectives, and colors—an irresistible challenge for any artist.

143. Spring-fed Racey Ponds at Shenandoah University in Winchester.

This scene was painted from the second-floor of Shenandoah University's Davis Hall, and it contained my favorite subject matter: trees overhanging water, in this case with an unusual foreground of shoreline geometry.

144. Shenandoah University's Health and Life Sciences Building reflects the continued growth of the university from its humble roots as a small college and conservatory of music in Dayton in the Upper Valley, having moved from there to Winchester in 1960.

145. John Handley High School in Winchester was endowed by the namesake judge from Scranton, Pennsylvania, whose generosity to a city he never lived in also resulted in the construction of the Beaux Arts Handley Library downtown.

146. The Triangle Diner, under renovation, in Winchester is one of the few extant Virginia diners, which are more commonplace north of the Potomac River in the great Northeast megalopolis with its plethora of factory towns. The Triangle Diner was built in Elizabeth, New Jersey, in 1948 by the Jerry O'Mahony Diner Company, which at one time was the largest manufacturer of dining cars in the U.S.

147. Amherst Diner, now Lynette and Jerri's Diner, in Winchester. Unlike the Triangle Diner, which was a prefabricated dining car frequently seen in Northern factory towns, the Amherst Diner is a bricks-and-mortar concern that is more lunch counter than diner.

This painting is all about space and angles.

148. The village of Opequon is situated along its namesake creek and grew out of a second-quarter of the eighteenth-century Scots-Irish settlement.

The carving out of forms, with paint, made this scene challenging. While I wanted to get to the beautiful, leafless tree with hanging buckeyes on the left, I felt that I first needed to solve the accurate depiction of the crossroads, with the low bridge and the rectangular church sign facing the road. I enjoyed the afternoon solving these puzzles.

149. Front view of Belle Grove Plantation, a National Historic Landmark and property of the National Trust for Historic Preservation on the site of the Battle of Cedar Creek (October 19, 1864).

150. These railroad tracks at Strasburg once belonged to the Manassas Gap Railroad, one of four antebellum railroads to service the Shenandoah Valley. Signal Knob (2,106 feet elevation) is the northern peak of Massunutten Mountain.

151. The building that once served as the Strasburg Railroad Depot for the Southern Railway was originally built as the Strasburg Stone and Earthenware Manufacturing Company and has served as the Strasburg Museum since 1970. Strasburg was called "Pot Town," due to the influence of its pottery industry, and the pieces once produced here are highly sought after by antique collectors today.

152. Originally built as a hospital and operated since 1915 as a hotel, Hotel Strasburg was one of several historic and cultural attractions in Strasburg and nearby Middletown operated by the late Washington banker and real estate broker Leo M. Bernstein, which included the Museum of American Presidents, Stonewall Jackson Museum at Hupp's Hill, Crystal Caverns, Strasburg Antiques Emporium, Wayside Inn, and Wayside Theater.

153. Up and down the Valley are parked ice cream and custard stands such as the Ice Cream Depot in Strasburg that have become permanent fixtures, even as most only operate in the warmer months of the year.

154. Autumn on the North Fork of the Shenandoah River south of Strasburg. Horses have long been a part of life in the Valley, whether for work or sport.

155. The North Fork of the Shenandoah River at its confluence with Tumbling Run, a tributary near Fishers Hill.

156. Wintertime view of Signal Knob at the northern terminus of Massanutten Mountain and the North Fork of the Shenandoah River near Tumbling Run.

157. The linearity of Massanutten Mountain—a characteristic of mountain ranges in the Ridge and Valley Physiographic Province—is on display near Tumbling Run and Fishers Hill.

Sometimes the painting done in the late of the day is the sweetest.

158–159. The North Fork of the Shenandoah River at Narrow Passage, located just south of Woodstock, with and without its iconic swinging bridge. Intended as an escape valve for residents marooned by flooding of the many low-water bridges over the Shenandoah River and its forks, swinging bridges are excellent for watching wildlife and as platforms for diving when the river is deep enough. The swinging bridge here is a favorite of residents and tourists alike.

I found that the addition of a few adept lines (for the bridge) and strokes of color representing people could transform a pure landscape into a genre painting. On another occasion in the fall, I met a reporter from TV3 in Winchester while painting on the VA 55 bridge over the Shenandoah River near Strasburg. He wanted to do an interview, so I invited him to meet me at the swinging bridge near Tumbling Run. He produced a story of how I painted this work from that swinging bridge about thirty feet over the Shenandoah River. The interview (posted on March 6, 2016) can be seen on YouTube: "Andrei Kushnir Painting on the Swinging Bridge, Shenandoah River."

160. (Top) Burnshire Dam on the North Fork of the Shenandoah River, near Woodstock; (bottom) wintertime at Narrow Passage.

The winter scene in the bottom painting was painted from inside the stone building (then undergoing construction) that appears in the two paintings of Narrow Passage on Page 158. The owner of the building kindly invited me to paint from the second-floor window, so I could get this good view. After standing all day on snow and ice-covered ground, I was in heaven!

161. Spring on the North Fork of the Shenandoah River at Narrow Passage.

This view was painted from the outdoor balcony of the same stone building from which I painted the winter view on the preceding page. I felt I was capturing a quintessential Shenandoah Valley springtime scene.

162–163. Carnival rides at the Shenandoah County Fair, which have been a delight of children for generations. While the original function of county fairs was to showcase prowess in agriculture and homemaking skills, focus began to shift away exclusively from the exhibition sheds to encompass the midway after the 1893 World's Fair in Chicago cultivated public interest in traveling carnivals and their attendant sideshows.

An artist could undertake a lifetime project just painting the variety of scenes available at the Shenandoah County Fair—amusement rides, games of chance, livestock pens and barns, horse races, concert arenas, food stalls, the cast of characters who work at the fair, and the attendees. My paintings of the Shenandoah County Fair are souvenirs of one of the most fun days I have had in the Valley. I enjoyed delicious local barbecue and homemade ice cream, great exhibits, and people watching. The variety of livestock is amazing, and the owners are often nearby to offer their tales of life on the farm. My favorite exhibit area was the "poultry" building, full of clucking, quacking, squawking, screeching, and other noises of the bird variety. Upon entering for the first time, I called everyone I knew to so they could hear the cacophony! These paintings of the Shenandoah County Fair just flew off my brushes!

164. The Alms House in Shenandoah County was the last remaining alms house in Virginia still serving its original function—caring for community members in need—until it succumbed to fire on April 13, 2014.

I needed permission to paint at this site and was met by an elderly woman who then sat on the hood of a pick-up truck and read The Holy Bible. *Only the chirping of the birds and rustling of tree leaves disturbed the silence, while I set up and worked on this lovely, secluded location. I thought the site would make an excellent subject for a series of paintings, but the historic home burned down the next year. Lesson for the artist: Act NOW.*

165. Shenandoah County was, and remains, a stronghold of the Lutheran Church in the Valley. Bethel Lutheran Church near Hamburg was originally constructed in 1861 and completed in 1867 as the result of a schism with nearby Zion Lutheran Church, which dates back to 1781. The Bethel congregants were desirous of adhering to the Virginia Synod with the Zion congregants wishing to adhere to the more conservative Tennessee Synod.

Note the chicken coop to the right of the church. As I was setting up to do this painting on a Sunday morning, the pastor came out, and we chatted. He said he was going to go back and tell the congregation that an artist was painting a picture of their church that very day!

166–167. Morning (page 166, top) late-afternoon (page 166, bottom), and evening (page 167) views at Red Banks, a favorite fishing spot of locals along the North Fork of the Shenandoah River between Edinburg and Mount Jackson.

The painting on the bottom of page 166 is a study I made before beginning work on the large "Shenandoah River at Red Banks" painting, which was going to be an "afternoon" painting. I painted the top work on one especially beautiful autumn morning, having driven to the location but learning that rain was to arrive that afternoon. Thus, the exquisite clouds in this painting were the precursors to rain. The view on page 167 is the scene from the other side of the low bridge from which I painted "Shenandoah River at Red Banks."

168. Bridge over the North Fork of the Shenandoah River near Mt. Jackson.

169. Rudes Hill, the high ground on the south side of the 2,000-acre ensemble of prime farmland soils known as Meems Bottom, was the scene of two engagements—1863 and 1864—during the Civil War.

170–171. The covered bridge at Meems Bottom, on the North Fork of the Shenandoah River just north of New Market, is one of only eight extant covered bridges in Virginia, two of which are located in the Shenandoah Valley. The riparian corridor adjacent to the covered bridge is protected in perpetuity by a conservation easement held by Valley Conservation Council, the region's preeminent non-profit land trust and conservation advocacy organization.

172–173. Morning views from the overlook of the North Fork of the Shenandoah River at New Market Battlefield State Historical Park.

174. Southern Kitchen Restaurant in New Market has been serving up local favorites such as fried chicken and country ham since it opened for business in 1955.

175. Shenvalee Golf Resort in New Market commenced operations in grand fashion, with golfing legend Bobby Jones opening the first nine holes in 1927.

As evening approached, the mayflies came out—very irritating—and I was painting while being eaten alive by mosquitoes.

176. Sunset view of Massanutten Peak from the Old Valley Turnpike (Valley Road) north of Harrisonburg.

I painted this scene from a hilltop cemetery (the West Haven Memorial Gardens) on my way home one evening after a rain.

177. Designed by accomplished Staunton architect T. J. Collins and completed in 1897, the Rockingham County Courthouse is the fifth courthouse to stand

on the site since 1778, when Rockingham County was created from Augusta County. The so-called "Harrisonburg Square," surrounded by businesses on all sides and with streets radiating northeast, east, southeast, southwest, west, and northwest, may have originated in Ulster, Ireland, carried to Pennsylvania, and diffused southward and westward with migration. Indeed, the centrally located courthouse square in the counties of the South and Midwest, with its ornate edifice, is a marked departure from the New England states with their de-emphasized county government structure and asymmetrical and less commercialized town green.

I moved the historic springhouse a few feet to the right of its actual location in order to create a better perspective of the courthouse scene, just as other artists during the nineteenth century did in their renderings.

178. The Edith J. Carrier Arboretum at James Madison University has become an oasis of green surrounded by Harrisonburg's burgeoning residential and commercial developments.

179. Named after President Woodrow Wilson, who was born in Staunton, Wilson Hall at James Madison University was constructed in 1931 and is a prominent feature of the so-called Bluestone Area of campus—comprised of the original campus buildings from 1908.

180. Mount Crawford was established along the Old Philadelphia Wagon Road, later called the Valley Turnpike, then Valley Road, and now U.S. 11.

181. Like Mount Crawford, Mount Sidney is a village laid out in a linear fashion along the Valley Turnpike to service the local farming community. Some front yards were reduced when the road was widened to become U.S. 11.

182. Restored to its former grandeur, the restoration of the Stonewall Jackson Hotel in downtown Staunton is an outstanding example of a private-public partnership, in which half of the $21,000,000 cost to restore the structure and build the adjacent conference center was covered by private developers and half by the City of Staunton. State and federal historic rehabilitation tax credits administered by the Virginia Department of Historic Resources and National Park Service, respectively, were utilized to help offset the developer's tax liability, ensuring that projects of this nature come to fruition.

Making a painting of the Stonewall Jackson Hotel in historic Staunton presented a challenge because of all of the various planes to depict: the different street levels, the situation of the hotel into the hillside, and the difficult visual angle of the sign atop the hotel. The eye must follow the street downward on the left side of the painting but must be directed upward on the right side of the painting.

183. Known as the "Queen City of the Shenandoah," Staunton has long been a transportation hub located at the intersection of several major roads and railroads. AMTRAK serves the city three times a week, with service to Chicago and Washington, D.C.

184. The American Shakespeare Center (top) and Zynodoa Restaurant and New Performing Arts Center, formerly the Dixie Theater (bottom), in downtown Staunton. Staunton's rebirth as a downtown destination has received local, state, and national recognition.

185. Thomas Woodrow Wilson served not only as the 28th President of the United States but as Governor of New Jersey, President of Princeton University, and a professor at Princeton, Wesleyan University, and Bryn Mawr College during his career. Together with Wilson, William Howard Taft and Teddy Roosevelt comprised the so-called "Progressive Presidents" who advocated social reforms and environmental protections, although Wilson has recently been criticized because of his segregationist optics. Wilson's birthplace stands in Staunton along with his presidential library.

186. Twin dairy barns and matching milkhouses at the Frontier Culture Museum in Staunton. The museum focuses on the cultural origins of the Valley's settlers in an open-air museum featuring historic farmhouses moved from England, Ireland, Germany, and various parts of the Valley, along with re-created American Indian and West African villages. The museum is located on a former dairy farm, which is historic in its own right, given the long history of agricultural innovation in the Valley, as evidenced by the use of cutting-edge dairy architecture that was en vogue during the second quarter of the twentieth century.

187. Augusta Farm Cooperative in Staunton is one of a number of locally owned cooperatives still operating in the Valley that endeavor to supply seed, feed, fencing, and tools to local farmers and rural landowners. In the left foreground is an abandoned poultry

house of the type used before large, concentrated animal-feeding operations dominated the poultry industry and a trend that avant-garde farmers such as nationally known Joel Salatin, of Augusta County, are bucking.

I just had to paint this site, which, to me, represented the passage of time. On a hill overlooking the modern structures of the Augusta Farm Cooperative in Staunton stood this ancient chicken coop. What a contrast!

188. View of the Shenandoah Valley from McCormick Gap Overlook on the Blue Ridge Parkway.

189. (Top) Agriculture still dominates much of the Upper Valley, such as this farm along Raphine Road, near Gibbs Falls in Rockbridge County. (Bottom) Hull's Drive-In Theater, north of Lexington, is one of two drive-ins still operating in the Valley, the other being the Family Drive-In Theatre near Stephens City in Frederick County. Hull's, built by W. C. Atkins, opened on August 6, 1950, closed in 1999, was granted non-profit status in 2000 in order to help preserve the historic landmark, and reopened in July 2000.

As I worked on the painting of Hull's Drive-In Theater (bottom), the owner of Goad's Auto Body Shop, located next door, came out and gave me a ball cap! The mechanics came by and told me they thought I was hiding prizes behind some bushes for a cable TV show. When they saw I was painting, they offered directions to other scenic places in the Valley. Such are the curious adventures of the plein-air painter.

190. Designated a National Historic Landmark—those nationally significant historic places designated by the U.S. Secretary of the Interior because they possess exceptional value or quality in illustrating or interpreting the heritage of the United States—Washington and Lee University in Lexington grew out of Augusta Academy near Greenville, which was reestablished at Timber Ridge in Rockbridge County, reestablished again west of downtown Lexington, and renamed Liberty Hall Academy before moving to its present location in Lexington and renamed Washington College. After General Robert E. Lee's tenure as its president following the Civil War, the institution was renamed Washington and Lee.

191. Designated a National Historic Landmark in 1965, the Virginia Military Institute Barracks in Lexington was designed by noted architect Alexander Jackson Davis in the Gothic Revival style and completed in 1851. It was burned by order of Union General David Hunter, and the partially destroyed structure was rebuilt thereafter.

Portfolio III

197. View of the Valley's agricultural landscapes from Oak Ridge (1,220 feet elevation), near Columbia Furnace.

198. Saint Paul's Lutheran Church in Jerome (top) and the small hamlet of Jerome (elevation 1,191 feet), as seen from Alum Springs Road (bottom).

199. (Top) Shrine Mont at Orkney Springs is a conference and retreat center owned by the Episcopal Diocese of Virginia since 1979, which encompasses an outdoor shrine built in 1925 and the Orkney Springs Hotel, the first portion of which was built in 1853 and the largest portion built in 1873. (Bottom) A small hamlet located a few miles northeast of Orkney Springs, Basye has been synonymous with Bryce's Mountain Resort (later shortened to Bryce Resort) since its establishment in 1909. A four-season resort with sprawling modern infrastructure and associated vacation homes, a few early twentieth-century buildings from the original complex are extant.

These two resort towns, one historic (top) and one modern, are hidden gems in the Shenandoah Valley that I would never have discovered but for my quest to paint in every corner of the Valley.

200–201. Views of Massanutten Mountain (left) and the Allegheny Mountains near Timberville.

These two views were painted from both sides of the road, looking in opposite (east-west) directions.

202–203. Evening views along the North Fork of the Shenandoah River in Timberville, looking west (page 202, top) and east (page 202, bottom). One of the few Valley towns located on the Shenandoah River, Timberville is situated along the "Middle Road"—what locals call the road west of the Valley Turnpike but east of the "Back Road," which flanks the eastern slope of Little North Mountain.

These three views were painted from both sides of the bridge at Timberville.

204. Entrance to the Town of Timberville over the bridge that spans the North Fork of the Shenandoah River, one of the few Shenandoah Valley towns to be situated on its namesake waterbody.

205. The Timberville Historic District has few modern intrusions and was listed in the Virginia Landmarks Register in 2012 and National Register of Historic Places in 2013.

206. A marked departure from the proliferation of chain stores in nearby Harrisonburg, Broadway's downtown, much like nearby Timberville, has defied homogenization and speaks to a bygone era when locals obtained much of their daily goods from nearby establishments rather than driving to regional shopping venues.

I chose this location in Broadway, because it included both the street and railroad tracks running parallel to it. As I worked, a local artist came by and gave me her card. Kids played around the apartment building in the middle of the painting until dinnertime, when they all went inside within seconds, before I could put them into the painting. I suddenly realized they were gone when silence descended on the scene.

207. The John Kline House in Broadway was home to the prominent Church of the Brethren preacher, who was martyred when bushwackers murdered him during the Civil War. Rockingham County trails only Lancaster County, Pennsylvania, for the largest number of Brethren congregations in the nation.

208–209. The North Fork of the Shenandoah River rises just west of the hamlet of Fulks Run in the front ranges of the Allegheny Mountains.

One would never guess from the painting of the North Fork on page 208—made on VA 259 between Fulks Run and Cootes Store at Brocks Gap (elevation 1,073 feet)—that I was positioned in a parking lot behind a restaurant! The painting on page 209 was created from one of my favorite painting sites: under a bridge, shielded from the sun, safe from rain, and unnoticed by passersby.

210–211. Originally called Mountain Valley, the village of Singers Glen (page 210) was renamed due to the printing press located here that produced hymnals, including *Harmonia Sacra* (1832), which was one of the most widely distributed and, perhaps, oldest continually used hymnal published in the nation. Succeeded by the Ruebush-Kieffer Company of Dayton, Rockingham County was the foremost publisher of seven-note scale of shape notes during the late-nineteenth century and attributed as the birthplace of both Southern Gospel and Shape-Note Singing. Supplanted by chain stores located in regional shopping hubs such as nearby Harrisonburg, the architecturally sophisticated T. Funk and Sons Store in Singers Glen (page 211) is a relic of a bygone era when general stores served local villagers and surrounding farms.

The view was taken from the front porch of the Funk General Store in Singers Glen, which appears on page 211.

212. The Singers Glen home of Mennonite Joseph Funk, who established a prominent printing press on the property that produced the acclaimed hymnbook *Harmonia Sacra* along with a number of other books containing religious songs. Funk also established a number of singing schools in the area.

I was very excited to paint in Singers Glen, the site of the home of Joseph Funk, one of the first American composers and publisher of the Harmonia Sacra, a Mennonite hymnal still used. He is sometimes called the founder of Southern Gospel music. In scoping out this charming town, I quickly identified the sites to be painted and came across Mr. Larry Gray, who, via his mother, is a descendant of the Funk side of the family. He noted that many of the residents of Singers Glen are descendants and gave me a brief history of the town. When I told him I intended to do a painting of Joseph Funk's well-marked house, he mentioned that, under the white siding of the present-day house, is the original log-cabin home. I thought that fact was interesting—much of what we see or think we know is only surface. Singers Glen is certainly a hidden gem.

213. This century-old Foursquare house is surrounded by grain elevators and railroad tracks, a mobile home park, an Exxon gas station, and (opposite) Eastern Mennonite University: a rich cultural landscape. It served as the original office of the Center for American Places, a nonprofit organization, when it was located in Harrisonburg. Founded in 1990 by George F. Thompson, the Center (renamed the Center for the Study of Place in 2007) has been one of the foremost publishers of geography, history, architecture, art, and photography books in the world.

When I parked next to this Foursquare house, the original site of George F. Thompson's renowned Center for American Places, and told the young man (who had just finished mowing the lawn) that I would like to paint his house, he asked, "Where are your ladders?" When I said I actually wanted to paint a PICTURE of the house, he said he was happy he had just cut the grass!

214. Eastern Mennonite University in Harrisonburg (bottom) and EMU's soccer fields and Massanutten Mountain (top). EMU is one of five institutions of higher education in the nation that are affiliated with the Mennonite Church USA. Not surprisingly, they are located in the counties and states that contain the greatest numbers of adherents.

215. Shenandoah Valley Livestock Sales in Harrisonburg has been in operation since 1935 and joins the long-tenured livestock auctions in Front Royal, Winchester, and Staunton as the brick-and-mortar outlets for Valley farmers to market their feeder cattle. A number of other livestock auctions, such as the one formerly north of Woodstock, are no long extant. While auction days are not quite the spectacle that they used to be before the advent of social media, they still occupy an important place in the culture of the agricultural community.

216. Dry River, a tributary of North River, at Rawley Springs, is surrounded by mature forests that include white pine, a remnant of the last Ice Age.

217. Aptly named Blue Hole is a favorite swimming hole located in the Dry River at Rawley Springs.

This local swimming hole in Rawley Springs, is difficult to get to, as you must scamper down a steep incline from a pull-off on the side of U.S. 33. A resident just past the site allowed me to walk to the Blue Hole through his property, for which I was very grateful on an incredibly hot and humid day. I could not believe people were jumping off the big rock into a little sliver of deeper water, but apparently it is safe enough. About midway into my painting, a rain shower came up, and I flipped the canvas over to protect it and waited for twenty minutes or so for the rain to stop before completing the painting.

218–219. Buck Bowman Stadium in Clover Hill is home of the Clover Hill Bucks of the Rockingham County Baseball League. This has been the Bucks' home ever since they entered league play in 1954. The rare, surviving wooden grandstand of Buck Bowman Stadium (opening night: July 1, 1954) is the crown jewel of the Rockingham County Baseball League (RCBL). The RCBL is one of the oldest continuously operating baseball leagues in the nation, having been established in 1924.

I love this baseball park and enjoyed every minute painting the infield from the seats in right field and from inside the wooden grandstand. Later that month, my wife and I attended a game here and enjoyed the nostalgic feel of the place and the people.

220. The Daniel Harrison House in Dayton is one of the oldest houses in the Valley. Traditionally dated ca.1746–1749, updates to the front facade (replacement and enlargement of windows and the door openings) during the late-nineteenth century obscure what was likely an otherwise austere appearance typical of Valley houses during the mid-eighteenth-century.

As I painted this view, an elderly lady from across the road came by and told me her husband was the last person born in this historic house.

221. Dayton Farmer's Market is a favorite among residents and visitors alike for fresh bakery items, bulk foods, meats, and locally produced handicrafts. Together with a substantial Mennonite presence among its purveyors, the market is analogous to the type commonplace in Lancaster County, Pennsylvania, whence many of the current purveyors' ancestors migrated to the Valley during the eighteenth century.

I learned long ago that, if you want to include something that might move away in a painting, to paint it immediately. Thus, after blocking in the major forms, my first brushstrokes were of the Mennonite carriage and horse. Sure enough, five minutes after painting them into the picture, they were gone.

222. The former mill pond of Silver Lake Mill (top) and the Silver Lake Mill building, historically known as Rife's Mill and, subsequently, Bowman's Mill (bottom). The previous flour mill and adjacent sawmill and miller's house were burned by General George Custer under orders of General Philip Sheridan in 1864 and replaced by the present structures shortly thereafter. The mill continued serving its original purpose, until twenty years ago, but it has been retrofitted for use as a gift shop.

As I arrived at Silver Lake Mill, rain began to fall, so I set up on the mill's back-loading area (depicted at the center of the bottom painting) and painted Silver Lake as the rainclouds lifted (the top painting). Afterwards, in the gorgeous afternoon light, I focused on capturing the mill itself, trying to depict accurately its unique beauty as well as its idyllic surroundings.

223. Pleasant View Mennonite Church near Dayton. Rockingham County and the City of Harrisonburg rank among the top-five localities in the U.S. for the number of adherents to the Mennonite Church.

As I arrived and walked to the site from which I painted this scene (the church sits on a hill and is surrounded by farmland), I could hear the pastor giving a "fire and brimstone" sermon. I noticed there were several fathers standing outside the church holding and cradling their infant children and made sure to include them into the painting. After the service, many of the older kids who had been in the church came over and watched me work. I asked them what they were going to do that day, and one responded they were going to their cousins' house for a big Sunday meal and to spend time with their families.

224. The former Ottobine Country Store, now Krossroads Kuntry Store. Daily fishing permits can be secured here on a first-come, first-serve basis for access to excellent angling on privately owned streams, but you need to rise early to be among the lucky few.

As late as the 1960s, a wooden structure that would not have been out of place during the nineteenth century stood on this spot. The current Ottobine Country Store hands out a picture of that building in a brochure. Today's combination store and gas station certainly projects a different image, but the friendly folks inside are no less welcoming than their predecessors.

225. Horse and buggy are still commonplace in the Mennonite country of Rockingham County. Skilled agriculturalists, Mennonites have historically been recruited by various national governments to settle in their midst and ply their trade. Many of the Valley's Mennonites are of Swiss-German ancestry, having immigrated to Pennsylvania and subsequently to Virginia in search of good land at a good price and the opportunity to live free of the religious persecution they experienced in their European homelands. Rockingham County, home to the largest number of Mennonite congregations in Virginia, is the most prosperous agricultural county in the Commonwealth.

Note the Mennonite horse and buggy at the extreme right in this painting.

226. Bridgewater College, located in its namesake town, is one of six colleges in the United States affiliated with the Church of the Brethren. The Brethren, along with the Mennonites, Amish, and Hutterites, are Germanic Anabaptist groups who sought freedom of worship in the New World after being persecuted in Europe for their belief in adult rather than infant baptism and pacifism.

227. Edgebriar Park, along the North River, in Bridgewater. The North River is one of two tributaries of the South Fork of the Shenandoah River.

228–229. Mossy Creek is one of Virginia's (and America's) most celebrated trout streams. Creeks like Mossy that traverse soils underlain by limestone are more productive trout fisheries than non-limestone lands, since the former are conducive to sustaining insect and crustacean populations that are critical for trout feeding. This fly-fishing-only stream offers brook, rainbow, and brown trout and is accessible to the public via a signed permit card through an arrangement with private landowners and the Virginia Department of Game and Inland Fisheries.

This portion of Mossy Creek, one of the famed trout-fishing spots in the Valley, is on private property. I received an invitation from the gracious owner to paint here after being run off another section of the creek—apparently one of the few places in the world where artists are prohibited from painting!

When I first arrived and parked my van in the public parking turn-out along the creek, I noticed a sign: "Public use of this area is for fishing only . . . all other uses are prohibited." I thought to myself that painting, being the nondestructive activity it is, certainly would not be included in the prohibition. So I crossed the pony truss bridge depicted in the painting on page 229 and found a nice spot from which I could get a good view of the creek and the surroundings. Soon, another car pulled up, and a lady and her son got out and began fishing near the bridge. I was completing my painting, when a big, white pickup truck stopped on the bridge, and a man yelled something to the lady I could not hear. She then walked over to me and said the fellow told her it was ok for her and her son to fish, but I WAS NOT ALLOWED TO PAINT HERE! I had heard of artists being protective and even secretive about their favorite painting spots, so why not anglers?

I packed up, drove to Bridgewater (where I could get a cell signal), and called the Virginia Department of Game and Inland Fisheries. I was advised that that site had been the subject of considerable negotiations with local anglers and that it would probably cause the least amount of aggravation to everyone involved if I painted at some other place along the creek. They even provided me with phone numbers of neighbors in the area who would LOVE for an artist to paint along their section of the famed creek. After leaving a few phone messages, I drove to the site of the historic Henry Miller farm, just down the road, and began a painting of the big farmstead there (page 230). In time, a van pulled up, and a man got out and asked, "Are you Andrei Kushnir?" After my recent experience, I didn't know if I should say yes or run. After acknowledging that, yes, I was Andrei, he welcomed me to paint along a stretch of Mossy Creek along his property. Thus, all turned out well, resulting in two paintings and a great story.

230. An amalgamation of Germanic and British building traditions, the architecturally refined Henry Miller Farm, south of Bridgewater in the Mossy Creek area of Augusta County, is a tangible manifestation of agricultural and industrial prosperity. In addition to purportedly accumulating 30,000 acres of land during his lifetime, Miller established Mossy Creek Iron Works during the late-eighteenth century and served as an iron master.

231. Late winter in Middlebrook, a linear village in south-central Augusta County settled during the late-eighteenth century. Bisected by Middlebrook Road, which became the Staunton-Lexington Turnpike, the route offered a more westerly connection to the two county seats than did the Valley Turnpike. The renowned Polyface Farm, owned by Joel Salatin, is located nearby, and the historic district—listed on the National Register of Historic Places in 1983—encompases 102 contributing buildings and sites.

About halfway through working on this painting in remote Middlebrook, a cold rain started to fall. I drove my van up to the spot and opened the tailgate so that it hung over the painting. While I got very wet, I was able to complete this painting, which I thought to title "The Middle of March in Middlebrook."

232–233. Like Middlebrook, Brownsburg was a linear village established during the late-eighteenth century that straddled the Staunton-Lexington Turnpike. It became a historic district on the National Register of Historic Places in 1973, with forty-two historic buildings. And a true sense of place abounds here.

I just love this little hamlet of Brownsburg! It is as close as one can get to reliving the past, with so many historic buildings.

234. The Allegheny Mountains of the Virginias, once the epicenter of healing springs on the East Coast, spawned a number of renowned resorts such as Rockbridge Alum Springs, which grew up around the springs that offered an elixir to various ailments. The dramatically situated pavilion into which the springs flow, built into the face of a cliff, instantly conveys its purpose. It is topped by a statute of Hygeia, the goddess of health in Greek and Roman mythology.

While there seemed to be no mosquitoes anywhere else at the Rockbridge Alum Springs, at the creek in front of the defunct spring house they were plentiful. I lost a lot of blood here.

235. The waterfall at Jordan's Point Park in Lexington is located on an island in the Maury River, a tributary of the James River.

236. Lee Chapel, at Washington and Lee University in Lexington, is the final resting place of Confederate General Robert E. Lee. After the Civil War, Lee served as the president of Washington College, which was subsequently renamed Washington and Lee in his honor. Buried just outside the chapel walls is Lee's trusty horse, Traveller.

237. The Virginia Military Institute in Lexington, known as the "West Point of the South," has been associated with many great military leaders since its founding in 1839, the likes of which include Generals George C. Marshall, George S. Patton, and Thomas J. "Stonewall" Jackson.

Land and Life in the Shenandoah Valley

238. View of the old Jacob Bushong Farm (1818) on the outskirts of New Market, including the forebay barn (left), old orchard (center), and restored family farmhouses and outbuildings (right). On May 15, 1864, on this farm, a makeshift Confederate army of approximately 4,090 men (under the command of Major General John C. Breckinridge who, prior to the Civil War, was the 14th Vice President of the United States, 1857–1861), defeated an organized Union force of approximately 6,275 men (under the command of

Major General Franz Siegel, who was born in Germany) and forced their retreat to Strasburg. In one of the most courageous acts of the war, 247 cadets from the Virginia Military Institute marched eighty-four miles from campus in Lexington to bolster the Confederate line in the strategic battle. To this day, VMI Cadets re-create the march each May—in period uniforms and accoutrements—to honor those 247 cadets "who served and sacrificed their lives for their institution, their state, and their nation."

241. Wintertime along the South Fork of the Shenandoah River, west of Elkton.

242. The South Fork of the Shenandoah River at Red Banks on a winter morning.

247. Blue Ball is a mountain peak (1,070 feet elevation) in the Blue Ridge Mountains adjacent to the Shenandoah River near Asbhy Gap through which settlers crossed into the Shenandoah Valley (present-day U.S. 17/50) from the Virginia Piedmont. Its unusual name bestowed on it as early as 1736, the base of this cone-shaped peak is where the road through Ashby Gap (elevation 1,029 feet) originally crossed the Shenandoah River before being subsequently realigned.

It is interesting to note that the magnificent tree in this study seems to bend in a different direction from the same tree in the larger painting (page 82). After I made this study, I decided to move my location just a bit in order to include the farm that appears in the larger work. From the new angle, the tree seems to bend the other way! Same tree, different perspective.

248. Morning view of Front Royal and the U.S. 340/522 bridge from Guard Hill Road near Riverton, where the South and North Forks merge into the Main Stem of the Shenandoah River.

251. Wintertime along the Potomac River at Berkeley Springs, west of its confluence with the Shenandoah River at Harpers Ferry.

252. A rainy day view of the Seven Bends of the North Fork of the Shenandoah River from the Woodstock Fire Lookout Tower on Massanutten Mountain (1,873 feet elevation), off VA 758. The top of the tower offers a 360° view of the Main Valley, Fort Valley, and the distant Allegheny and Blue Ridge Mountains.

After painting the 16" x 20" work depicting beautiful morning clouds and the scene at Red Banks, rain came in, so I decided to go to the Woodstock fire tower, since I knew there was a good view there, as well as a roof on the structure. However, once I got to the fire tower (via a long, crooked gravel road, running through the woods on the side of the mountain), I found company—a mother and her daughter came up the ladder to the platform to discuss the girls school issues, and a couple of hikers arrived to chat about sports! It would have been a great setting for a play. I also found that, despite the roof, the wind blew the rain all over the place. The spectacular view was shrouded in mist and clouds, but I think the painting captured the scene perfectly.

254. The White House Farm on Kauffmans Mill Road, near Luray in Page County, is located within the original 5,000-acre land grant that opened up Page Valley to the earliest European settlement, "Massanutton." Martin Kauffman came here during the early 1730s from his previous home in Lancaster, Pennsylvania, and his son, Martin Kauffman II, built the Rhenish-style White House (ca. 1760) as a residence and Mennonite meeting house. It was listed on the Virginia Landmarks Register in 1977.

256. The South Fork of the Shenandoah River at Port Republic, which long served as a center of commerce at the head of navigation, where the South River and Middle Rivers merge to form the South Fork. Many a grist mill was built here as early as 1745, and the town's historic architecture remains largely intact as part of a designated historic district on the Virginia Landmarks Register and National Register of Historic Places.

258. Natural Chimneys is a popular park with a campground, pool, and hiking trails. Located along the North River near Mt. Solon in Augusta County, the rock "chimneys," for which the park is named, are as tall as 120 feet and represent some 500,000,000 years of geological work, beginning when the region was under water. Over time, what once was a cave-like landscape eroded, leaving the more resistant rock chimneys we see today. The park has also hosted, on the third Saturday of every August since 1821, an annual jousting tournament, claimed to be the oldest continuous sporting event in the nation.

261. Soaking in the warm healing waters in Berkeley Springs, West Virginia, has been a tradition since colonial times. George Washington favored the locale as early as the 1740s.

262. The Cowbane Prairie Natural Area Preserve near Stuarts Draft is a sixty-three acre preserve of outstanding examples of wet prairies, mesic prairies, and calcareous spring marshes that are rare today but were once common in the Valley. Eleven rare plants grow here.

266. Looking toward the Piedmont (eastern) side of the Blue Ridge Mountains from the Blue Ridge Parkway at Rockfish Gap (1,903 feet elevation).

270. Signal Knob (2,106 feet elevation) in Shenandoah and Warren Counties is the northernmost peak of Massanutten Mountain and part of the George Washington National Forest. Hikers in the Massanutten Range enjoy trails known to be less crowded than those in Shenandoah National Park. Expansive views of the Valley and the Town of Strasburg await those who hike to the peak.

This painting, from a wide bridge on VA 55 over the Shenandoah's North Fork, was a hair-raising experience. Huge trucks sped by only a few feet away. I finished this somewhat serene-looking painting on site but vowed never to take this kind of risk again.

273. View of Massanutten Mountain (2,690 feet elevation) near Tumbling Run, a tributary of the North Fork of the Shenandoah River south of Strasburg.

274. A distant view of Massanutten Mountain and the Shenandoah Valley, as seen from the Skyline Drive.

277 The Henrietta Furnace at Shenandoah Alum Springs, a popular summer resort featuring healing springs founded in 1853 near Basye (page 199, bottom), was first built in 1852 by Samuel and John Myers and destroyed in 1864 during the Civil War. It stands today as it did then, in this condition. Pig-iron furnaces and forges were key drivers of the Valley's industrial prowess before and after the Civil War, but the Valley's iron industry, like the Commonwealth's, did not extend far into the twentieth century.

278. The two-story Thomas Hudson House, likely built ca. 1800 by Henry Baughman, was executed in native limestone and remains virtually unchanged since it was erected. Situated among the first ridges of the Allegheny Mountains to the west, the landscape around Hudson Cross Roads offers a true glimpse into the past in which little has changed visually from the nineteenth century.

281. Truck stops along I-81, such as the one here at Exit 200 near Fairfield, juxtapose modern, homogeneous architecture against the serene Blue Ridge Mountains in the background.

282. The Shenandoah Valley and South Fork of the Shenandoah River from Gooney Run Overlook on the Skyline Drive near Front Royal.

285. Ferry Hill Plantation, near Sharpsburg, Maryland, overlooks the Potomac River, with a view toward Shepherdstown, West Virginia. This area was a major crossing by ferry since 1775 for people, especially German migrants from the Southeastern Pennsylvania region, wanting to settle in the Shenandoah Valley. Ferry Hill was the boyhood home of Henry Kyd Douglas, youngest member of Confederate General Thomas J. "Stonewall" Jackson's staff and author of the acclaimed memoir *I Rode with Stonewall*, published posthumously in 1946.

286. Greenway Court, a National Historic Landmark near White Post in Clarke County, was the estate and hunting lodge of Thomas Fairfax, the largest landowner of the Shenandoah Valley in 1748, when the estate was built. The surviving buildings on the site include a replacement red-brick house and a limestone land office, from which George Washington began his early career as a surveyor.

289. The pastures, barns, and fences of Long Branch Plantation, a former wheat plantation named after Long Branch stream in Millwood, are part of a present-day, 400-acre private preserve that features the 1811 mansion built by owner Robert Carter Burwell's slaves. Burwell incorporated the classical principles of design recommended by Benjamin Henry Latrobe, architect of the U.S. Capitol in Washington, D.C.

293. Commercial sprawl along U.S. 33 in Harrisonburg is ongoing, with no end in sight. Such development became possible after Interstate 81 opened a 7.5-mile segment in the city in 1963, when the city's population was approximately 12,500, compared to more than 53,000 today. Harrisonburg is now the largest city in the Valley and the twelfth-largest city in Virginia, and the population of the Harrisonburg, Virginia, Metropolitan Statistical Area now exceeds 130,000.

294. View of the Potomac River from the Bavarian Inn in Shepherdstown, West Virginia. The earliest Euro-American immigration into the Shenandoah

Valley from the north came by way of two ferry crossings: one at Pack Horse Ford near this site and the other at Ferry Hill (page 285).

297. The Valley Turnpike and Bethlehem Stone Church at Tenth Legion south of New Market. The church (far right), built in 1845, is the oldest stone church in Rockingham County, and it replaced an earlier Quaker meeting house. Reportedly, the church also served as a temporary hospital during the Civil War. The neo-Gothic brick building (1952) now serves as the primary edifice for the fellowship. The stone structure was listed on the National Register of Historic Places in 1985.

300. Mennonites built meeting houses in the frontier lands of present-day Page County as early as 1740. Among the few survivors is Mauck's Meeting House (also known as Mill Creek Church) in Hamburg, near Luray. Built of rare planked-log construction and featuring a central chimney and both half and full notching, the structure was added to the National Register of Historic Places in 1976.

304. The founders of Augusta Stone Presbyterian Church near Fort Defiance, established in 1790, were Scots-Irish pioneers who first landed in America at historic New Castle, Delaware, along the Delaware River. The impressive stone building honored today was completed in 1749, making it the oldest Presbyterian house of worship in continuous use in Virginia. Its first minister, Rev. John Craig, who was born in Donegore, County Antrim, Ireland, was the first ordained Presbyterian minister to settle in the Valley.

I created this painting of the church on a sparking late-autumn afternoon, which I thought was fitting for the subject. The storm that blew through the area earlier in the day really cleared the air. The structures depicted at the left of the church are of the Augusta Military Academy, which closed in 1984.

307. (Top) An original log church was built on this site in Millwood ca. 1740–1750. The current stone church, known as Old Chapel, was completed in 1793, making it the oldest Episcopal house of worship still in use west of the Blue Ridge Mountains. It was listed on the National Register of Places in 1973. (Bottom) During the mid-1800s, Staunton attracted a number of Jewish merchants from present-day Germany and Prussia. The Temple House of Israel, still active in downtown Staunton, was founded in 1876, and the current Moorish Revival synagogue, designed by noted architect T. J. Collins, was built in 1925.

310. Picnicking in the Marker-Miller Orchards near Winchester, which remains a center for apple storage and processing in the Valley. The Shenandoah Valley was one of the nation's—and certainly Virginia's—premier apple growing regions as early as the third quarter of the nineteenth century, and today Virginia ranks sixth among apple-producing states, with nearly half of the state's production coming from Frederick County alone, of which Winchester is the county seat. The annual Apple Blossom Festival in Winchester during the first weekend of May is a major regional event.

315. (Top) A wood-framed Pennsylvania Bank Barn, part of the historic Bushong Farm on the grounds of New Market Battlefield. (Bottom) A stone Pennsylvania Barn on the Lick Run Plantation (1770) near Bedington in Berkeley County, West Virginia.

316. The Edinburg (or Grandstaff) Mill, an architectural gem since its construction in 1848 by George Grandstaff, was barely saved from a fire during Union General Philip Sheridan's "Burning of the Valley" campaign in 1864 and barely saved from neglect, until a "Save the Mill" campaign, begun in 2000, helped restore the amazing structure. The mill was listed on the National Register of Historic Places in 1979.

320. Although not the equivalent of Route 66, Route 11 (U.S. 11) has its own automobile culture. Taking advantage of that iconography, a fabulous recipe, and an old-style, kettle-cooked technique, Route 11 Potato Chips cooked up its first batch of salted chips in 1992. The original store and kitchen were located in an old feedstore in Middletown, but the small business became so popular it expanded and moved its factory to Mt. Jackson in 2008.

324. The Standard Lime and Stone Quarry, located along the Shenandoah River near Millville, south of Harpers Ferry, long mined crushed limestone here and produced furnace lime, lime flux, and rock wool. A planned town emerged here, including housing for large number of Italian-American workers.

326. In 1987, Coors Brewing, of Golden, Colorado, built its first brewery east of the Rocky Mountains here in Elkton, at the base of the Blue Ridge Mountains, along the South Fork of the Shenandoah River, where Coors beer was blended, packaged, and distributed to Eastern markets. A central location in the East, close access to Interstate 81, and a reliable source of quality water all contributed to Coors locating the plant here. MillerCoors assumed ownership after a merger in 2008.

After being denied entrance to the brewery by the guards, I painted this view from the side of the road. I was determined to capture a surprising industry in the Valley and to paint an homage to one of my favorite beverages.

328. The village of Brownsburg was listed as a historic district in the National Register of Historic Places in 1973, due to the integrity of its predominantly nineteenth-century architecture. The Brownsburg Academy, a private Presbyterian school for young men (1850–1877), is among the town's most prized edifices.

331. (Top) In 1882, former slaves and free blacks of the Berryville area built this grade school, the Josephine City School, which ceased being used for educational purposes in 1971 but was completely renovated in 2002 to make way, in 2003, for it becoming Clarke County African American Cultural Center, the first museum devoted to the history of Clarke County's African-American community. Individually listed in 1995 on the National Register of Historic Places, it is also part of the forty-acre Josephine City Historic District. (Bottom) Founded in Staunton in 1842 as Augusta Female Seminary, the fifty-five acre school became Mary Baldwin College in 1923 and Mary Baldwin University in 2016. Mary Baldwin is the oldest institution of higher education for women in the U.S. affiliated with the Presbyterian Church, and its affiliation with the American Shakespeare Center and Heifetz International Music Institute in Staunton is well-known.

334. The Wayside Inn, in Middletown, has been serving the public along the Valley Turnpike (U.S. 11) since 1797. Today, the inn includes twenty-two guest rooms and suites, a popular tavern, and formal dining.

337. L'Auberge Provençale Bed and Breakfast, near White Post, is the creation of innkeeper Celeste Borel and Chef Alain Borel. For more than thirty years, it has been regarded as one of Virginia's finest restaurants and inns.

338. Mrs. Rowe's Restaurant and Bakery in Staunton has been a favorite roadside eatery for locals and travelers alike since 1947. Founded by the late Mildred Rowe, the restaurant serves around a half-million customers a year, all of whom enjoy the home-style cooking and amazing pies.

340. Willow Shade was built in 1851 near Gore in Frederick County. It was the childhood home of renowned novelist Willa Cather (1873–1947) before her family moved to Red Cloud, Nebraska in 1883. The house was listed on the Virginia Landmarks Register in 1989 and the National Register of Historic Places in 1990.

343. Mount Airy (also known as the Major James Crawford House), built in Verona ca. 1840, today is known as the Grandma Moses House, in honor of the American artist and her husband, Thomas Salmon Moses, who owned the house from 1901–1902. Although it was listed on the Virginia Landmarks Register and the National Register of Historic Places in 2012, it requires significant restoration.

This property is not open to the public, and I had to have an Augusta County supervisor take me here. The site contains a beautiful overlook view of neighboring farmland, much like that which Grandma Moses liked to paint. I couldn't resist painting that view myself, before a terrific thunderstorm chased me away from the scene.

344. (Top) Four stools comprise the Statler Brothers Tribute Monument in the historic Wharf Area of Staunton. The Statler Brothers, a revered vocal quartet from Staunton (1955–2002), won Top Vocal Group of the Year awards in 1972–1980 and 1984, and they were inducted into the Gospel Hall of Fame in 2007 and the Country Music Hall of Fame in 2008. (Bottom) Located in a working-class neighborhood in Winchester, on 608 Kent Street, country music legend Patsy Cline lived in this two-story house from 1948–1957. In 2005, it was listed on the Virginia Landmarks Register and National Register of Historic Places.

I wanted to make a painting of the Patsy Cline House on Kent Street in Winchester so decided to paint the entire block, for several reasons: The house will not likely change in the distant future (because of Patsy's fame), but the other houses (and the entire ambiance of the street) may well look different someday; and I wanted to get the maroon-colored motorcycle on the porch of the house next door on the left into the painting—a fitting symbol of the character of the place.

347. (Top) Dating back to 1963, the Shenandoah Valley Music Festival in historic Orkney Springs (page 199, top) has brought a wide variety of summer music concerts to the Shenandoah Valley, from chamber music and symphonic concerts to bluegrass, county, folk, and soul. The main section of the Orkney Springs Hotel, historically known as the Virginia House, is a cavernous 66,000 square feet (or 1.5 acres). Built in 1873 and restored in 1987, it was listed on the Virginia Landmark Register in 1975 and the National Register of Historic Places in 1976. (Bottom) The first season for the Lime Kiln Theater in Lexington was 1984, and ever since fabulous musical and theatrical events have taken place in this former limestone quarry with excellent acoustics.

348. In 1886, the Shenandoah County Agricultural Society organized a fair for October 4–7, 1887, to showcase the Valley's agricultural bounty and homemaking skills. It is part of a larger county-fair tradition in the region that contains four of Virginia's top-five agricultural counties.

352. The rich history of the Battle of New Market (May 15, 1864) is recorded and presented at New Market Battlefield State Historical Park and Virginia Museum of the Civil War (formerly the VMI Hall of Valor). Casualties and losses were 841 Union (13.4 percent) and 531 Confederate (13.0 percent); of the 247 teenage cadets from Virginia Military Institute who fought here, ten were killed and thirty-seven were wounded (19.0 percent).

358. Watermelon Park and Campground, along VA 621 near Berryville in Clarke County.

362. Gypsy Hill Park in Staunton began as the site of the community's water supply, which was fed by several nearby springs. Over time, the park was enlarged to its current 214 acres, and it is one of Staunton's most treasured public assets. During times of racial segregation, Staunton in 1946 developed a second park (Montgomery Hall Park) on a former estate for exclusive use by the African-American community. That park was finally honored in 2015 with a formal dedication of a highway marker from the Virginia Department of Historic Resources.

384. The Museum of the Shenandoah Valley in Winchester sits on land (214 acres) originally claimed by James Wood, founder of Winchester in 1735. The 50,000-square-foot building, designed in 2005 by acclaimed architect Michael Graves, provides multiple state-of-the-art spaces in which the art, history, and culture of the Valley are beautifully presented.

I will always be honored to have had a solo exhibition of my paintings of the Valley at the Museum of the Shenandoah Valley, one of the region's great venues.

408. The Confederate Soldiers Monument on East Main Street in Luray, sculpted by the renowned Herbert Barbee, was unveiled on July 21, 1898. Many statues and memorials honoring the Confederacy, here and throughout the South, were erected at this period of time.

412. Self-portrait of the artist.

Even in the cold, painting en plein air *is a gift.*

*Luray in April**

OIL ON PANEL, 8" X 12," APRIL 26, 2015 (PAINTING #224).

Artist's Acknowledgments

The Shenandoah Valley always triggered my visual inspiration, going back to when I started painting in oils in 1980. Views of the Valley from the Skyline Drive were among my earliest paintings. I loved the long views of the fields and forests, with Massanutten Mountain and the North Mountains in the background, a perfect foil for creating hazy Valley views and colorful sunsets. After joining and exhibiting with the Front Royal Blue Ridge Arts Council during the 1990s, I learned of the new Shenandoah River/Raymond R. "Andy" Guest Jr. State Park, and so I started an in-depth exploration of the banks of the river's South Fork and created the first landscapes in this collection.

It was only after meeting with and listening to Jeffrey Everett that I began exploring a richer visual subject—actually going into the Valley to capture more than surface impressions and scenic views of the Shenandoah River and Valley. This step took quite a bit of thought. I had loved standing along the beautiful river or high in the bordering mountains, surrounded by nature, and creating landscape paintings of scenery rivaling that depicted by artists from the Hudson River School. But Jeff, who grew up in the Valley, inflamed my curiosity by talking of places with names such as Red Banks, Meems Bottom, Singers Glen, and Rudes Hill, and he enticed me further by describing the delightful meals one could sample at eateries like the Southern Kitchen in New Market, Mrs. Rowe's in Staunton, and the Amherst Diner in Winchester. After standing all day on a windy hill in the Blue Ridge Mountains, what could sound better?

And so I began painting views along the North Fork of the Shenandoah, at first within sight of the river but quickly including images of the hamlets, bridges, farm buildings, graveyards, cities, natural wonders, schools, churches, roads, and restaurants from one end of the Valley to the other. Jeff often provided specific locations, maps, and contextual material, which helped me understand the sites. Upon sampling the variety of landscapes and subject matter, I realized how artistically challenging these new places would be. Here was a world in many instances untouched by the twenty-first century, and now I had the opportunity not only to interpret them as an artist, but to record in action and, in some cases, mid-transformation.

Meeting historian Warren Hofstra was another momentous development. He provided even more exotic-sounding locations to seek out—Watermelon Park, Blue Ball Mountain, Blandy Farm, Bears Den, and White Post. I began reading his books about the fascinating history and geography of the Valley (for instance, how Indians, who wanted to attack another group south of Virginia, routinely obtained writs—passes—to travel through European settled areas to do it!). I became reacquainted with the music of Patsy Cline, the expressive singer from Winchester. Warren's love of and respect for the Valley and its history are so deep and profound, I am honored that he sensed my enthusiastic artistic engagement with the Valley enough to write the introductory essay to this book.

William M. S. Rassmussen, the Lead Curator of the Virginia Historical Society with whom I became acquainted during the "Painted History" exhibition of my works previously held at that venerable institution in Richmond and who had contributed to the catalog memorializing that exhibit, provided welcomed encouragement, especially to my seeking out places in the Valley that, perhaps, had not recently received much attention by artists, the media, and even the local populace. His previous published work, *The Virginia Landscape*, with co-author James C. Kelly (Howell Press, 2000), is still the seminal work about landscape painting in Virginia, and, thus, I am deeply honored by his contribution to this project.

Finally, through Warren, I met George F. Thompson, a unique and acclaimed publisher whose mission in life is to bring to publication books of lasting value about the spaces and places of the world that surround us, from the everyday to the wondrous. From the get-go, George completely understood that this project could become a major book, and he added his own recommendations for places to paint. I am forever grateful that he steadfastly maintained that this book is, first and foremost, an artist's exploration of the natural and cultural landscapes of the Shenandoah Valley, and his talent in sequencing the paintings is evident on every page.

As the book took its final shape and George recommended the addition of an afterword, Warren Hofstra made it possible to enlist Edward Ayers, the esteemed historian and author and the former president of the University of Richmond, to write the concluding essay. His love of the Valley and insights into its lingering impact on those who know it offer a unique way to consider the Shenandoah Valley in our own lives, just as he shares the impact the Valley has had on his own.

One might say that I initially came to the Valley for the famed scenery but stayed for the food, music, history, and friendship of the people who inhabit this wonderful region. The idyllic, peaceful, bucolic, and mostly agrarian landscape, where village and country folks interdependently respect each other, also appealed to my Ukrainian-American roots. And so, apart from Jeff, Warren, Bill, George, and Ed, I express my deep appreciation to the many, many residents of the Shenandoah Valley who made my travels into the Valley—during a ten-year period and over many thousands of miles—more comfortable and pleasant by their friendliness and generosity. Thus, they shared the adventure with me. Notable among these folks were Kym Crump, Timothy Fitzgerald, Elwood Funkhauser, James E. Gander, Steven Glazier, Larry Gray, General William L. Hammack, Gretchen Hazard, Judy and Don Hensley, William E. Huffman, Ryan Klopf, Joe Kraemer, Joseph Lukowski, Sandy and Bobby Pumphrey, Ernesto Santiago, Wanda and Peter Shoemaker, Michael Snyder, Sidney and Sara Stern, Jenni Vincent, and Anthony Widmer.

I also wish to thank Michele Martin Taylor, for her longstanding friendship and advice; Walter Jackson and Hussam Albeik, for their dedicated friendship, advice, and assistance over the years on this project and others; Mikki Soroczak, for her excellent editorial and research assistance; Purna Makaram, for his excellent copyediting and proofreading; Morgan Pfaelzer, for her cartographic skills; and David Skolkin, for his incredible book design.

Deep appreciation is extended to the following patrons and friends, whose help made the publication of this book possible: Elizabeth J. Angel; Lois E. and Michael J. Boland; Michael S. Crawmer; Patricia Coffey; M. Blair Corkran; Deirdre E. Donahue and James L. Dahlberg; Robert L. Fagan; Jeffrey S. and Christy Fulcher; Alma H. and Harry F. Gates, Jr.; Theodore Hirt; Marika Jurach and Vitalij Garber; Barbara and Kendall LePoer; Audur V. Kugajevsky; Alice M. Merrill; Kenneth L. McVearry; Christian R. and Helen M. Miles; Jakob and Charlotte H. Nielsen; Robert K. Oaks; Ronald Rosenfeld; Laura R. Rubinstein and Tamburai M'ndnge-Pfu; Lucantonio N. Salvi; John and Linda Sillin; Shelley R. Slade; Henry and Judith M. Sondheimer; Marilyn and Hugh South; Sid Stern; James B. Watts; and Brent and Katie Wiesel. Heartfelt thanks are also expressed to the following collectors who granted permission to include images of their paintings for this book: Mike and Meg Croxon; Deirdre E. Donahue and James L. Dahlberg; E. Hall and Betsy Johnstone; John and Barbara Kosogof; and Amy Gilbert and Steven Newpol.

Finally, I offer special thanks to my brothers, Walter and Anatolij Kushnir, and to Walter's late wife, Larysa, for their unending and dedicated support of this and other art projects over the years. My gratitude for their love, trust, and confidence knows no bounds.

Self-Portrait

OIL ON CANVAS, 9" X 12," JANUARY 23, 2005.

About the Author and the Essayists

ANDREI KUSHNIR has painted in oils since 1980, with a particular focus on the American landscape rendered *en plein air* (painting out of doors). He is particularly well known for his plein-air paintings of the Potomac River and Chesapeake and Ohio (C&O) canal, both near his home in Maryland, but he has painted throughout the United States—in particular Virginia's Shenandoah Valley and Crooked Run Valley; the shorelines of Maine, New York, Cape Hatteras, and Florida's Gulf Coast; Colorado, New Mexico, and Arizona—as well as in New Zealand, Italy, and the Netherlands. His paintings have been exhibited widely in numerous juried and invitational shows selected by curators at the Corcoran Gallery of Art, Hirshorn Museum, National Gallery of Art, and National Museum of American Art, all in Washington, D.C. Other exhibitions include the Virginia Historical Society, where he was the first living artist accorded such an exhibit; University Club, of Washington, D.C.; Taylor and Sons Fine Art, of Washington, D.C.; Rehoboth (Delaware) Art League; Museum of the Shenandoah Valley, where, in 2016, he was the first living artist accorded such an exhibit; South Florida State College Museum of Florida's Art and Culture, in Avon Park, FL; James Madison University's Duke Gallery of Fine Art; and Capitol Hill Art League, of Washington, D.C. The artist's paintings are also in the permanent collections of the Virginia Historical Society; U.S. Coast Guard; University of Maryland University College Maryland Artist Collection; Museum of Florida's Art and Culture; and District of Columbia's Commission of Arts and Humanities, among others.

Kushnir was elected a signature member of the National Oil and Acrylic Painters Society, and he is also an elected member of the Washington Society of Landscape Painters in Washington, D.C., and the Salmagundi Club, of New York City; Oil Painters of America; Miniature Painters, Sculptors and Gravers Society, of Washington, D.C., where he served as a vice president; Capitol Hill Art League; Blue Ridge Arts Council, of Front Royal, Virginia; and Alexandria and Fairfax, Virginia, Art Leagues. He has also served as an Official U.S. Coast Guard Artist.

Kushnir is the author of seven publications of his work: *Oh, Shenandoah: Paintings of the Historic Valley and River* (2016), *River Visions* (2013), *Painted Seasons* (2010), *Potomac River School*

(2009), *Painted History* (2004), *American Light, 2001* (2001), and *My River* (1999). Kushnir's paintings have also appeared in *Rock Creek Park* (2003) and *Along the Potomac: Images of America* (2000). Articles about Kushnir and his work have been published in *The Washington Times*, *The Washington Post*, *The Ukrainian Weekly*, *The Register Guard* (Oregon), *The Northern Virginia Daily*, *The Nature Conservancy Magazine*, *The Montgomery Gazette* (Maryland), *The Longboat Observer* (Florida), *The Journal* (West Virginia), *Hill Rag* (Washington, D.C.), *Highlander Today* (Florida), *The Gloucester Matthews Gazette Journal* (Virginia), *The Gasparilla Gazette* (Florida), *élan Magazine*, and *The Baltimore Sun*, among others.

Edward L. Ayers is the Tucker-Boatwright Professor of the Humanities and President Emeritus (2007-2015) of the University of Richmond who, in 2013, was awarded the National Humanities Medal by President Barack Obama. He is the author and editor of eleven books, among them *The Promise of the New South: Life after Reconstruction* (1992; 2007), which was a finalist for both the National Book Award and the Pulitzer Prize, and *In the Presence of Mine Enemies: War in the Heart of America, 1859–1863* (2003), which won the Bancroft Prize of the American Historical Association, awarded to the best book in English about the Americas since 1492.

Dana Hand Evans has been Executive Director of the Museum of the Shenandoah Valley since 2011. Previously, she was Executive Director (2002–2011) of the Wilton House Museum and the National Society of the Colonial Dames of America in the Commonwealth of Virginia.

Jeffrey C. Everett, raised in the Shenandoah Valley, has been a leading land conservation and historic preservation consultant since 1994. He has held appointments as Chief of Agricultural Resources in the Farmland Preservation Program of the New Jersey Department of Agriculture (since 2012), Deputy Farmland Preservation Manager for Carroll County, Maryland (2007–2011), and Cultural Landscapes Inventory Coordinator for the National Park Service (2001–2005).

Warren R. Hofstra is the Stewart Bell Professor of History at Shenandoah University and the author and editor of six books, among them *The Planting of New Virginia: Settlement and Landscape in the Shenandoah Valley* (2004), *The Great Valley Road: Shenandoah Landscapes from Prehistory to the Present,* with Karl B. Raitz, (2010), and *Sweet Dreams: The World of Patsy Cline* (2013).

William M. S. Rasmussen is Lead Curator and Lora M. Robins Curator of Art at the Virginia Historical Society and the author and co-author of eight books, among them *Old Virginia: The Pursuit of a Pastoral Ideal*, with Robert S. Tilton (2003), and *The Virginia Landscape: A Cultural History*, with James C. Kelly (2002), and *George Washington: The Man behind the Myths*, with Robert S. Tilton (1999), whih recovered the Award of Merit from the American Association for State and local History.

About the Book

Oh, Shenandoah: Paintings of the Historic Valley and River was brought to publication in an edition of 1,300 hardcover copies. The text was set in Adobe Caslon, the paper is Kinmari, 157 gsm weight, and the book was professionally printed and bound by P. Chan & Edward, Inc. in China.

Project Director and Publisher: George F. Thompson
Editorial and Research Assistant: Mikki Soroczak
Manuscript Editor and Proofreader: Purna Makaram
Book Design and Production: David Skolkin

About the Exhibitions:
This book was developed in partnership with the Museum of the Shenandoah Valley, which presented a solo exhibition of seventy-one paintings entitled *Painting the Valley: Works by Andrei Kushnir*. The exhibit was curated by Corwyn Garman, who organized Andrei Kushnir's work into three sections: "A Sense of Place," "Life in the Valley," and "Learning the Landscape." The exhibition opened on April 1, 2016, and closed on September 11, 2016. A second solo exhibition of Kushnir's paintings was featured at the Duke Hall Gallery of Fine Art at James Madison University. It was curated by Gary Freeburg and was open from May 1, 2017 to June 23, 2017. The publisher and artist extend their respective gratitude to both institutions for their support of this book and project.

Published 2016. First hardcover edition.
Printed in China on acid-free paper.

George F. Thompson Publishing, L.L.C.
217 Oak Ridge Circle
Staunton, VA 24401-3511, U.S.A.
www.gftbooks.com

24 23 22 21 20 19 18 17 16 1 2 3 4 5

The Library of Congress Preassigned Control Number is 2015956255.

ISBN: 978-1-938086-41-0